M000265939

Apache Solr Search Patterns

Leverage the power of Apache Solr to power up your business by navigating your users to their data quickly and efficiently

Jayant Kumar

[PACKT] open source ✳
PUBLISHING   community experience distilled

BIRMINGHAM - MUMBAI

Apache Solr Search Patterns

Copyright © 2015 Packt Publishing

All rights reserved. No part of this book may be reproduced, stored in a retrieval system, or transmitted in any form or by any means, without the prior written permission of the publisher, except in the case of brief quotations embedded in critical articles or reviews.

Every effort has been made in the preparation of this book to ensure the accuracy of the information presented. However, the information contained in this book is sold without warranty, either express or implied. Neither the author nor Packt Publishing, and its dealers and distributors will be held liable for any damages caused or alleged to be caused directly or indirectly by this book.

Packt Publishing has endeavored to provide trademark information about all of the companies and products mentioned in this book by the appropriate use of capitals. However, Packt Publishing cannot guarantee the accuracy of this information.

First published: April 2015

Production reference: 1210415

Published by Packt Publishing Ltd.
Livery Place
35 Livery Street
Birmingham B3 2PB, UK.

ISBN 978-1-78398-184-7

www.packtpub.com

Credits

Author
Jayant Kumar

Reviewers
Ramzi Alqrainy
Damiano Braga
Omar Shaban

Commissioning Editor
Edward Bowkett

Acquisition Editor
Vinay Argekar

Content Development Editor
Sumeet Sawant

Technical Editor
Tanmayee Patil

Copy Editors
Janbal Dharmaraj
Pooja Iyer

Project Coordinator
Akash Poojary

Proofreaders
Ting Baker
Simran Bhogal
Safis Editing

Indexer
Monica Ajmera Mehta

Graphics
Sheetal Aute
Ronak Dhruv

Production Coordinator
Shantanu N. Zagade

Cover Work
Shantanu N. Zagade

About the Author

Jayant Kumar is an experienced software professional with a bachelor of engineering degree in computer science and more than 14 years of experience in architecting and developing large-scale web applications.

Jayant is an expert on search technologies and PHP and has been working with Lucene and Solr for more than 11 years now. He is the key person responsible for introducing Lucene as a search engine on www.naukri.com, the most successful job portal in India.

Jayant is also the author of the book *Apache Solr PHP Integration*, *Packt Publishing*, which has been very successful.

Jayant has played many different important roles throughout his career, including software developer, team leader, project manager, and architect, but his primary focus has been on building scalable solutions on the Web. Currently, he is associated with the digital division of HT Media as the chief architect responsible for the job site www.shine.com.

Jayant is an avid blogger and his blog can be visited at http://jayant7k.blogspot.in. His LinkedIn profile is available at http://www.linkedin.com/in/jayantkumar.

I would like to thank the guys at Packt Publishing for giving me the opportunity to write this book. Special thanks to Vinay Argekar and Mohammed Fahad from Packt Publishing for keeping me engaged and dealing with my drafts and providing feedback at all stages.

I would like to thank my wife, Nidhi, and my parents for taking care of our kids while I was engaged in writing this book. And finally, I would like to thank my kids, Ashlesha and Banhishikha, for bearing with me while I was writing this book.

About the Reviewers

Ramzi Alqrainy is one of the most recognized experts within artificial intelligence and information retrieval fields in the Middle East. He is an active researcher and technology blogger with a focus on information retrieval.

He is a Solr engineer at Lucidworks and head of technology of www.openSooq.com, where he capitalizes on his solid experience in open source technologies in scaling up the search engine and supportive systems.

His experience in Solr, Elasticsearch, Spark, Mahout, and Hadoop stack contributed directly to the business growth through the implementations and projects that helped the key people to slice and dice information easily throughout the dashboards and data visualization solutions.

By developing more than eight full stack search engines, he was able to solve many complicated challenges about agglutination and stemming in the Arabic language.

He holds a master's degree in computer science, was among the first rank in his class, and was listed on the honor roll. His website address is http://ramzialqrainy.com. His LinkedIn profile is http://www.linkedin.com/in/ramzialqrainy. He can be contacted at ramzi.alqrainy@gmail.com.

I would like to thank my parents and sisters for always being there for me.

Damiano Braga is a senior software engineer at Trulia, where he helps the company to scale the search infrastructure and make search better. He's also an open source contributor and a conference speaker.

Prior to Trulia, he studied at and worked for the University of Ferrara (Italy), where he completed his master's degree in computer science engineering.

Omar Shaban is a software architect and software engineer with a passion for programming and open source. He began programming as a youngster in 2001. He is the lead maintainer of PHP's PECL Solr Extension and a proud PHP member.

Omar enjoys resolving complex problems, designing web applications architecture, and optimizing applications' performance. He is interested in Natural Language Processing (NLP) and machine learning.

www.PacktPub.com

Support files, eBooks, discount offers, and more

For support files and downloads related to your book, please visit www.PacktPub.com.

Did you know that Packt offers eBook versions of every book published, with PDF and ePub files available? You can upgrade to the eBook version at www.PacktPub.com and as a print book customer, you are entitled to a discount on the eBook copy. Get in touch with us at service@packtpub.com for more details.

At www.PacktPub.com, you can also read a collection of free technical articles, sign up for a range of free newsletters and receive exclusive discounts and offers on Packt books and eBooks.

https://www2.packtpub.com/books/subscription/packtlib

Do you need instant solutions to your IT questions? PacktLib is Packt's online digital book library. Here, you can search, access, and read Packt's entire library of books.

Why subscribe?

- Fully searchable across every book published by Packt
- Copy and paste, print, and bookmark content
- On demand and accessible via a web browser

Free access for Packt account holders

If you have an account with Packt at www.PacktPub.com, you can use this to access PacktLib today and view 9 entirely free books. Simply use your login credentials for immediate access.

Table of Contents

Preface

Apache Solr is the most widely used full text search solution. Almost all the websites today use Solr to provide the search function. Development of the search feature with a basic Solr setup is the starting point. At a later stage, most developers find it imperative to delve into Solr to provide solutions to certain problems or add specific features. This book will provide a developer working on Solr with a deeper insight into Solr. The book will also provide strategies and concepts that are employed in the development of different solutions using Solr. You will not only learn how to tweak Solr, but will also understand how to use it to handle big data and solve scalability problems.

What this book covers

Chapter 1, Solr Indexing Internals, delves into how indexing happens in Solr and how analyzers and tokenizers work during index creation.

Chapter 2, Customizing the Solr Scoring Algorithm, discusses different scoring algorithms in Solr and how to tweak these algorithms and implement them in Solr.

Chapter 3, Solr Internals and Custom Queries, discusses in-depth how relevance calculation happens and how scorers and filters work internally in Solr. This chapter will outline how to create custom plugins in Solr.

Chapter 4, Solr for Big Data, focuses on churning out big data for analysis purposes, including various faceting concepts and tools that can be used with Solr in order to plot graphs and charts.

Chapter 5, Solr in E-commerce, discusses the problems faced during the implementation of Solr in an e-commerce website and the related strategies and solutions.

Chapter 6, Solr for Spatial Search, focuses on spatial capabilities that the current and previous Solr versions possess. This chapter will also cover important concepts such as indexing and searching or filtering strategies together with varied query types that are available with a spatial search.

Chapter 7, Using Solr in an Advertising System, discusses the problems faced during the implementation of Solr to search in an advertising system and the related strategies and solutions.

Chapter 8, AJAX Solr, focuses on an AJAX Solr feature that helps reduce dependency on the application. This chapter will also cover an in-depth understanding of AJAX Solr as a framework and its implementation.

Chapter 9, SolrCloud, provides the complete procedure to implement SolrCloud and examines the benefits of using a distributed search with SolrCloud.

Chapter 10, Text Tagging with Lucene FST, focuses on the basic understanding of an FST and its implementation and guides us in designing an algorithm for text tagging, which can be implemented using FSTs and further integrated with Solr.

What you need for this book

You will need a Windows or Linux machine with Apache configured to run the web server. You will also need the Java Development Kit (JDK) installed together with an editor to write Java programs. You will need Solr 4.8 or higher to understand the procedures.

Who this book is for

Basic knowledge of working with Solr is required to understand the advanced topics discussed in this book. An understanding of Java programming concepts is required to study the programs discussed in this book.

Conventions

In this book, you will find a number of styles of text that distinguish between different kinds of information. Here are some examples of these styles and an explanation of their meanings.

Code words in text, database table names, folder names, filenames, file extensions, pathnames, dummy URLs, user input, and Twitter handles are shown as follows: "The `mergeFactor` class controls how many segments a Lucene index is allowed to have before it is coalesced into one segment."

A block of code is set as follows:

```
//Create collection of documents to add to Solr server
SolrInputDocument doc1 = new SolrInputDocument();
document.addField("id",1);
document.addField("desc", "description text for doc 1");
```

When we wish to draw your attention to a particular part of a code block, the relevant lines or items are set in bold:

```
//Create collection of documents to add to Solr server
SolrInputDocument doc1 = new SolrInputDocument();
document.addField("id",1);
document.addField("desc", "description text for doc 1");
```

Any command-line input or output is written as follows:

```
java -jar post.jar *.xml
```

New terms and **important words** are shown in bold. Words that you see on the screen, in menus or dialog boxes, appear as follows: "In the index, we can see that the token **Harry** appears in both documents."

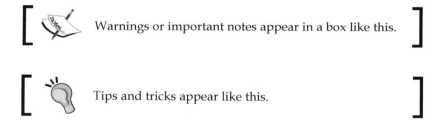

> Warnings or important notes appear in a box like this.

> Tips and tricks appear like this.

Reader feedback

Feedback from our readers is always welcome. Let us know what you think about this book—what you liked or may have disliked. Reader feedback is important for us to develop titles that you really get the most out of.

To send us general feedback, simply send an e-mail to feedback@packtpub.com, and mention the book title on the subject line of your message.

If there is a topic that you have expertise in and you are interested in either writing or contributing to a book, see our author guide on www.packtpub.com/authors.

Customer support

Now that you are the proud owner of a Packt book, we have a number of things to help you to get the most from your purchase.

Downloading the example code

You can download the example code files for all Packt books you have purchased from your account from `http://www.packtpub.com`. If you purchase this book elsewhere, you can visit `http://www.packtpub.com/support` and register to have the files e-mailed directly to you.

Errata

Although we have taken care to ensure the accuracy of our content, mistakes do happen. If you find a mistake in any of our books—maybe a mistake in the text or the code—we would be grateful if you reported this to us. By doing so, you can save other readers from frustration and help us improve the subsequent versions of this book. If you find any errata, please report them by visiting `http://www.packtpub.com/submit-errata`, selecting your book, clicking on the **Errata Submission Form** link, and entering the details of your errata. Once your errata are verified, your submission will be accepted and the errata will be uploaded on our website, or added to any list of existing errata, under the Errata section of that title.

To view the previously submitted errata, go to `https://www.packtpub.com/books/content/support` and enter the name of the book in the search field. The required information will appear under the **Errata** section.

Piracy

Piracy of copyright material on the Internet is an ongoing problem across all media. At Packt, we take the protection of our copyright and licenses very seriously. If you come across any illegal copies of our works, in any form, on the Internet, please provide us with the location address or website name immediately so that we can pursue a remedy.

Please contact us at `copyright@packtpub.com` with a link to the suspected pirated material.

We appreciate your help in protecting our authors, and our ability to bring you valuable content.

Questions

You can contact us at questions@packtpub.com if you are having a problem with any aspect of the book, and we will do our best to address it.

1
Solr Indexing Internals

This chapter will walk us through the indexing process in Solr. We will discuss how input text is broken and how an index is created in Solr. Also, we will delve into the concept of **analyzers** and **tokenizers** and the part they play in the creation of an index. Second, we will look at multilingual search using Solr and discuss the concepts used for measuring the quality of an index. Third, we will look at the problems faced during indexing while working with large amounts of input data. Finally, we will discuss **SolrCloud** and the problems it solves. The following topics will be discussed throughout the chapter. We will discuss use cases for Solr in e-commerce and job sites. We will look at the problems faced while providing search in an e-commerce or job site:

- Solr indexing fundamentals
- Working of analyzers, tokenizers, and filters
- Handling a multilingual search
- Measuring the quality of search results
- Challenges faced in large-scale indexing
- Problems SolrCloud intends to solve
- The e-commerce problem statement

The job site problem statement – Solr indexing fundamentals

The index created by Solr is known as an inverted index. An inverted index contains statistics and information on terms in a document. This makes a term-based search very efficient. The index created by Solr can be used to list the documents that contain the searched term. For an example of an inverted index, we can look at the index at the back of any book, as this index is the most accurate example of an inverted index. We can see meaningful terms associated with pages on which they occur within the book. Similarly, in the case of an inverted index, the terms serve to point or refer to documents in which they occur.

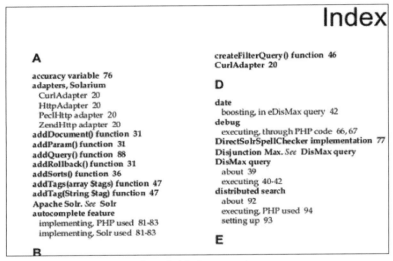

Inverted index example

Let us study the Solr index in depth. A Solr index consists of documents, fields, and terms, and a document consists of strings or phrases known as terms. Terms that refer to the context can be grouped together in a field. For example, consider a product on any e-commerce site. Product information can be broadly divided into multiple fields such as product name, product description, product category, and product price. Fields can be either stored or indexed or both. A stored field contains the unanalyzed, original text related to the field. The text in indexed fields can be broken down into terms. The process of breaking text into terms is known as **tokenization**. The terms created after tokenization are called tokens, which are then used for creating the inverted index. The tokenization process employs a list of token filters that handle various aspects of the tokenization process. For example, the tokenizer breaks a sentence into words, and the filters work on converting all of those words to lowercase. There is a huge list of analyzers and tokenizers that can be used as required.

Let us look at a working example of the indexing process with two documents having only a single field. The following are the documents:

Document Id	Text
1	Harry Potter And The Half Blood Prince
2	Harry Potter And The Deathly Hallows

Documents with Document Id and content (Text)

Suppose we tell Solr that the tokenization or breaking of terms should happen on whitespace. Whitespace is defined as one or more spaces or tabs. The tokens formed after the tokenization of the preceding documents are as follows:

Document Id	Text						
1	Harry	Potter	And	The	Half	Blood	Prince
2	Harry	Potter	And	The	Deathly	Hallows	

Tokens in both documents

The inverted index thus formed will contain the following terms and associations:

Token	Document Id
Harry	1, 2
Potter	1, 2
And	1, 2
The	1, 2
Half	1
Blood	1
Prince	1
Deathly	2
Hallows	2

Inverted index

In the index, we can see that the token **Harry** appears in both documents. If we search for Harry in the index we have created, the result will contain documents **1** and **2**. On the other hand, the token **Prince** has only document **1** associated with it in the index. A search for **Prince** will return only document **1**.

Let us look at how an index is stored in the filesystem. Refer to the following image:

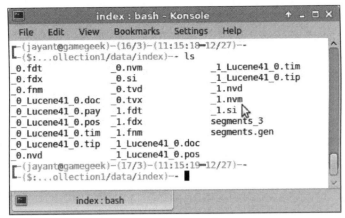

Index files on disk

For the default installation of Solr, the index can be located in the `<Solr_directory>/example/solr/collection1/data`. We can see that the index consists of files starting with `_0` and `_1`. There are two `segments*` files and a `write.lock` file. An index is built up of sub-indexes known as segments. The `segments*` file contains information about the segments. In the present case, we have two segments namely `_0.*` and `_1.*`. Whenever new documents are added to the index, new segments are created or multiple segments are merged in the index. Any search for an index involves all the segments inside the index. Ideally, each segment is a fully independent index and can be searched separately.

Lucene keeps on merging these segments into one to reduce the number of segments it has to go through during a search. The merger is governed by `mergeFactor` and `mergePolicy`. The `mergeFactor` class controls how many segments a Lucene index is allowed to have before it is coalesced into one segment. When an update is made to an index, it is added to the most recently opened segment. When a segment fills up, more segments are created. If creating a new segment would cause the number of lowest-level segments to exceed the `mergeFactor` value, then all those segments are merged to form a single large segment. Choosing a `mergeFactor` value involves a trade-off between indexing and search. A low `mergeFactor` value indicates a small number of segments and a fast search. However, indexing is slow as more and more mergers continue to happen during indexing. On the other hand, maintaining a high value of `mergeFactor` speeds up indexing but slows down the search, since the number of segments to search increases. Nevertheless, documents can be pushed to newer segments on disk with fewer mergers. The default value of `mergeFactor` is 10. The `mergePolicy` class defines how segments are merged together. The default method is `TieredMergePolicy`, which merges segments of approximately equal sizes subject to an allowed number of segments per tier.

Let us look at the file extensions inside the index and understand their importance. We are working with Solr Version 4.8.1, which uses Lucene 4.8.1 at its core. The segment file names have Lucene41 in them, but this string is not related to the version of Lucene being used.

 The index structure is almost similar for Lucene 4.2 and later.

The file types in the index are as follows:

- segments.gen, segments_N: These files contain information about segments within an index. The segments_N file contains the active segments in an index as well as a generation number. The file with the largest generation number is considered to be active. The segments.gen file contains the current generation of the index.

- .si: The segment information file stores metadata about the segments. It contains information such as segment size (number of documents in the segment), whether the segment is a compound file or not, a checksum to check the integrity of the segment, and a list of files referred to by this segment.

- write.lock: This is a write lock file that is used to prevent multiple indexing processes from writing to the same index.

- .fnm: In our example, we can see the _0.fnm and _1.fnm files. These files contain information about fields for a particular segment of the index. The information stored here is represented by **FieldsCount**, **FieldName**, **FieldNumber**, and **FieldBits**. **FieldCount** is used to generate and store ordered number of fields in this index. If there are two fields in a document, FieldsCount will be 0 for the first field and 1 for the second field. FieldName is a string specifying the name as we have specified in our configuration. FieldBits are used to store information about the field such as whether the field is indexed or not, or whether term vectors, term positions, and term offsets are stored. We study these concepts in depth later in this chapter.

- .fdx: This file contains pointers that point a document to its field data. It is used for stored fields to find field-related data for a particular document from within the field data file (identified by the .fdt extension).

- .fdt: The field data file is used to store field-related data for each document. If you have a huge index with lots of stored fields, this will be the biggest file in the index. The fdt and fdx files are respectively used to store and retrieve fields for a particular document from the index.

- `.tim`: The term dictionary file contains information related to all terms in an index. For each term, it contains per-term statistics, such as document frequency and pointers to the frequencies, skip data (the `.doc` file), position (the `.pos` file), and payload (the `.pay` file) for each term.

- `.tip`: The term index file contains indexes to the term dictionary file. The `.tip` file is designed to be read entirely into memory to provide fast and random access to the term dictionary file.

- `.doc`: The frequencies and skip data file consists of the list of documents that contain each term, along with the frequencies of the term in that document. If the length of the document list is greater than the allowed block size, the skip data to the beginning of the next block is also stored here.

- `.pos`: The positions file contains the list of positions at which each term occurs within documents. In addition to terms and their positions, the file also contains part payloads and offsets for speedy retrieval.

- `.pay`: The payload file contains payloads and offsets associated with certain term document positions. Payloads are byte arrays (strings or integers) stored with every term on a field. Payloads can be used for boosting certain terms over others.

- `.nvd` and `.nvm`: The normalization files contain lengths and boost factors for documents and fields. This stores boost values that are multiplied into the score for hits on that field.

- `.dvd` and `.dvm`: The per-document value files store additional scoring factors or other per-document information. This information is indexed by the document number and is intended to be loaded into main memory for fast access.

- `.tvx`: The term vector index file contains pointers and offsets to the `.tvd` (term vector document) file.

- `.tvd`: The term vector data file contains information about each document that has term vectors. It contains terms, frequencies, positions, offsets, and payloads for every document.

- `.del`: This file will be created only if some documents are deleted from the index. It contains information about what files were deleted from the index.

- `.cfs` and `.cfe`: These files are used to create a compound index where all files belonging to a segment of the index are merged into a single `.cfs` file with a corresponding `.cfe` file indexing its subfiles. Compound indexes are used when there is a limitation on the system for the number of file descriptors the system can open during indexing. Since a compound file merges or collapses all segment files into a single file, the number of file descriptors to be used for indexing is small. However, this has a performance impact as additional processing is required to access each file within the compound file.

For more information please refer to: `http://lucene.apache.org/core/4_6_0/core/org/apache/lucene/codecs/lucene46/package-summary.html`.

Ideally, when an index is created using Solr, the document to be indexed is broken down into tokens and then converted into an index by filling relevant information into the files we discussed earlier. We are now clear with the concept of tokens, fields, and documents. We also discussed payload. Term vectors, frequencies, positions, and offsets form the term vector component in Solr. The term vector component in Solr is used to store and return additional information about terms in a document. It is used for fast vector highlighting and some other features like *"more like this"* in Solr. Norms are used for calculating the score of a document during a search. It is a part of the scoring formula.

Now, let us look at how analyzers, tokenizers, and filters work in the conversion of the input text into a stream of tokens or terms for both indexing and searching purposes in Solr.

Working of analyzers, tokenizers, and filters

When a document is indexed, all fields within the document are subject to analysis. An analyzer examines the text within fields and converts them into token streams. It is used to pre-process the input text during indexing or search. Analyzers can be used independently or can consist of one tokenizer and zero or more filters. Tokenizers break the input text into tokens that are used for either indexing or search. Filters examine the token stream and can keep, discard, or convert them on the basis of certain rules. Tokenizers and filters are combined to form a pipeline or chain where the output from one tokenizer or filter acts as an input to another. Ideally, an analyzer is built up of a pipeline of tokenizers and filters and the output from the analyzer is used for indexing or search.

Let us see the example of a simple analyzer without any tokenizers and filters. This analyzer is specified in the schema.xml file in the Solr configuration with the help of the `<analyzer>` tag inside a `<fieldtype>` tag. Analyzers are always applied to fields of type `solr.TextField`. An analyzer must be a fully qualified Java class name derived from the Lucene analyzer `org.apache.lucene.analysis.Analyzer`. The following example shows a simple whitespace analyzer that breaks the input text by whitespace (space, tab, and new line) and creates tokens, which can then be used for both indexing and search:

```
<fieldType name="whitespace" class="solr.TextField">
  <analyzer class="org.apache.lucene.analysis.WhitespaceAnalyzer"/>
</fieldType>
```

Downloading the example code

You can download the example code files from your account at
http://www.packtpub.com for all Packt Publishing books that
you have purchased. If you purchased this book elsewhere, you
can visit http://www.packtpub.com/support and register
yourself to have the files e-mailed directly to you.

A custom analyzer is one in which we specify a tokenizer and a pipeline of filters.
We also have the option of specifying different analyzers for indexing and search
operations on the same field. Ideally, we should use the same analyzer for indexing
and search so that we search for the tokens that we created during indexing.
However, there might be cases where we want the analysis to be different during
indexing and search.

The job of a tokenizer is to break the input text into a stream of characters or strings,
or phrases that are usually sub-sequences of the characters in the input text. An
analyzer is aware of the field it is configured for, but a tokenizer is not. A tokenizer
works on the character stream fed to it by the analyzer and outputs tokens. The
tokenizer specified in schema.xml in the Solr configuration is an implementation
of the tokenizer factory - org.apache.solr.analysis.TokenizerFactory.

A filter consumes input from a tokenizer or an analyzer and produces output in
the form of tokens. The job of a filter is to look at each token passed to it and to pass,
replace, or discard the token. The input to a filter is a token stream and the output is
also a token stream. Thus, we can chain or pipeline one filter after another. Ideally,
generic filtering is done first and then specific filters are applied.

An analyzer can have only one tokenizer. This is because the input to a
tokenizer is a character stream and the output is tokens. Therefore, the
output of a tokenizer cannot be used by another.

In addition to tokenizers and filters, an analyzer can contain a char filter. A char
filter is another component that pre-processes input characters, namely adding,
changing, or removing characters from the character stream. It consumes and
produces a character stream and can thus be chained or pipelined.

Let us look at an example from the schema.xml file, which is shipped with the
default Solr:

```
<fieldType name="text_general" class="solr.TextField"
positionIncrementGap="100">
    <analyzer type="index">
```

```
      <tokenizer class="solr.StandardTokenizerFactory"/>
      <filter class="solr.StopFilterFactory" ignoreCase="true"
words="stopwords.txt" />
      <filter class="solr.LowerCaseFilterFactory"/>
    </analyzer>
    <analyzer type="query">
      <tokenizer class="solr.StandardTokenizerFactory"/>
      <filter class="solr.StopFilterFactory" ignoreCase="true"
words="stopwords.txt" />
      <filter class="solr.SynonymFilterFactory"
synonyms="synonyms.txt" ignoreCase="true" expand="true"/>
      <filter class="solr.LowerCaseFilterFactory"/>
    </analyzer>
</fieldType>
```

The field type specified here is named `text_general` and it is of type `solr.TextField`. We have specified a position increment gap of 100. That is, in a multivalued field, there would be a difference of 100 between the last token of one value and first token of the next value. A multivalued field has multiple values for the same field in a document. An example of a multivalued field is tags associated with a document. A document can have multiple tags and each tag is a value associated with the document. A search for any tag should return the documents associated with it. Let us see an example.

Doc id	Text	Tags
1	Harry Potter And The Half Blood Prince	Harry potter series, book, half blood prince
2	Harry Potter And The Deathly Hallows	Book, harry potter series, deathly hallows

Example of multivalued field – documents with tags

Here each document has three tags. Suppose that the tags associated with a document are tokenized on comma. The tags will be multiple values within the index of each document. In this case, if the position increment gap is specified as `0` or not specified, a search for **series book** will return the first document. This is because the token series and book occur next to each other in the index. On the other hand, if a `positionIncrementGap` value of `100` is specified, there will be a difference of 100 positions between `series` and `book` and none of the documents will be returned in the result.

In this example, we have multiple analyzers, one for indexing and another for search. The analyzer used for indexing consists of a `StandardTokenizer` class and two filters, `stop` and `lowercase`. The analyzer used for the `search` (query) consists of three filters, stop, synonym, and lowercase filters.

The standard tokenizer splits the input text into tokens, treating whitespace and punctuation as delimiters that are discarded. Dots not followed by whitespace are retained as part of the token, which in turn helps in retaining domain names. Words are split at hyphens (-) unless there is a number in the word. If there is a number in the word, it is preserved with hyphen. @ is also treated as a delimiter, so e-mail addresses are not preserved.

The output of a standard tokenizer is a list of tokens that are passed to the stop filter and lowercase filter during indexing. The `stop filter` class contains a list of **stop words** that are discarded from the tokens received by it. The lowercase filter converts all tokens to lowercase. On the other hand, during a search, an additional filter known as **synonym filter** is applied. This filter replaces a token with its synonyms. The synonyms are mentioned in the `synonyms.txt` file specified as an attribute in the filter.

Let us make some modifications to the `stopwords.txt` and `synonyms.txt` files in our Solr configuration and see how the input text is analyzed.

Add the following two words, each in a new line in the `stopwords.txt` file:

```
and
the
```

Add the following in the `synonyms.txt` file:

```
King => Prince
```

We have now told Solr to treat `and` and `the` as stop words, so during analysis they would be dropped. During the search phrase, we map `King` to `Prince`, so a search for `king` will be replaced by a search for `prince`.

In order to view the results, perform the following steps:

- Open up your Solr interface, select a core (say collection1), and click on the **Analysis** link on the left-hand side.
- Enter the text of the first document in text box marked field value (index).
- Select the field name and field type value as `text`.
- Click on **Analyze values.**

		Harry	Potter	And	The	Half	Blood	Prince
ST	text	Harry	Potter	And	The	Half	Blood	Prince
	raw_bytes	[48 61 72 72 79]	[50 6f 74 74 65 72]	[41 6e 64]	[54 68 65]	[48 61 6c 66]	[42 6c 6f 6f 64]	[50 72 69 6e 63 65]
	start	0	6	13	17	21	26	32
	end	5	12	16	20	25	31	38
	type	<ALPHANUM>	<ALPHANUM>	<ALPHANUM>	<ALPHANUM>	<ALPHANUM>	<ALPHANUM>	<ALPHANUM>
	position	1	2	3	4	5	6	7
SF	text	Harry	Potter			Half	Blood	Prince
	raw_bytes	[48 61 72 72 79]	[50 6f 74 74 65 72]			[48 61 6c 66]	[42 6c 6f 6f 64]	[50 72 69 6e 6e 65 65]
	position	1	2			5	6	7
	start	0	6			21	26	32
	end	5	12			25	31	38
	type	<ALPHANUM>	<ALPHANUM>			<ALPHANUM>	<ALPHANUM>	<ALPHANUM>
LCF	text	harry	potter			half	blood	prince
	raw_bytes	[68 61 72 72 79]	[70 6f 74 74 65 72]			[68 61 6c 66]	[62 6c 6f 6f 64]	[70 72 69 6e 6e 65 65]
	position	1	2			5	6	7
	start	0	6			21	26	32
	end	5	12			25	31	38
	type	<ALPHANUM>	<ALPHANUM>			<ALPHANUM>	<ALPHANUM>	<ALPHANUM>

Solr analysis for indexing

We can see the complete analysis phase during indexing. First, a standard tokenizer is applied that breaks the input text into tokens. Note that here **Half-Blood** was broken into **Half** and **Blood**. Next, we saw the stop filter removing the stop words we mentioned previously. The words **And** and **The** are discarded from the token stream. Finally, the lowercase filter converts all tokens to lowercase.

During the search, suppose the query entered is **Half-Blood** and **King**. To check how it is analyzed, enter the value in **Field Value** (Query), select the `text` value in the **FieldName / FieldType**, and click on **Analyze values**.

		Half	Blood	and	king
ST	text	Half	Blood	and	king
	raw_bytes	[48 61 6c 66]	[42 6c 6f 6f 64]	[61 6e 64]	[6b 69 6e 67]
	start	0	5	11	15
	end	4	10	14	19
	type	<ALPHANUM>	<ALPHANUM>	<ALPHANUM>	<ALPHANUM>
	position	1	2	3	4
SF	text	Half	Blood		king
	raw_bytes	[48 61 6c 66]	[42 6c 6f 6f 64]		[6b 69 6e 67]
	position	1	2		4
	start	0	5		15
	end	4	10		19
	type	<ALPHANUM>	<ALPHANUM>		<ALPHANUM>
SF	text	Half	Blood		prince
	raw_bytes	[48 61 6c 66]	[42 6c 6f 6f 64]		[70 72 69 6e 6e 65 63 65
	positionLength	1	1		1
	type	<ALPHANUM>	<ALPHANUM>		SYNONYM
	start	0	5		15
	end	4	10		19
	position	1	2		3
LCF	text	half	blood		prince
	raw_bytes	[68 61 6c 66]	[62 6c 6f 6f 64]		[70 72 69 6e 6e 65 63 65
	position	1	2		3
	start	0	5		15
	end	4	10		19
	type	<ALPHANUM>	<ALPHANUM>		SYNONYM
	positionLength	1	1		1

Solr analysis during a search

We can see that during the search, as before, **Half-Blood** is tokenized as **Half** and **Blood**, **And** and is dropped in the stop filter phase. **King** is replaced with **prince** during the synonym filter phase. Finally, the lowercase filter converts all tokens to lowercase.

An important point to note over here is that the lowercase filter appears as the last filter. This is to prevent any mismatch between the text in the index and that in the search due to either of them having a capital letter in the token.

The Solr analysis feature can be used to analyze and check whether the analyzer we have created gives output in the desired format during indexing and search. It can also be used to debug if we find any cases where the results are not as expected.

What is the use of such complex analysis of text? Let us look at an example to understand a scenario where a result is expected from a search but none is found. The following two documents are indexed in Solr with the custom analyzer we just discussed:

Doc id	Text
1	Project management
2	Project manager

After indexing, the index will have the following terms associated with the respective document ids:

Term	Doc Id	
Project	1	2
Management	1	
Manager		2

A search for project will return both documents **1** and **2**. However, a search for manager will return only document 2. Ideally, manager is equal to management. Therefore, a search for manager should also return both documents. This intelligence has to be built into Solr with the help of analyzers, tokenizers, and filters. In this case, a synonym filter mentioning manager, management, manages as synonyms should do the trick. Another way to handle the same scenario is to use **stemmers**. Stemmers reduce words into their stem, base, or root form. In this chase, the stem for all the preceding words will be manage. There is a huge list of analyzers, tokenizers, and filters available with Solr by default that should be able to satisfy any scenario we can think of.

For more information on analyzers, tokenizers, and filters, refer to: `http://wiki.apache.org/solr/AnalyzersTokenizersTokenFilters`

`AND` and `OR` queries are handled by respectively performing an intersection or union of documents returned from a search on all the terms of the query. Once the documents or hits are returned, a scorer calculates the relevance of each document in the result set on the basis of the inbuilt **Term Frequency-Inverse Document Frequency (TF-IDF)** scoring formula and returns the ranked results. Thus, a search for `Project AND Manager` will return only the *2nd* document after the intersection of results that are available after searching both terms on the index.

It is important to remember that text processing during indexing and search affects the quality of results. Better results can be obtained by high-quality and well thought of text processing during indexing and search.

> TF-IDF is a formula used to calculate the relevancy of search terms in a document against terms in existing documents. In a simple form, it favors a document that contains the term with high frequency and has lower occurrence in all the other documents.
>
> In a simple form, a document with a high TF-IDF score contains the search term with high frequency, and the term itself does not appear as much in other documents.
>
> More details on TF-IDF will be explained in *Chapter 2, Customizing a Solr Scoring Algorithm.*

Handling a multilingual search

Content is produced and consumed in native languages. Sometimes even normal-looking documents may contain more than one language. This makes language an important aspect for search. A user should be able to search in his or her language. Each language has its own set of characters. Some languages use characters to form words, while some use characters to form sentences. Some languages do not even have spaces between the characters forming sentences. Let us look at some examples to understand the complexities that Solr should handle during text analysis for different languages.

Suppose a document contains the following sentence in English:

```
Incorporating the world's largest display screen on the slimmest of
bodies the Xperia Z Ultra is Sony's answer to all your recreational
needs.
```

The question here is whether the words `world's` and `Sony's` should be indexed. If yes, then how? Should a search for `Sony` return this document in the result? What would be the stop words here—the words that do not need to be indexed? Ideally, we would like to ignore stop words such as `the`, `on`, `of`, `is`, `all`, or `your`. How should the document be indexed so that `Xperia Z Ultra` matches this document? First, we need to ensure that `z` is not a stop word. The search should contain the term `xperia z ultra`. This would break into `+xperia OR z OR ultra`. Here `xperia` is the only mandatory term. The results would be sorted in such a fashion that the document (our document) that contains all three terms will be at the top. Also, ideally we would like the search for `world` or `sony` to return this document in the result. In this case, we can use the `LetterTokenizerFactory` class, which will separate the words as follows:

```
World's => World, s
Sony's => Sony, s
```

Then, we need to pass the tokens through a stop filter to remove stop words. The output from the stop filter passes through a lowercase filter to convert all tokens to lowercase. During the search, we can use a `WhiteSpaceTokenizer` and a `LowerCaseFilter` tokenizer to tokenize and process our input text.

In a real-life situation, it is advisable to take multiple examples with different use cases and work around the scenarios to provide the desired solutions for those use cases. Given that the numbers of examples are large, the derived solution should satisfy most of the cases.

If we translate the same sentence into German, here is how it will look:

Die Einbeziehung der weltweit größten Display-Bildschirm auf der flachste der Körper das Xperia Z Ultra ist Sonys Antwort auf alle Ihre Freizeit-Bedürfnisse.

German

Solr comes with an inbuilt field type for German - `text_de`, which has a `StandardTokenizer` class followed by a `lowerCaseFilter` class and a `stopFilter` class for German words. In addition, the analyzer has two German-specific filters, `GermanNormalizationFilter` and `GermanLightStemFilter`. Though this text analyzer does a pretty good job, there may be cases where it will need improvement.

Let's translate the same sentence into Arabic and see how it looks:

دمج أكبر شاشة عرض في العالم على الأقل سمكا من الهيئات اريكسون Z الترا هو الجواب سوني لجميع الاحتياجات الترفيهية الخاصة بك.

Arabic

Note that Arabic is written from right to left. The default analyzer in the Solr schema configuration is `text_ar`. Again tokenization is carried out with `StandardTokenizer` followed by `LowerCaseFilter` (used for non-Arabic words embedded inside the Arabic text) and the Arabic `StopFilter` class. This is followed by the Arabic Normalization filter and the Arabic Stemmer. Another aspect used in Arabic is known as a diacritic. A diacritic is a mark (also known as glyph) added to a letter to change the sound value of the letter. Diacritics generally appear either below or above a letter or, in some cases, between two letters or within the letter. Diacritics such as ' in English do not modify the meaning of the word. In contrast, in other languages, the addition of a diacritic modifies the meaning of the word. Arabic is such a language. Thus, it is important to decide whether to normalize diacritics or not.

Let us translate the same sentence into Japanese and see what we get:

のXperia Zはウルトラボディの最薄で、世界最大のディ
スプレイ画面を組み込むことは、すべてあなたのレクリ
エーションのニーズにソニーの答えです。

Japanese

Now that the complete sentence does not have any whitespace to separate the words, how do we identify words or tokens and index them? The Japanese analyzer available in our Solr schema configuration is `text_ja`. This analyzer identifies the words in the sentence and creates tokens. A few tokens identified are as follows:

Token	Pronounciation (en)	Indexed ?
ボディ	bodi	Yes
の	no	No (stop word)
は	wa	No (stop word)
Xperia	xperia	Yes
ソニー	soni	Yes

Japanese tokens

It also identifies some of the stop words and removes them from the sentence.

As in English, there are other languages where a word is modified by adding a suffix or prefix to change the tense, grammatical mood, voice, aspect, person, number, or gender of the word. This concept is called inflection and is handled by stemmers during indexing. The purpose of a stemmer is to change words such as indexing, indexed, or indexes into their base form, namely index. The stemmer has to be introduced during both indexing and search so that the stems or roots are compared during both indexing and search.

The point to note is that each language is unique and presents different challenges to the search engine. In order to create a language-aware search, the steps that need to be taken are as follows:

- **Identification of the language**: Decide whether the search would handle the dominant language in a document or find and handle multiple languages in the document.

- **Tokenization**: Decide the way tokens should be formed from the language.

- **Token processing**: Given a token, what processing should happen on the token to make it a part of the index? Should words be broken up or synonyms added? Should diacritics and grammars be normalized? A stop-word dictionary specific to the language needs to be applied.

Token processing can be done within Solr by using an appropriate analyzer, tokenizer, or filter. However, for this, all possibilities have to be thought through and certain rules need to be formed. The default analyzers can also be used, but it may not help in improving the relevance factor of the result set. Another way of handling a multilingual search is to process the document during indexing and before providing the data to Solr for indexing. This ensures more control on the way a document can be indexed.

The strategies used for handling a multilingual search with the same content across multiple languages at the Solr configuration level are:

- **Use one Solr field for each language**: This is a simple approach that guarantees that the text is processed the same way as it was indexed. As different fields can have separate analyzers, it is easy to handle multiple languages. However, this increases the complexity at query time as the input query language needs to be identified and the related language field needs to be queried. If all fields are queried, the query execution speed goes down. Also, this may require creation of multiple copies of the same text across fields for different languages.

- **Use one Solr core per language**: Each core has the same field with different analyzers, tokenizers, and filters specific to the language on that core. This does not have much query time performance overhead. However, there is significant complexity involved in managing multiple cores. This approach would prove complex in supporting multilingual documents across different cores.

- **All languages in one field**: Indexing and search are much easier as there is only a single field handling multiple languages. However, in this case, the analyzer, tokenizer, and filter have to be custom built to support the languages that are expected in the input text. The queries may not be processed in the same fashion as the index. Also, there might be confusion in the scoring calculation. There are cases where particular characters or words may be stop words in one language and meaningful in another language.

 Custom analyzers are built as Solr plugins. The following link gives more details regarding the same: `https://wiki.apache.org/solr/SolrPlugins#Analyzer`.

The final aim of a multilingual search should be to provide better search results to the end users by proper processing of text both during indexing and at query time.

Measuring the quality of search results

Now that we know what analyzers are and how text analysis happens, we need to know whether the analysis that we have implemented provides better results. There are two concepts in the search result set that determine the quality of results, **precision** and **recall**:

- **Precision**: This is the fraction of retrieved documents that are relevant. A precision of 1.0 means that every result returned by the search was relevant, but there may be other relevant documents that were not a part of the search result.

$$precision = \frac{|\{\text{relevant documents}\} \cap \{\text{retrieved documents}\}|}{|\{\text{retrieved documents}\}|}$$

Precision equation

- **Recall**: This is the fraction of relevant documents that are retrieved. A recall of 1.0 means that all relevant documents were retrieved by the search irrespective of the irrelevant documents included in the result set.

$$recall = \frac{|\{\text{relevant documents}\} \cap \{\text{retrieved documents}\}|}{|\{\text{relevant documents}\}|}$$

Recall equation

Another way to define precision and recall is by classifying the documents into four classes between relevancy and retrieval as follows:

	Relevant	Irrelevant
Retrieved	A	B
Not retrieved	C	D

Precision and recall

We can define the formula for precision and recall as follows:

```
Precision = A / (A union B)
Recall = A / (A union C)
```

We can see that as the number of irrelevant documents or **B** increases in the result set, the precision goes down. If all documents are retrieved, then the recall is perfect but the precision would not be good. On the other hand, if the document set contains only a single relevant document and that relevant document is retrieved in the search, then the precision is perfect but again the result set is not good. This is a trade-off between precision and recall as they are inversely related. As precision increases, recall decreases and vice versa. We can increase recall by retrieving more documents, but this will decrease the precision of the result set. A good result set has to be a balance between precision and recall.

We should optimize our results for precision if the hits are plentiful and several results can meet the search criteria. Since we have a huge collection of documents, it makes sense to provide a few relevant and good hits as opposed to adding irrelevant results in the result set. An example scenario where optimization for precision makes sense is **web search** where the available number of documents is huge.

On the other hand, we should optimize for recall if we do not want to miss out any relevant document. This happens when the collection of documents is comparatively small. It makes sense to return all relevant documents and not care about the irrelevant documents added to the result set. An example scenario where recall makes sense is **patent search**.

Traditional accuracy of the result set is defined by the following formula:

```
Accuracy = 2*((precision * recall) / (precision + recall))
```

This combines both precision and recall and is a harmonic mean of precision and recall. Harmonic mean is a type of averaging mean used to find the average of fractions. This is an ideal formula for accuracy and can be used as a reference point while figuring out the combination of precision and recall that your result set will provide.

Let us look at some practical problems faced while searching in different business scenarios.

The e-commerce problem statement

E-commerce provides an easy way to sell products to a large customer base. However, there is a lot of competition among multiple e-commerce sites. When users land on an e-commerce site, they expect to find what they are looking for quickly and easily. Also, users are not sure about the brands or the actual products they want to purchase. They have a very broad idea about what they want to buy. Many customers nowadays search for their products on Google rather than visiting specific e-commerce sites. They believe that Google will take them to the e-commerce sites that have their product.

The purpose of any e-commerce website is to help customers narrow down their broad ideas and enable them to finalize the products they want to purchase. For example, suppose a customer is interested in purchasing a mobile. His or her search for a mobile should list mobile brands, operating systems on mobiles, screen size of mobiles, and all other features as facets. As the customer selects more and more features or options from the facets provided, the search narrows down to a small list of mobiles that suit his or her choice. If the list is small enough and the customer likes one of the mobiles listed, he or she will make the purchase.

The challenge is also that each category will have a different set of facets to be displayed. For example, searching for books should display their format, as in paperpack or hardcover, author name, book series, language, and other facets related to books. These facets were different for mobiles that we discussed earlier. Similarly, each category will have different facets and it needs to be designed properly so that customers can narrow down to their preferred products, irrespective of the category they are looking into.

The takeaway from this is that categorization and feature listing of products should be taken care of. Misrepresentation of features can lead to incorrect search results. Another takeaway is that we need to provide multiple facets in the search results. For example, while displaying the list of all mobiles, we need to provide facets for a brand. Once a brand is selected, another set of facets for operating systems, network, and mobile phone features has to be provided. As more and more facets are selected, we still need to show facets within the remaining products.

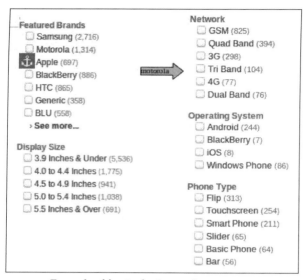

Example of facet selection on Amazon.com

Another problem is that we do not know what product the customer is searching for. A site that displays a huge list of products from different categories, such as electronics, mobiles, clothes, or books, needs to be able to identify what the customer is searching for. A customer can be searching for samsung, which can be in mobiles, tablets, electronics, or computers. The site should be able to identify whether the customer has input the author name or the book name. Identifying the input would help in increasing the relevance of the result set by increasing the precision of the search results. Most e-commerce sites provide search suggestions that include the category to help customers target the right category during their search.

Amazon, for example, provides search suggestions that include both latest searched terms and products along with category-wise suggestions:

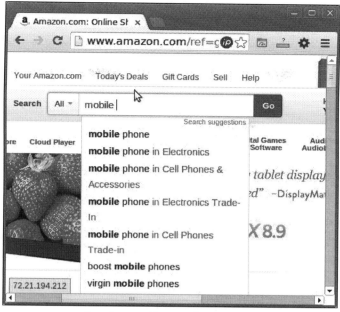

Search suggestions on Amazon.com

It is also important that products are added to the index as soon as they are available. It is even more important that they are removed from the index or marked as sold out as soon as their stock is exhausted. For this, modifications to the index should be immediately visible in the search. This is facilitated by a concept in Solr known as **Near Real Time Indexing and Search** (**NRT**). More details on using Near Real Time Search will be explained later in this chapter.

The job site problem statement

A job site serves a dual purpose. On the one hand, it provides jobs to candidates, and on the other, it serves as a database of registered candidates' profiles for companies to shortlist.

A job search has to be very intuitive for the candidates so that they can find jobs suiting their skills, position, industry, role, and location, or even by the company name. As it is important to keep the candidates engaged during their job search, it is important to provide facets on the abovementioned criteria so that they can narrow down to the job of their choice. The searches by candidates are not very elaborate. If the search is generic, the results need to have high precision. On the other hand, if the search does not return many results, then recall has to be high to keep the candidate engaged on the site. Providing a personalized job search to candidates on the basis of their profiles and past search history makes sense for the candidates.

On the recruiter side, the search provided over the candidate database is required to have a huge set of fields to search upon every data point that the candidate has entered. The recruiters are very selective when it comes to searching for candidates for specific jobs. Educational qualification, industry, function, key skills, designation, location, and experience are some of the fields provided to the recruiter during a search. In such cases, the precision has to be high. The recruiter would like a certain candidate and may be interested in more candidates similar to the selected candidate. The `more like this` search in Solr can be used to provide a search for candidates similar to a selected candidate.

NRT is important as the site should be able to provide a job or a candidate for a search as soon as any one of them is added to the database by either the recruiter or the candidate. The promptness of the site is an important factor in keeping users engaged on the site.

Challenges of large-scale indexing

Let us understand how indexing happens and what can be done to speed it up. We will also look at the challenges faced during the indexing of a large number of documents or bulky documents. An e-commerce site is a perfect example of a site containing a large number of products, while a job site is an example of a search where documents are bulky because of the content in candidate resumes.

During indexing, Solr first analyzes the documents and converts them into tokens that are stored in the RAM buffer. When the RAM buffer is full, data is flushed into a segment on the disk. When the numbers of segments are more than that defined in the `MergeFactor` class of the Solr configuration, the segments are merged. Data is also written to disk when a commit is made in Solr.

Let us discuss a few points to make Solr indexing fast and to handle a large index containing a huge number of documents.

Using multiple threads for indexing on Solr

We can divide our data into smaller chunks and each chunk can be indexed in a separate thread. Ideally, the number of threads should be twice the number of processor cores to avoid a lot of context switching. However, we can increase the number of threads beyond that and check for performance improvement.

Using the Java binary format of data for indexing

Instead of using XML files, we can use the Java bin format for indexing. This reduces a lot of overhead of parsing an XML file and converting it into a binary format that is usable. The way to use the Java bin format is to write our own program for creating fields, adding fields to documents, and finally adding documents to the index. Here is a sample code:

```
//Create an instance of the Solr server
String SOLR_URL = "http://localhost:8983/solr"
SolrServer server = new HttpSolrServer(SOLR_URL);

//Create collection of documents to add to Solr server
SolrInputDocument doc1 = new SolrInputDocument();
document.addField("id",1);
document.addField("desc", "description text for doc 1");

SolrInputDocument doc2 = new SolrInputDocument();
document.addField("id",2);
document.addField("desc", "description text for doc 2");

Collection<SolrInputDocument> docs = new
ArrayList<SolrInputDocument>();
docs.add(doc1);
docs.add(doc2);

//Add the collection of documents to the Solr server and commit.
server.add(docs);
server.commit();
```

Here is the reference to the API for the `HttpSolrServer` program `http://lucene.apache.org/solr/4_6_0/solr-solrj/org/apache/solr/client/solrj/impl/HttpSolrServer.html`.

 Add all files from the `<solr_directory>/dist` folder to the classpath for compiling and running the `HttpSolrServer` program.

Using the ConcurrentUpdateSolrServer class for indexing

Using the ConcurrentUpdateSolrServer class instead of the HttpSolrServer class can provide performance benefits as the former uses buffers to store processed documents before sending them to the Solr server. We can also specify the number of background threads to use to empty the buffers. The API docs for ConcurrentUpdateSolrServer are found in the following link: http://lucene. apache.org/solr/4_6_0/solr-solrj/org/apache/solr/client/solrj/impl/ ConcurrentUpdateSolrServer.html

The constructor for the ConcurrentUpdateSolrServer class is defined as:

```
ConcurrentUpdateSolrServer(String solrServerUrl, int queueSize, int
threadCount)
```

Here, queueSize is the buffer and threadCount is the number of background threads used to flush the buffers to the index on disk.

Note that using too many threads can increase the context switching between threads and reduce performance. In order to optimize the number of threads, we should monitor performance (docs indexed per minute) after each increase and ensure that there is no decrease in performance.

Solr configuration changes that can improve indexing performance

We can change the following directives in solrconfig.xml file to improve indexing performance of Solr:

- ramBufferSizeMB: This property specifies the amount of data that can be buffered in RAM before flushing to disk. It can be increased to accommodate more documents in RAM before flushing to disk. Increasing the size beyond a particular point can cause swapping and result in reduced performance.

- maxBufferedDocs: This property specifies the number of documents that can be buffered in RAM before flushing to disk. Make this a large number so that commit always happens on the basis of the RAM buffer size instead of the number of documents.

- useCompoundFile: This property specifies whether to use a compound file or not. Using a compound file reduces indexing performance as extra overhead is required to create the compound file. Disabling a compound file can create a large number of file descriptors during indexing.

The default number of file descriptors available in Linux is 1024. Check the number of open file descriptors using the following command:

```
cat /proc/sys/fs/file-max
```

Check the hard and soft limits of file descriptors using the `ulimit` command:

```
ulimit -Hn
ulimit -Sn
```

To increase the number of file descriptors system wide, edit the file `/etc/sysctl.conf` and add the following line:

```
fs.file-max = 100000
```

The system needs to be rebooted for the changes to take effect.

To temporarily change the number of file descriptors, run the following command as root:

```
Sysctl -w fs.file-max = 100000
```

- **mergeFactor**: Increasing the `mergeFactor` can cause a large number of segments to be merged in one go. This will speed up indexing but slow down searching. If the merge factor is too large, we may run out of file descriptors, and this may even slow down indexing as there would be lots of disk I/O during merging. It is generally recommended to keep the merge factor constant or lower it to improve searching.

Planning your commit strategy

Disable the `autocommit` property during indexing so that commit can be done manually. Autocommit can be a pain as it can cause too frequent commits. Instead, committing manually can reduce the overhead during commits by decreasing the number of commits. Autocommit can be disabled in the `solrconfig.xml` file by setting the `<autocommit><maxtime>` properties to a very large value.

Another strategy would be to configure the `<autocommit><maxtime>` properties to a large value and use the `autoSoftCommit` property for short-time commits to disk. Soft commits are faster as the commit is not synced to disk. Soft commits are used to enable near real time search.

We can also use the `commitWithin` tag instead of the `autoSoftCommit` tag. The former forces documents to be added to Solr via soft commit at certain intervals of time. The `commitWithin` tag can also be used with hard commits via the following configuration:

```
<commitWithin><softCommit>false</softCommit></commitWithin>
```

Avoid using the `autoSoftCommit` / `autoCommit` / `commitWithin` tags while adding bulk documents as it has a major performance impact.

Using better hardware

Indexing involves lots of disk I/O. Therefore, it can be improved by using a local file system instead of a remote file system. Also, using better hardware with higher IO capability, such as **Solid State Drive (SSD)**, can improve writes and speed up the indexing process.

Distributed indexing

When dealing with large amounts of data to be indexed, in addition to speeding up the indexing process, we can work on distributed indexing. Distributed indexing can be done by creating multiple indexes on different machines and finally merging them into a single, large index. Even better would be to create the separate indexes on different Solr machines and use Solr sharding to query the indexes across multiple shards.

For example, an index of 10 million products can be broken into smaller chunks based on the product ID and can be indexed over 10 machines, with each indexing a million products. While searching, we can add these 10 Solr servers as shards and distribute our search queries over these machines.

The SolrCloud solution

SolrCloud provides the high availability and failover solution for an index spanning over multiple Solr servers. If we go ahead with the traditional master-slave model and try implementing a sharded Solr cluster, we will need to create multiple master Solr servers, one for each shard and then slaves for these master servers. We need to take care of the sharding algorithm so that data is distributed across multiple shards. A search has to happen across these shards. Also, we need to take care of any shard that goes down and create a failover setup for the same. Load balancing of search queries is manual. We need to figure out how to distribute the search queries across multiple shards.

SolrCloud handles the scalability challenge for large indexes. It is a cluster of Solr servers or cores that can be bound together as a single Solr (cloud) server. SolrCloud is used when there is a need for highly scalable, fault-tolerant, distributed indexing and search capabilities. With SolrCloud, a single index can span across multiple Solr cores that can be on different Solr servers. Let us go through some of the concepts of SolrCloud:

- **Collection**: A logical index that spans across multiple Solr cores is called a collection. Thus, if we have a two-core Solr index on a single Solr server, it will create two collections with multiple cores in each collection. The cores can reside on multiple Solr servers.

- **Shard**: In SolrCloud, a collection can be sliced into multiple shards. A shard in SolrCloud will consist of multiple copies of the slice residing on different Solr cores. Therefore, in SolrCloud, a collection can have multiple shards. Each shard will have multiple Solr cores that are copies of each other.

- **Leader**: One of the cores within a shard will act as a leader. The leader is responsible for making sure that all the replicas within a shard are up to date.

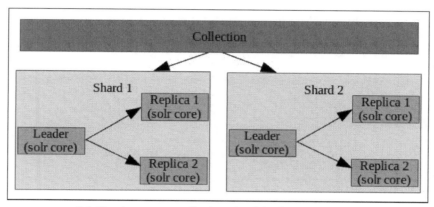

SolrCloud concepts – collection, shard, leader, replicas, core

SolrCloud has a central configuration that can be replicated automatically across all the nodes that are part of the SolrCloud cluster. The central configuration is maintained using a configuration management and coordination system known as Zookeeper. Zookeeper provides reliable coordination across a huge cluster of distributed systems. Solr does not have a master node. It uses Zookeeper to maintain node, shard, and replica information based on configuration files and schemas. Documents can be sent to any server, and Zookeeper will be able to figure out where to index them. If a leader for a shard goes down, another replica is automatically elected as the new leader using Zookeeper.

If a document is sent to a replica during indexing, it is forwarded to the leader. On receiving the document at a leader node, the SolrCloud determines whether the document should go to another shard and forwards it to the leader of that shard. The leader indexes the document and forwards the index notification to its replicas.

SolrCloud provides automatic failover. If a node goes down, indexing and search can happen over another node. Also, search queries are load balanced across multiple shards in the Solr cluster. Near Real Time Indexing is a feature where, as soon as a document is added to the index, the same is available for search. The latest Solr server contains commands for soft commit, which makes documents added to the index available for search immediately without going through the traditional commit process. We would still need to make a hard commit to make changes onto a stable data store. A soft commit can be carried out within a few seconds, while a hard commit takes a few minutes. SolrCloud exploits this feature to provide near real time search across the complete cluster of Solr servers.

It can be difficult to determine the number of shards in a Solr collection in the first go. Moreover, creating more shards or splitting a shard into two can be tedious task if done manually. Solr provides inbuilt commands for splitting a shard. The previous shard is maintained and can be deleted at a later date.

SolrCloud also provides the ability to search the complete collection of one or more particular shards if needed.

SolrCloud removes all the hassles of maintaining a cluster of Solr servers manually and provides an easy interface to handle distributed search and indexing over a cluster of Solr servers with automatic failover. We will be discussing SolrCloud in *Chapter 9, SolrCloud*.

Summary

In this chapter, we went through the basics of indexing in Solr. We saw the structure of the Solr index and how analyzers, tokenizers, and filters work in the conversion of text into searchable tokens. We went through the complexities involved in multilingual search and also discussed the strategies that can be used to handle the complexities. We discussed the formula for measuring the quality of search results and understood the meaning of precision and recall. We saw in brief the problems faced by e-commerce and job websites during indexing and search. We discussed the challenges faced while indexing a large number of documents. We saw some tips on improving the speed of indexing. Finally, we discussed distributed indexing and search and how SolrCloud provides a solution for implementing the same.

2
Customizing the Solr Scoring Algorithm

In this chapter, we will go through the relevance calculation algorithm used by Solr for ranking results and understand how relevance calculation works with reference to the parameters in the algorithm. In addition to this, we will look at tweaking the algorithm and create our own algorithm for scoring results. Then, we will add it as a plugin to Solr and see how the search results are ranked. We will discuss the problems with the default algorithm used in Solr and define a new algorithm known called the information gain model. This chapter will incorporate the following topics:

- The relevance calculation algorithm
- Building a custom scorer
- Drawback of the TF-IDF model
- The information gain model
- Implementing the information gain model
- Options to TF-IDF similarity
- BM25 similarity
- DFR similarity

Relevance calculation

Now that we are aware of how Solr works in the creation of an inverted index and how a search returns results for a query from an index, the question that comes to our mind is how Solr or Lucene (the underlying API) decides which documents should be at the top and how the results are sorted. Of course, we can have custom sorting, where we can sort results based on a particular field. However, how does sorting occur in the absence of any custom sorting query?

The default sorting mechanism in Solr is known as relevance ranking. During a search, Solr calculates the relevance score of each document in the result set and ranks the documents so that the highest scoring documents move to the top. Scoring is the process of determining how relevant a given document is with respect to the input query. The default scoring mechanism is a mix of the **Boolean model** and the **Vector Space Model (VSM)** of information retrieval. The binary model is used to figure out documents that match the query set, and then the VSM is used to calculate the score of each and every document in the result set.

In addition to the VSM, the Lucene scoring mechanism supports a number of pluggable models, such as probabilistic models and language models. However, we will focus on the VSM as it is a default scoring algorithm, and it works pretty well for most of the cases. The VSM requires that the document and queries are represented as weighted vectors in a multidimensional space where each distinct index item is a dimension and weights are TF-IDF values. The TF-IDF formula is the core of the relevance calculation in Lucene. The practical scoring formula used in Lucene is shown in the following image:

$$score(q,d) = coord(q,d) \cdot queryNorm(q) \cdot \sum_{t \text{ in } q} \left(tf(t \text{ in } d) \cdot idf(t^2) \cdot t.getBoost() \cdot norm\ t,d \right)$$

The default implementation of the `tf-idf` equation for Lucene is known as default similarity (the class is `DefaultSimilarity` inside Lucene). Let us look at the terms in the equation before understanding how the formula works:

- `tf(t in d)`: This is the term frequency, or the number of times term `t` (in the query) appears in document `d`. Documents that have more occurrences for a given term will have a higher score. The default implementation for this part of the equation in the `DefaultSimilarity` class is the square root of frequency.

- `idf(t)`: This is the inverse document frequency, or the inverse of the number of documents in which term t appears, also known as the inverse of **DocFreq**. This means that a term that occurs in fewer documents is a rare term and results in a higher score. The implementation in the `DefaultSimilarity` class is as follows:

  `idf(t) = 1+log(numDocs / (docFreq+1))`

- `t.getBoost()`: This is the search time boost of term t in query q as specified in the query syntax.

- `norms(t,d)`: This function is a product of index time boosts and the length normalization factor. During indexing, a field can be boosted by calling the `field.setBoost()` function before adding the field to the document. This is known as index time boost. Length normalization (`lengthNorm`) is computed on the basis of the number of tokens in a field for a document. The purpose of `lengthNorm` factor is to provide a higher score for shorter fields. Once calculated, this cannot be modified during a search.

- `coord(q,d)`: This function is a score factor that specifies the number of query terms that are found in a document. A document that has more of the query's terms will have a higher score than that of another document that has fewer query terms.

- `queryNorm(q)`: This function is used to make the scores between queries comparable. As this is the same factor for all documents, it does not affect the document ranking but just makes the scores from different queries or indexes comparable.

Boosting is used to change the score of documents retrieved from a search. There is index time boosting and search time or query time boosting of documents. Index time boosting is used to boost fields in documents permanently. Once a document is boosted during index time, the boost is stored with the document. Therefore, after the search completes and during relevancy calculation, the stored boost is taken into consideration. Search time or query time boosting is dynamic. Certain fields can be boosted in the query that can result in certain documents getting a higher relevancy score than others. For example, we can boost the score of books by adding the parameter `cat:book^4` in the query. This boosting will make the score of books relatively higher than the score of other items in the index.

For details on the scoring algorithm, please go through the following documentation: `https://lucene.apache.org/core/4_6_0/core/org/apache/lucene/search/similarities/TFIDFSimilarity.html`.

Building a custom scorer

Now that we know how the default relevance calculation works, let us look at how to create a custom scorer. The default scorer used for relevance calculation is known as `DefaultSimilarity`. In order to create a custom scorer, we will need to extend `DefaultSimilarity` and create our own similarity class and eventually use it in our Solr schema. Solr also provides the option of specifying different similarity classes for different `fieldTypes` configuration directive in the schema. Thus, we can create different similarity classes and then specify different scoring algorithms for different `fieldTypes` as also a different global `Similarity` class.

Let us create a custom scorer that disables the IDF factor of the scoring algorithm. Why would we want to disable the IDF? The IDF boosts documents that have query terms that are rare in the index. Therefore, if a query contains a term that occurs in fewer documents, the documents containing the term will be ranked higher. This does not make sense for certain fields, such as name, designation, or age.

The default implementation for `idf` function can be found in the Lucene source code inside the `org.apache.lucene.search.similarities.DefaultSimilarity` class:

```
public float idf(long docFreq, long numDocs) {
    return (float)(Math.log(numDocs/(double)(docFreq+1)) + 1.0);
}
```

In this code snippet, `numDocs` is the total number of documents in the collection and `docFreq` is the number of documents that have the specific term from the query. To customize the IDF, we would extend the `DefaultSimilarity` class and create a `NoIDFSimilarity` class that returns 1 for `idf` as indicated by the following code:

```
public class NoIDFSimilarity extends DefaultSimilarity {
  @Override
  public float idf(long docFreq, long numDocs) {
    return 1.0f;
  }
}
```

The `NoIDFSimilarity` class can be used where we would like to ignore the commonality of a term across the entire collection. If we do not consider the rareness of a term in the algorithm, both common and rare terms in the entire index will have the same ranking. This makes sense when a search is on a targeted field, such as a name, a category, or an e-mail address, where the rareness of the term does not make much sense.

Let us compile our customized similarity classes and implement them in our schema. For this, we need the `lucene-core-4.6.0.jar` file, which can be found in the `<solr folder>/example/solr-webapp/webapp/WEB-INF/lib/` folder. Run the following command to compile the `NoIDFSimilarity.java` file:

```
javac -cp /opt/solr-4.6.0/example/solr-webapp/webapp/WEB-INF/lib/lucene-core-4.6.0.jar:. -d . NoIDFSimilarity.java
```

 The commands here are for Linux systems. For Windows systems, use Windows path format while executing the commands.

This will compile the Java file into the `com.myscorer` folder. Now create a `myscorer.jar` file for the package `com.myscorer` by running the `jar` command on the created folder `com`:

```
jar -cvf myscorer.jar com
```

The JAR file needs to be placed with the Lucene JAR file in our Solr library:

```
cp myscorer.jar /opt/solr-4.6.0/example/solr-webapp/webapp/WEB-INF/lib/
```

In order to check the scorer, let us index all files in the Solr default installation under the `exampledocs` folder. In Solr 4.6, execution of the following commands inside the `exampledocs` folder will result in indexing of all files:

```
java -jar post.jar *.xml
java -Dtype=text/csv -jar post.jar *.csv
java -Dtype=application/json -jar post.jar *.json
```

This step will index all the XML files along with the `books.csv` and `books.json` files into the index. The index should contain approximately 46 documents. This can be verified by running the following query on the Solr query interface: `http://localhost:8983/solr/collection1/select?q=*:*`

Search for `ipod` in the field `text` with the `DefaultSimilarity` class and note the score and order of a few documents that appear on the top.

Also, note that the `debugQuery=true` parameter in the query gives the name of the similarity class used. `[DefaultSimilarity]` in this case.

```
http://localhost:8983/Solr/collection1/select/q=text:ipod&fl=*&debugQ
uery=true
```

Search for ipod using DefaultSimilarity

Now let's modify our `schema.xml` file and put `NoIDFSimilarity` as the default similarity class to be used and observe how our search behaves. Add the following line to the end of `schema.xml` file and restart Solr:

```
<similarity class="com.myscorer.NoIDFSimilarity"/>
```

This will change the similarity for all fields in our schema to the `NoIDFSimilarity` class. On running the same query again, we can see that scores of the documents have changed. Also, the similarity class is now `[NoIDFSimilarity]`.

Solr will need to be restarted whenever schema.xml or solrconfig.xml file is changed. Only then will the changes be visible in Solr.

```
<str name="parsedquery_toString">text:ipod</str>
▼<lst name="explain">
  ▼<str name="IW-02">
      0.4330127 = (MATCH) weight(text:ipod in 4)
      [NoIDFSimilarity], result of: 0.4330127 = fieldWeight in
      4, product of: 1.7320508 = tf(freq=3.0), with freq of:
      3.0 = termFreq=3.0 1.0 = idf(docFreq=3, maxDocs=46) 0.25
      = fieldNorm(doc=4)
  </str>
  ▼<str name="F8V7067-APL-KIT">
      0.25 = (MATCH) weight(text:ipod in 3) [NoIDFSimilarity],
      result of: 0.25 = fieldWeight in 3, product of: 1.0 =
      tf(freq=1.0), with freq of: 1.0 = termFreq=1.0 1.0 =
      idf(docFreq=3, maxDocs=46) 0.25 = fieldNorm(doc=3)
  </str>
  ▼<str name="MA147LL/A">
      0.09375 = (MATCH) weight(text:ipod in 5)
      [NoIDFSimilarity], result of: 0.09375 = fieldWeight in 5,
      product of: 1.0 = tf(freq=1.0), with freq of: 1.0 =
      termFreq=1.0 1.0 = idf(docFreq=3, maxDocs=46) 0.09375 =
      fieldNorm(doc=5)
  </str>
```

Search for ipod using NoIDFSimilarity

Let us create another custom scorer where length normalization is disabled. The default implementation for the lengthNorm function can be found in the Lucene source code inside the org.apache.lucene.search.similarities. DefaultSimilarity class:

```
public float lengthNorm(FieldInvertState state) {
    final int numTerms;
    if (discountOverlaps)
      numTerms = state.getLength() - state.getNumOverlap();
    else
      numTerms = state.getLength();
    return state.getBoost() * ((float) (1.0 / Math.sqrt(numTerms)));
}
```

In a broad sense, this extracts the number of terms in a field and returns `Boost *` `(1/sqrt(number of terms))` so that shorter fields have a higher boost. In order to disable boosting due to shorter field length, either consider the number of terms as 1 for this algorithm or return 1 irrespective of the number of terms and the boost on the field. Let us create our own implementation of `DefaultSimilarity` known as `NoLengthNormSimilarity` where we will simply return the boost for the field and discard any calculations with respect to the number of terms in the field. The code will override the `lengthNorm` function as follows:

```
public class NoLengthNormSimilarity extends DefaultSimilarity {
  // return field's boost irrespective of the length of the field.
  @Override
  public float lengthNorm(FieldInvertState state) {
    return state.getBoost();
  }
}
```

 The purpose of creating a similarity class without length normalization is to treat documents with different number of terms in their field similarly.

Thus, a document with say 5 tokens will be treated as equal to another document with say 50, 500, or 5000 tokens. Now, in a search for **WiFi router**, two products, say **Netgear R6300 WiFi router** and **D-Link DSL-2750U Wireless N ADSL2 4-Port WiFi router**, will have the same boost. Earlier with the default similarity, the **Netgear R6300 WiFi router** would have had a higher boost as it had a smaller number of terms than that in **D-Link DSL-2750U Wireless N ADSL2 4-Port WiFi router**. On the negative side, a document with a field having the Netgear R6300 WiFi router will have the same boost as another document with the field having the following text:

```
Experience blazing speeds upto 300Mbps of wireless speed while you
upload and download data within a matter of seconds when you use this
WiFi router.
```

A user searching for a Wi-Fi router is specifically searching for a product rather than a description of the product. Hence, it would make more sense if we use the `NoLengthNormSimilarity` class in our product names in an e-commerce website.

It is possible to use two different similarity classes for two different `fieldTypes` in Solr. To implement this, we need a global similarity class that can support the specification of the `fieldType` level similarity class implementation. This is provided by `solr.SchemaSimilarityFactory`.

Simply add this similarity class at the global level at the end of `schema.xml` file as follows, which will replace the earlier similarities we had introduced:

```
<similarity class="solr.SchemaSimilarityFactory"/>
```

Specify the `fieldType` level similarity classes in the section where `fieldType` is defined. For example, we can add `NoLengthNormSimilarity` to `fieldType` text_general and `NoIDFSimilarity` to text_ws, as follows:

```
<fieldType name="text_ws" class="solr.TextField"
positionIncrementGap="100">
    <analyzer>
        <tokenizer class="solr.WhitespaceTokenizerFactory"/>
        <filter class="solr.EnglishMinimalStemFilterFactory"/>
    </analyzer>
    <similarity class="com.myscorer.NoIDFSimilarity"/>
</fieldType>


<fieldType name="text_general" class="solr.TextField"
positionIncrementGap="100">
    <analyzer type="index">
        <tokenizer class="solr.StandardTokenizerFactory"/>
        <filter class="solr.StopFilterFactory" ignoreCase="true"
words="stopwords.txt" />
        <filter class="solr.LowerCaseFilterFactory"/>
    </analyzer>
    <analyzer type="query">
        <tokenizer class="solr.StandardTokenizerFactory"/>
        <filter class="solr.StopFilterFactory" ignoreCase="true"
words="stopwords.txt" />
        <filter class="solr.SynonymFilterFactory" synonyms="synonyms.
txt" ignoreCase="true" expand="true"/>
        <filter class="solr.LowerCaseFilterFactory"/>
    </analyzer>
    <similarity class="com.myscorer.NoLengthNormSimilarity"/>
</fieldType>
```

This can be tested by restarting Solr and running the Solr query again with `debugQuery=true`, which is similar to what we did before for testing `NoIDFSimilarity`.

There are a few other similarity algorithms that are available in Solr. The details are available in the following API documents: `http://lucene.apache.org/solr/4_6_0/solr-core/org/apache/solr/search/similarities/package-summary.html`.

Some of these similarities, such as `SweetSpotSimilarity`, have an option of specifying additional parameters for different `fieldTypes`. This can be specified in `schema.xml` file while defining the similarity class implementation for `fieldType` by adding additional parameters during definition. A sample implementation is as shown in the following code snippet:

```
<fieldType name="text_baseline" class="solr.TextField" indexed="true"
stored="false">
   <analyzer
class="org.apache.lucene.analysis.standard.StandardAnalyzer"/>
   <similarity class="solr.SweetSpotSimilarityFactory">
     <!-- TF -->
     <float name="baselineTfMin">6.0</float>
     <float name="baselineTfBase">1.5</float>
     <!-- plateau norm -->
     <int name="lengthNormMin">3</int>
     <int name="lengthNormMax">5</int>
     <float name="lengthNormSteepness">0.5</float>
   </similarity>
</fieldType>
```

We will discuss some of these similarity algorithms later in this chapter.

Drawbacks of the TF-IDF model

Suppose, on an e-commerce website, a customer is searching for a jacket and intends to purchase a jacket with a unique design. The keyword entered is `unique jacket`. What happens at the Solr end?

`http://solr.server/solr/clothes/?q=unique+jacket`

Now, `unique` is a comparatively rare keyword. There would be fewer items or documents that mention unique in their description. Let us see how this affects the ranking of our results via the TF-IDF scoring algorithm. A relook at the scoring algorithm with respect to this query is shown in the following diagram:

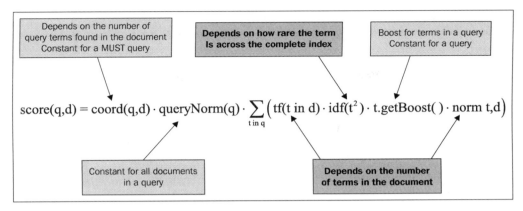

Depends on the number of query terms found in the document Constant for a MUST query

Depends on how rare the term Is across the complete index

Boost for terms in a query Constant for a query

$$\text{score(q,d)} = \text{coord(q,d)} \cdot \text{queryNorm(q)} \cdot \sum_{t \text{ in } q} \left(\text{tf(t in d)} \cdot \text{idf}(t^2) \cdot \text{t.getBoost( )} \cdot \text{norm t,d} \right)$$

Constant for all documents in a query

Depends on the number of terms in the document

A relook at the TF-IDF scoring algorithm

The following parameters in the scoring formula do not affect the ranking of the documents in the query result:

- `coord(q,d)`: This would be constant for a MUST query. Herein we are searching for both `unique` and `jacket`, so all documents will have both the keywords and the `coord(q,d)` value will be the same for all documents.

- `queryNorm(q)`: This is used to make the scores from different queries comparable, as it is a constant value and does not affect the ranking of documents.

- `t.getBoost()`: This is the search time boost for term `t` specified in query `q`. Again this is constant for all documents, as it depends on the query terms and not on the document content.

The following parameters depend on the term in a document and affect the ranking of the documents in the result set:

- `tf(t in d)`: This is the term frequency and depends directly on the terms in the document. As the content within the documents varies so does the frequency and the score.

- `norm(t,d)`: This contains the index time boost and length normalization information. Index time boosts are constant for boosted fields. If a document contains a boosted field that has the searched term, it will contribute more to the final score. Length normalization moves documents with shorter field lengths to the top. Therefore, a term occurring in a shorter field in the document will contribute more to the score.

- `idf(t)`: This is a measure of the rarity of the term across the index. If a searched term occurs in fewer documents, it will contribute more to the score than a searched term occurring in more number of documents.

Coming back to our earlier example, a search for a `unique jacket`, the term `unique` will have fewer occurrences than the term `jacket`, so the IDF of `unique` will be more than that of `jacket`:

```
idf(unique) > idf(jacket)
```

Thus, the scores of documents with `unique` in them will be more and they will be ranked higher. What if a document has multiple occurrences of the term `unique`?

```
score("A unique book on selecting unique jackets") > score("This is
an unique jacket. Better than other jackets")
```

However, `unique` is an attribute. It actually does not tell us anything useful about the product being searched. We can make the same argument for other keywords such as `nice`, `handmade`, or `comfortable`. These are low-information words that can be used for matching but can lead to unusual ranking of the search results. The problem we saw was due to the IDF factor of the TF-IDF algorithm. The IDF gives importance to the rareness of a term but ignores the usefulness of the term.

Another problem that is likely to arise because of the IDF is while dealing with a large and sharded index. The IDF of a term in each shard can be different. Let us see how. Suppose an index has **2** shards, `sh1` and `sh2`. The total number of documents in the index including both shards is say n out of which `sh1` contains k documents and `sh2` contains `n-k` documents.

The formula for the IDF of term `t`, which we saw earlier was:

```
idf(t) = 1+log(numDocs / (docFreq+1))
```

Suppose we search for the term `jacket` across both the shards. Let us see what happens to the IDF of `jacket` on shards `sh1` and `sh2` and the entire index.

Shard `sh1` has *k* documents each having different frequencies for the term jacket. The IDF of the term jacket on `sh1` would be calculated separately as follows:

Sh1	Doc #	Doc$_1$	Doc$_2$	....	Doc$_{k-1}$	Doc$_k$
	frequency	1	3	...	0	5

$$IDF_{Sh1}(jacket) = 1 + log(k / (sumof(freq \text{ "jacket" for } k \text{ documents})+1))$$

IDF for jacket on shard sh1

Shard `sh2` had the remaining (n-k) documents. Again the frequency of the term jacket will be different across each document in shard `sh2` as compared to that in shard `sh1`. The IDF of the term jacket for `sh2` will be different from that for `sh1`.

Sh2	Doc #	Doc_{k+1}	Doc_{k+2}	....	Doc_{n-1}	Doc_n
	frequency	0	4	...	1	1

$$IDF_{sh2}(jacket) = 1 + \log(\ (n\text{-}k) \ / \ (sumof(freq \ \text{"jacket" for} \ (n\text{-}k) \ documents)+1) \ )$$

IDF for jacket on shard sh2

What about the actual IDF for the term jacket across the entire index? If the index had not been sharded, the calculation of IDF for the term jacket would have depended on its frequency across n documents in the entire index.

$$IDF(jacket) = 1 + \log\left(n / \left(sumof\left(freq \text{ "jacket" for } n \text{ documents}\right)+1\right)\right)$$

IDF of jacket on the entire index

Therefore, the IDF of the term jacket is different across `sh1`, `sh2`, and the entire index:

$$IDF_{sh1}(jacket) \mathrel{!}= IDF_{sh2}(jacket) \mathrel{!}= IDF(jacket)$$

Unequal IDF across sh1, sh2, and the entire index

This means that a search for a term across different shards can result in different scores for the same term. Moreover, the score would not match with what it should have been across the entire index. This can lead to unexpected scoring and ranking of results.

One way to handle this scenario is to implement a strategy such that all the shards share the index statistics with each other during scoring. However, this can be very messy and can lead to performance issues if the number of shards is large. Another way is to index the documents in a fashion such that the terms are equally distributed across all shards. This solution, too, is messy and mostly not feasible. As the number of documents is large, it may not be feasible to pre-process them and push them into certain shards. SolrCloud provides a better approach to handling this distribution of documents. We will have a look at it in *Chapter 9, SolrCloud*.

The information gain model

The information gain model is a type of machine learning concept that can be used in place of the inverse document frequency approach. The concept being used here is the probability of observing two terms together on the basis of their occurrence in an index. We use an index to evaluate the occurrence of two terms x and y and calculate the information gain for each term in the index:

- P(x): Probability of a term x appearing in a listing
- P(x|y): Probability of the term x appearing given a term y also appears

The information gain value of the term y can be computed as follows:

$$in\ fo(y) = \sum_{x \in X} \log\left(\frac{P(x|y)}{P(x)}\right) * P(x|y)$$

Information gain equation

This equation says that the more number of times term y appears with term x with respect to the total occurrence of term x, the higher is the information gain for that y.

Let us take a few examples to understand the concept.

In the earlier example, if the term unique appears with jacket a large number of times as compared to the total occurrence of the term jacket, then unique will have a higher score. However, unique can appear with other words as well, and jacket can appear without the word unique. On the basis of the number of times they conditionally appear together, the value of info("unique") will be calculated.

Another example is the term jacket that appears with almost all words and quite a large number of times. Almost all the jackets in the store will be labeled jacket along with certain terms that describe the jacket. Hence, jacket will have a higher information gain value.

Now, if we replace the IDF with the information gain model, the problem that we were facing earlier because of the rareness of the term unique will not occur. The information gain for the term unique will be much lower than the IDF of the term. The difference between the information gain values for the two terms, unique and jacket, will be higher than the difference between the terms' inverse document frequencies:

```
info("jacket")/info("unique") > idf("jacket")/idf("unique")
```

Therefore, after using information gain, instead of IDF, in our scoring formula, we obtain the following:

```
score("A unique book on selecting unique jackets") < score("This is
an unique jacket. Better than other jackets")
```

Information gain can also be used as an automatic stop word filter as terms that conditionally occur with many different terms in the index are bound to get a very low information gain value.

Implementing the information gain model

The problem with the information gain model is that, for each term in the index, we will have to evaluate the occurrence of every other term. The complexity of the algorithm will be of the order of square of the two terms, `square(xy)`. It is not possible to compute this using a simple machine. What is recommended is that we create a map-reduce job and use a distributed Hadoop cluster to compute the information gain for each term in the index.

Our distributed Hadoop cluster would do the following:

- Count all occurrences of each term in the index
- Count all occurrences of each co-occurring term in the index
- Construct a hash table or a map of co-occurring terms
- Calculate the information gain for each term and store it in a file in the Hadoop cluster

In order to implement this in our scoring algorithm, we will need to build a custom scorer where the IDF calculation is overwritten by the algorithm for deriving the information gain for the term from the Hadoop cluster. If we have a huge index, we will have information gain for most of the terms in the index. However, there can still be cases where the term is not available in the information gain files in the Hadoop cluster. In such cases, we would like to fall back on our original IDF algorithm or return a default value. This may result in some skewed value for the score, as the IDF values may not be comparable with information gain for any term.

Once we have the custom similarity ready, we will have to create a `copyField` parameter that implements the custom similarity we have built. And copy the earlier fields for which we want the similarity to be altered to this copyField we have created. The schema would then have multiple copies of the same field, each with different implementations of the similarity class.

In order to determine whether our implementation of the similarity class has been more beneficial to the users, we can perform **A/B testing**. We already have multiple copy fields, each with its own similarity class implementation. We can divide our app servers into two parts, one serving queries out of the field that implements the information gain model and another serving queries out of the field that implements the default IDF model. We can measure the response or conversion ratio (for an e-commerce site) from both the implementations and decide which implementation has been beneficial for us.

The A/B testing methodology is very useful in taking decisions based on data for which implementation has been successful for the business. We can test with live users where some users are exposed to a particular algorithm or flow, while others are exposed to a different algorithm or site flow. It is very important to put evaluation metrics in place so that the output of each test can be measured separately. A/B testing is the perfect way for implementing new concepts side by side and determining which concept is more successful.

Options to TF-IDF similarity

In addition to the default TF-IDF similarity implementation, other similarity implementations are available by default with Lucene and Solr. These models also work around the frequency of the searched term and the documents containing the searched term. However, the concept and the algorithm used to calculate the score differ.

Let us go through some of the most used ranking algorithms.

BM25 similarity

The **Best Matching (BM25)** algorithm is a probabilistic **Information Retrieval (IR)** model, while TF-IDF is a vector space model for information retrieval. The probabilistic IR model operates such that, given some relevant and non-relevant documents, we can calculate the probability of a term appearing in a relevant document, and this could be the basis of a classifier that decides whether the documents are relevant or not.

On a practical front, the BM25 model also defines the weight of each term as a product of some term frequency function and some inverse document frequency function and then uses the weight to calculate the score for the whole document with respect to the given query, as follows:

```
Score = function1(tf) * function2(idf)
```

The purpose of `function1(tf)` is to specify a limit on the factor contributing to the score for high-frequency terms. As the term frequency increases, the output of the function in BM25 approaches a limit. Therefore, for high-frequency terms, any further increase in the term frequency does not have much effect on the relevance. The output of the function is such that, for BM25, the increase in `tf` contribution to the score will be less than that in the TF-IDF model. This means given that the documents and queries are the same across the TF-IDF model and the BM25 model, the factor contributing to the score for term frequency in a document will be higher in the TF-IDF model than that in the BM25 model.

The BM25 model takes an initialization parameter `k1` that is used to control or normalize the term frequency. The default value for `k1` is `1.2`, and it can be changed by passing a separate value.

This is how `k1` theoretically affects the term frequency for the `ith` term in the BM25 algorithm:

```
tfi = tfi/(k1+tfi)
```

Another major factor that is used in BM25 is the average document length. BM25 uses document length to compensate for the fact that a longer document in general has more words and is thus more likely to have a higher term frequency, without necessarily being more pertinent to the term and thus no more relevant to the query. However, there may be other documents that have a wider scope and where the high term frequencies are justified. The BM25 similarity accepts another parameter `b` that is used to control to what degree the document length normalizes term frequency values. Parameter `b` is used in conjunction with document length `dl` and average document length `avdl` to calculate the actual term frequency.

To evaluate the full weight of the term, we need to multiply the term frequency with the IDF. BM25 does IDF differently than the default TF-IDF implementation. If `D` is the total number of documents in the collection and `di` is the number of documents containing the `ith` term in the query, IDFi (for the ith term) is calculated as follows:

```
IDFi = log(1 + ( (D-di+0.5) / (di+0.5) ))
```

The full weight of the term is calculated as follows:

```
Wi = IDFi * boost * TFi
```

In this case:

```
TFi = ((k1+1)*tfi) / (tfi + k1(1-b+(b*dl/avdl)))
```

The default TF-IDF similarity implementation in Lucene does not provide the custom term frequency normalization or document length normalization parameters. This is available in BM25. Tuning the normalization parameters k1 and b can result in better scoring and ranking of documents than that offered by the default TF-IDF similarity formula. It is generally recommended to keep the value of b between 0.5 and 0.8 and that of k1 between 1.2 and 2.

Again it depends on the document collection as to which similarity algorithm would produce better results. The BM25 algorithm is useful for short documents or fields. The best way to determine whether it is good for our collection is to use it in A/B testing with a copy of the same field.

We have already seen the scores for DefaultSimilarity and NoIDFSimilarity earlier in this chapter. Let us implement the BM25 similarity algorithm in our earlier index and see the results. Make the following changes to the schema.xml file. We have modified the values of k1 and b as 1.3 and 0.76, respectively, as follows:

```
<similarity class="solr.BM25SimilarityFactory">
        <float name="k1">1.3</float>
        <float name="b">0.76</float>
</similarity>
```

We will need to delete and re-index all the documents. To delete the documents, pass the delete command in the browser URL:

http://localhost:8983/solr/update?stream.body=<delete><query>*:*</query></delete>

http://localhost:8983/solr/update?stream.body=

To index the documents again from the exampledocs folder, run the following commands on the console:

```
java -jar post.jar *.xml
java -Dtype=text/csv -jar post.jar *.csv
java -Dtype=application/json -jar post.jar *.json
```

On running a search for `ipod` using BM25 similarity, we get the following output:

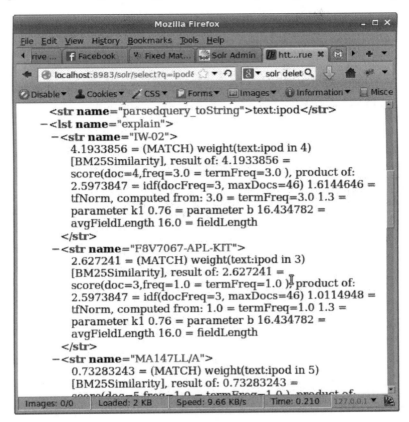

Scores for BM25Similarity

Note that the maximum and minimum scores for `BM25similarity` are `4.19` and `0.73`, respectively. On the other hand, the maximum and minimum scores for `DefaultSimilarity` are `1.49` and `0.32`, respectively. Changing the values of `k1` and `b` will change the scores.

BM25 scoring can be used for short documents. In an e-commerce environment, it can be applied to product names, while the default TF-IDF scoring can be used in product descriptions. Again, the scoring mechanism has to be tweaked by changing **k1** and **b** to obtain the expected search results.

BM25 similarity method reference:
`http://lucene.apache.org/core/4_6_0/core/`
`org/apache/lucene/search/similarities/`
`BM25Similarity.html`

DFR similarity

DFR stands for **Divergence From Randomness**. The DFR concept can be explained as follows. The more the divergence of the within-document term frequency from its frequency within the collection, the more the information carried by word t in document d. The DFR scoring formula contains three separate components — the basic model, the after effect, and an additional normalization component. To construct a DFR formula, we need to specify a value for all the three components mentioned previously.

Possible values for the basic model are:

- Be: Limiting form of the Bose-Einstein model
- G: Geometric approximation of the Bose-Einstein model
- P: Poisson approximation of the binomial model
- D: Divergence approximation of the binomial model
- I(n): Inverse document frequency
- I(ne): Inverse expected document frequency (combination of Poisson and IDF)
- I(F): Inverse term frequency (approximation of I(ne))

The possible values for the after effect are:

- L: Laplace's law of succession
- B: Ratio of two Bernoulli processes
- none: No first normalization

Additional normalization is also known as length normalization. It has the following options:

- H1: Uniform distribution of term frequency
  - parameter c (float): A hyper-parameter that controls the term frequency normalization with respect to the document length. The default is 1.

- **H2**: Term frequency density inversely related to length
  - ° parameter c (float): A hyper-parameter that controls the term frequency normalization with respect to the document length. The default is 1.

- **H3**: Term frequency normalization provided by a Dirichlet prior
  - ° parameter mu (float): Smoothing parameter μ. The default is 800

- **Z**: Term frequency normalization provided by a Zipfian relation
  - ° parameter z (float): Represents A/(A+1) where A measures the specificity of the language. The default is 0.3.

- **none**: No second normalization

In order to use the DFR similarity in Solr, we will need to add the solr. DFRSimilarityFactory class in our schema.xml file. A sample implementation of the DFR similarity is as follows:

```
<similarity class="solr.DFRSimilarityFactory">
  <str name="basicModel">G</str>
  <str name="afterEffect">B</str>
  <str name="normalization">H2</str>
  <float name="c">7</float>
</similarity>
```

We will need to restart Solr and then delete and index all the documents from the index. On running a search, we should be getting DFRSimilarity in our debug query output.

The DFR scoring algorithm provides a wide variety of tweaking options to choose from while defining the actual algorithm. It is important to choose the appropriate option or options and perform A/B testing to determine which one suits the data and the end user.

In addition to the above discussed similarity classes, we also have other lesser used similarity classes such as IBSimilarity, LMDirichletSimilarity, or LMJelinekMercerSimilarity. We also saw SweetSpotSimilarity earlier in this chapter.

 Reference to DFR similarity can be found at: http://lucene. apache.org/core/4_6_0/core/org/apache/lucene/ search/similarities/DFRSimilarity.html.

Summary

In this chapter, we saw the default relevance algorithm used by Solr and/or Lucene. We saw how the algorithm can be tweaked or overwritten to change the parameters that control the score of a document for a given query. We saw how to use multiple similarity classes for different fields within the same Solr schema. We explored the information gain model and saw the complexities involved in implementing the same. Furthermore, we saw additional alternatives to the default TF-IDF similarity available with Solr and Lucene. We went through the BM25 and DFR similarity models. We also understood that, in addition to selecting a similarity algorithm, we should perform A/B testing to determine which scoring algorithm the end users prefer and can be beneficial to the business.

In the next chapter, we will explore Solr internals and build some custom queries. In addition, we will understand how different parsers work in the creation of a Solr query and how the query actually gets executed. We will also write our own Solr plugin.

3
Solr Internals and Custom Queries

In this chapter, we will see how the relevance scorer works on the inverted index. We will understand how AND and OR clauses work in a query and look at how query filters and the minimum match parameter work internally. We will understand how the eDisMax query parser works. We will implement our own query language as a Solr plugin using which we will perform a proximity search. This chapter will give us an insight into the customization of the query logic and creation of custom query parsers as plugins in Solr. This chapter will cover the following topics:

- How a scorer works on an inverted index
- How OR and AND clauses work
- How the eDisMax query parser works
- The minimum should match parameter
- How filters work
- Using **Bibliographic Retrieval Services** (**BRS**) queries instead of **DisMax**
- Proximity search using **SWAN** (**Same, With, Adj, Near**) queries
- Creating a parboiled parser
- Building a Solr plugin for SWAN queries
- Integrating the SWAN plugin in Solr

Working of a scorer on an inverted index

We have, so far, understood what an inverted index is and how relevance calculation works. Let us now understand how a scorer works on an inverted index. Suppose we have an index with the following three documents:

Doc Id	Text
1	Apples are red in color
2	Oranges are orange in color
3	strawberries are red and not orange in color

3 Documents

To index the document, we have applied `WhitespaceTokenizer` along with the `EnglishMinimalStemFilterFactory` class. This breaks the sentence into tokens by splitting whitespace, and `EnglishMinimalStemFilterFactory` converts plural English words to their singular forms. The index thus created would be similar to that shown as follows:

Term	Doc Ids
apple	1
are	1, 2, 3
red	1, 3
in	1, 2, 3
color	1, 2, 3
orange	2, 3
strawberry	3
and	3
not	3

An inverted index

A search for the term **orange** will give documents **2** and **3** in its result. On running a debug on the query, we can see that the scores for both the documents are different and document **2** is ranked higher than document **3**. The term frequency of **orange** in document **2** is higher than that in document **3**.

However, this does not affect the score much as the number of terms in the document is small. What affects the score here is the `fieldNorm` value, which ranks shorter documents higher than longer documents.

 A debug can be run on a query by appending `debugQuery=true` to the Solr query.

```
▼<lst name="debug">
    <str name="rawquerystring">orange</str>
    <str name="querystring">orange</str>
    <str name="parsedquery">text:orange</str>
    <str name="parsedquery_toString">text:orange</str>
  ▼<lst name="explain">
    ▼<str name="2">
        0.4375 = (MATCH) weight(text:orange in 0)
        [DefaultSimilarity], result of: 0.4375 = fieldWeight in 0,
        product of: 1.0 = tf(freq=1.0), with freq of: 1.0 =
        termFreq=1.0 1.0 = idf(docFreq=2, maxDocs=3) 0.4375 =
        fieldNorm(doc=0)
      </str>
    ▼<str name="3">
        0.3125 = (MATCH) weight(text:orange in 0)
        [DefaultSimilarity], result of: 0.3125 = fieldWeight in 0,
        product of: 1.0 = tf(freq=1.0), with freq of: 1.0 =
        termFreq=1.0 1.0 = idf(docFreq=2, maxDocs=3) 0.3125 =
        fieldNorm(doc=0)
```

Relevance score

Inside the Lucene API, when a query is presented to the `IndexSearcher` class for search, `IndexReader` is opened and the query is passed to it and the result is collected in the `Collector` object — instance of `Collector` class. The `IndexSearcher` class also initializes the scorer and calculates the score for each document in the binary result set. This calculation is fast and it happens within a loop.

Working of OR and AND clauses

Let us see how the collector and scorer work together to calculate the results for both OR and AND clauses. Let us first focus on the OR clause. Considering the earlier index, suppose we perform the following search:

```
orange OR strawberry OR not
```

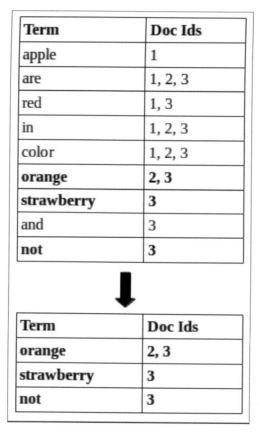

Term	Doc Ids
apple	1
are	1, 2, 3
red	1, 3
in	1, 2, 3
color	1, 2, 3
orange	**2, 3**
strawberry	**3**
and	3
not	**3**

Term	Doc Ids
orange	**2, 3**
strawberry	**3**
not	**3**

A search for orange OR strawberry OR not

On the basis of the terms in the query, **Doc Id 1** was rejected during the Boolean filtering logic. We will need to introduce the concept of **accumulator** here. The purpose of the accumulator is to loop through each term in the query and pass the documents that contain the term to the **collector**.

In the present case, when the accumulator looks for documents containing **orange**, it gets documents **2** and **3**. The output of the accumulator in this case is **2x1, 3x1**, where **2** and **3** are the document IDs and **1** is the number of times the term **orange** occurs in both the documents.Next, it will process the term **strawberry** where it will get document ID **3**. Now, the accumulator outputs **3x1** that adds to our previous output **3x1** and forms **3x2**, meaning that document ID **3** contains two of our input terms. The term **not** is processed in a similar fashion.

Sequence	Term	Doc Ids	Accumulator
1	orange	2, 3	2x1, 3x1
2	strawberry	3	2x1, 3x2
3	not	3	2x1, 3x3

An accumulator at work

Here **Sequence** denotes the sequence in which the terms are processed.

The **Collector** will get **Doc Id 2** with a score of **1**, as it occurs only in one document and **Doc Id 3** with a score of **3**. Therefore, the output from the collector will be as follows:

Collector	
Doc Id	**Score**
3	3
2	1

Document scores

In this case, since the score for **Doc Id 3** is higher, it will be ranked higher than *document* **2**. This type of search is known as a *"term at a time"* search, since we are processing documents for a term and we go through the terms in the query one by one to process the result.

The score here is a relative representation of frequency. It is not the actual score as per the equation shown in the following image that can be also found in *Chapter 2, Customizing the Solr Scoring Algorithm*:

$$\text{score(q,d)} = \text{coord(q,d)} \cdot \text{queryNorm(q)} \cdot \sum_{t \text{ in q}} \left(\text{tf(t in d)} \cdot \text{idf(t)}^2 \cdot \text{t.getBoost()} \cdot \text{norm(t,d)} \right)$$

Let us see how the AND clause works in filtering and ranking results. Let us perform an AND search with the following clause:

```
color AND red AND orange
```

While searching with the AND clause, first all terms matching the query are selected from the index. The collector then selects the document id corresponding to the first term and matches it against the document ids corresponding to the remaining terms.

Term	Doc Ids
apple	1
are	1, 2, 3
red	**1, 3**
in	1, 2, 3
color	**1, 2, 3**
orange	**2, 3**
strawberry	3
and	3
not	3

Term	Doc Ids
color	**1, 2, 3**
red	**1, 3**
orange	**2, 3**

Query: color AND red AND orange

In this case, **Doc Id 1** will be selected and matched against IDs corresponding to terms **red** and **orange**. Since no match is found with the term **orange**, the next document (**Doc Id 2**) corresponding to the term **color** will be selected, which is again not found in term **red**. Finally, **Doc Id 3** will be selected and it finds a match with the terms **red** and **orange**. The accumulator will output only document ID **3** in this case. This concept is known as *"doc at a time"* search, as we are processing documents instead of terms.

Collector	
Doc Id	**Score**
3	3

Document scores

In most cases, the query would be a mix of AND and OR clauses. Therefore, the algorithm for finding and ranking the results depends on the query parameters.

The *minimum should match* parameter, which is a part of the eDisMax query parser and discussed later in this book, is also an important factor in deciding the algorithm to be used for a search. In the case of an OR query, the *minimum should match* parameter is taken as 1, as only one term out of all the terms in our query should match. As seen in this case, the term at a time algorithm was used for search. The AND query results in a *minimum should match* parameter that is more than 1, and in this case, the *doc at a time* search was used.

The complexity of both the algorithms is shown in the following image:

Algorithms	Doc at time	Term at time
Complexity	$O(p\log q + n\log k)$	$O(p + n\log k)$
Memory	$q+k$	n

Algorithm complexity

In this case, the following needs to be noted:

- q: Number of terms in a query
  - Example: orange OR strawberry OR not

- p: Number of documents in terms matching the query

Term	Doc Ids	
orange	2, 3	p
strawberry	3	
not	3	

- k: Number of documents the accumulator collects for showing the first page
- n: Total number of documents that match the query

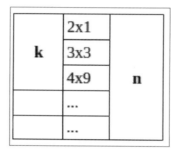

The eDisMax query parser

Let us understand the working of the eDisMax query parser. We will also look at the minimum should match parameter and filters in this section.

Working of the eDisMax query parser

Let us first refresh our memory about the different query modes in Solr. Query modes are ways to call different query parsers to process a query. Solr has different query modes that are specified by the defType parameter in the Solr URL. The defType parameter can also be changed by specifying a different defType parameter for the requestHandler property in the solrconfig.xml file. The popularly used query modes available in Solr are **DisMax (disjunction Max)** and eDisMax (**extended disjunction max**) in addition to the default (**no defType**) query mode. There are many other **queryModes** available, such as **lucene, maxscore**, and **surround**, but these are less used.

The query parser used by DisMax can process simple phrases entered by the user and search for individual terms across different fields using different boosts for different fields on the basis of their significance. The DisMax parser supports an extremely simplified subset of the Lucene query parser syntax. The eDisMax query parser, on the other hand, supports the full Lucene query syntax. It supports queries with AND, OR, NOT, +, and - clauses. It also supports pure negative nested queries such as +foo (-foo) that will match all documents. It lets the end user specify the fields allowed in the input query. We can also use the word shingles in a phrase boost (pf2 and pf3 parameters in Solr query) on the basis of the proximity of words.

Let us create a sample index and understand the working of a sample query in the eDisMax mode.

Index all files in the Solr default installation into the exampledocs folder. In Solr 4.6, execution of the following commands inside the exampledocs folder will result in the indexing of all files:

```
java -jar post.jar *.xml
java -Dtype=text/csv -jar post.jar *.csv
java -Dtype=application/json -jar post.jar *.json
```

This will index all the XML files along with the books.csv and books.json files into the index. The index should contain approximately 46 documents. It can be verified by running the following query on the Solr query interface:

```
http://localhost:8983/solr/collection1/select?q=*:*
```

A search for ipod usb charger with a boost of 2 on the name and a default boost on the text, along with a proximity boost on both the fields and a *minimum match* of 2, will form the following query:

```
http://localhost:8983/solr/collection1/select?q=ipod usb
charger&qf=text name^2&pf=text
name&mm=2&defType=dismax&debugQuery=true
```

The debug output shows how the eDisMax parser parses the query:

At the outermost level, the query (also known as the Boolean query) has 2 clauses:

- Clause 1:

```
+ (
(
DisjunctionMaxQuery((text:ipod | name:ipod^2.0))
DisjunctionMaxQuery((text:usb | name:usb^2.0))
DisjunctionMaxQuery((text:charger | name:charger^2.0))
) ~2
)
```

- Clause 2:

```
DisjunctionMaxQuery((text:"ipod usb charger" | name:"ipod usb
charger"))
```

The first clause has a + sign preceding it, which means that the first clause *must* match in every document returned in the result set. The second clause is an OR query that *should* match within the documents returned. Even if the clause does not find a match in the document, the document will be returned but with a lower score.

The first clause also has 3 sub-clauses. Each one *should* match with the documents in the result set. Also out of the 3 clauses, at least 2 *must* match, which we have specified by the mm=2 (minimum should match = 2) parameter in our Solr query. The mm=2 parameter in the Solr query is converted to the clause ~2 in our parsed query.

What does the clause `DisjunctionMaxQuery((text:ipod | name:ipod^2.0))` do? Here we search for ipod in the fields text and name and find the score in both the cases, that is the scores for ipod in text and ipod in name, and return the maximum of these two scores as the output of the DisjunctionMaxQuery clause. Why do we return the maximum score? Why not take the sum and return that as the score? Suppose, we are searching for usb charger in two fields, name and description. If we take the sum, then a document that has usb charger in the name and not in the description will have the same score as another document that has usb in both name and description but charger nowhere in these fields.

If still returning the maximum score is not something that makes sense in a particular scenario, we can use the tie parameter to decide how the final score of the query will be influenced by the scores of lower scoring compared to the higher scoring fields. A value of 0.0 means that only the maximum scoring subquery contributes to the final score. On the other hand, a value of 1.0 means that the final score will be a sum of individual subquery scores. In this case, the maximum scoring subquery loses its significance. Ideally, a value of 0.1 is preferred to have a mix of both scenarios.

The clause text:ipod is the smallest piece of the query, which is also known as a term query. This is where the tf-idf scoring we discussed above happens. This is encapsulated by the DisjunctionMaxQuery clause we just saw.

The second clause of the query, `DisjunctionMaxQuery((text:"ipod usb charger" | name:"ipod usb charger"))`, is again composed of two subqueries inside the DisjunctionMaxQuery clause. The query here is text:"ipod usb charger", which has multiple terms against a single field, and is known as a phrase query. It seeks all the documents that contain all the specified terms in the specified field and discards those documents where the terms are adjacent to each other in the specified order. In our case, the subquery will seek documents where the terms ipod, usb, and charger appear and in the field text and then check the order of the terms in the document. If the terms are adjacent to each other, the document is selected and ranked high.

Therefore, the interpretation of the query we saw earlier is as follows:

- Look for the documents that have two of the three terms `ipod`, `usb`, and `charger`. Search only the `name` and `text` fields. A document does not get a high score for matching any one of these terms in both fields.

- The `name` field is important, so it is boosted by `2`.

- If the documents from the previous section have the phrase `"ipod usb charger"` in the `text` or the `name` field, they are given higher scores.

The minimum should match parameter

We saw a brief preview of how the *minimum should match* parameter works in the earlier section. The default value of `mm` is `1` and it can be overwritten in `solrconfig.xml`. It can also be passed as a query parameter as we did in our example in the previous section.

When dealing with optional clauses, the `mm` parameter is used to decide how many of the optional clauses must match in a document for that document to be selected as a part of the result set. Note that the `mm` parameter can be a positive integer, a negative integer, or a percentage. Let us see all the options for specifying the `mm` parameter:

- **Positive integer**: A positive number `3` specifies that at least three clauses mush match irrespective of the total number of clauses in the query.

- **Negative integer**: A negative number `2` specifies that, out of the total number of clauses (n) in the query, the minimum number of matching clauses is `n-2`. Therefore, if the query has five clauses, `3` is the *must* match number.

- **Percentage**: A value of `75%` specifies that the matching clauses should constitute at least 75 percent of the total number of clauses in the query. A query with four clauses will have a minimum match number of `3` if `mm` is specified as `75%`.

- **Negative percentage**: A negative value of `-25%` indicates that the optional clauses constitute 25 percent of the total number of clauses. Therefore, if `mm=-25%` for four clauses, there should be at least three matching clauses.

- **Positive integer (> or <) percentage**: Let's take an example, say,`4<75%`. This means that, if the number of optional clauses in the query is less than or equal to `4`, then all of them must match. However, if the number of optional clauses is greater than `4`, say `8`, only 75 percent of the clauses or 6 clauses should match.

- **Multiple conditions**: These are used to define multiple conditions, each being valid for the number before it. For example, `2<-25% 9<-3` indicates that, if there are less than or equal to two clauses, all the clauses should match. If there are three to nine clauses, all but 25 percent are required. If there are more than nine clauses, all but three are required.

No matter what condition is specified and what number is derived during calculation, Solr will never use a value greater than the number of optional clauses or a value less than 1. That is, no matter what the calculated value for mm is, the minimum number of required matches would never be less than 1 or greater than the number of optional clauses.

The minimum should match parameter should be properly thought through for each use case. It is also important to have some sample user queries to figure out a particular formula for mm. The value of mm should be such that both precision and recall requirements for most queries are satisfied.

Minimum should match is an expensive algorithm during a search. There was a major bug fix in *Lucene version 4.3* that improved the performance of the minimum should match in DisMax queries. The bug fix is shown in the following figure:

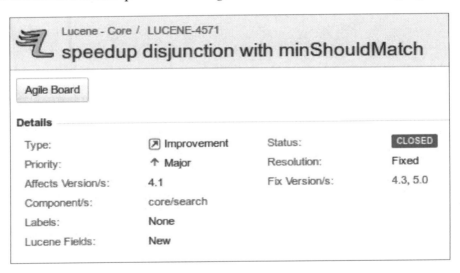

The improvement fix can be referred to in the following link: `https://issues.apache.org/jira/browse/LUCENE-4571`.

Working of filters

Filter queries do not affect the score of the documents in the result set. Filter queries cache the document IDs for inclusion or exclusion in a result set. This makes filter queries in Solr very fast. Since results obtained by using filter queries are not ranked, it is recommended to use filter queries to narrow down the result set rather than for the initial search itself.

Suppose that, in the index we created earlier, we are looking for a hard drive. The query for the same would be as follows:

```
http://localhost:8983/solr/collection1/select?q=hard drive&qf=name^2
text&pf=name&fl=id,name,score&defType=dismax&debugQuery=true
```

The result has the following three documents. Note that the scores are also printed.

```
▼<doc>
    <str name="id">SP2514N</str>
  ▼<str name="name">
     Samsung SpinPoint P120 SP2514N - hard drive - 250 GB -
     ATA-133
   </str>
    <float name="score">2.6919165</float>
  </doc>
▼<doc>
    <str name="id">6H500F0</str>
  ▼<str name="name">
     Maxtor DiamondMax 11 - hard drive - 500 GB - SATA-300
   </str>
    <float name="score">2.6919165</float>
  </doc>
▼<doc>
    <str name="id">0579B002</str>
    <str name="name">Canon PIXMA MP500 All-In-One Photo
    Printer</str>
    <float name="score">0.057317395</float>
  </doc>
```

Scores for documents in a query result

I am a brand conscious shopper and prefer the brand Samsung to other brands. Therefore, in this case, I would filter the search results on the basis of the brand field, which in our case is the field manu. The query would be as follows:

```
http://localhost:8983/solr/collection1/select?q=hard drive&qf=name^2
text&pf=name&fq=manu:samsung&fl=id,name,score&defType=dismax&debugQue
ry=true
```

The output clearly shows that the score of the document remained the same after applying the filter query:

Same score after applying the filter

As discussed earlier, the purpose of a filter query is to narrow down the result set. On an e-commerce site, the filter query should be used to narrow the result set on the basis of the facets. The first query should be an eDisMax query that gives results on the basis of the score of the documents. Once the results are in place, we would like to narrow them down but keep the results in the order that they were ranked. This is where filter queries make sense, as applying filter queries to the existing result set will narrow down the result and also keep the products in their previous order of ranking.

Suppose I am a customer and I am looking for a Levi's jeans in blue color. The query that I will enter would most probably be levis jeans blue. Here the search has to happen across multiple attributes of each product. The attributes that I have mentioned during my search are brand, category, and color. How should the search query be formed in this case? If we use the eDisMax query parser, all the terms will be searched in all the fields in my documents.

If I specify the query fields as `brand category color`, all the terms `levis`, `jeans`, and `blue` would be searched for all the three fields:

```
q = levis jeans blue
qf = brand category color
```

The matching documents would be found mostly when the following terms match: `brand:"levis"`, `category:"jeans"`, and `color:"blue"`. We would display the listing with the facets, say, `price` and `size`. A selection on the facet `size` would be treated as a filter query adding the `fq` parameter to our existing query:

```
fq = size:32
```

This will narrow down the result to a list of products that match my preferences. If the result is not too large to confuse me or too small with limited choices, I will most probably select a product and make a purchase. If the result is large enough, I can select more parameters from the facet `price` to narrow down the results further.

Using BRS queries instead of DisMax

Now that we know the internals of how DisMax queries work and how scoring happens in Solr, let's look at creating our own query syntax and parser for customizing our search. The question here is what is missing in eDisMax. Note that eDisMax provides a simple search syntax where we do not have to worry about the fields and the results are sorted by relevance. However, suppose the requirement is exactly opposite. The end user is an advanced user who knows the fields and what he or she is searching for. One such example is a search involving patents. The syntax for such a search is specified by BRS. In addition to `Fielded` and `Boolean` search, BRS also provides a proximity search with clauses such as `SAME` (in the same paragraph), `WITH` (in the same sentence), `ADJ` (adjacent with order), and `NEAR` (adjacent without order), along with parenthetical grouping. An example of a BRS query is as follows:

```
((galaxy ADJ samsung) SAME note) AND (mobile OR tablet)
```

BRS provides a rich search syntax generally devoid of facets, synonyms, stemming, and even relevancy sorting. Solr's eDisMax query syntax does not provide us with a very rich position-aware query syntax. BRS, on the other hand, is all about positions of words. We will creating our own Solr plugin for handling position-aware queries.

Building a custom query parser

Let us look at how we can build our own query parser. We will build a proximity query parser known as SWAN query where SWAN stands for Same, With, Adjacent, and Near. This query parser would use the SWAN relationships between terms to process the query and fetch the results.

Proximity search using SWAN queries

Solr provides position-aware queries via phrase slop queries. An example of a phrase slop is `"samsung galaxy"~4` that suggests `samsung` and `galaxy` must occur within 4 word positions of each other. However, this does not take care of the SWAN queries that we are looking for. Lucene has support for providing position-aware queries using `SpanQueries`. The classes that implement span queries in Lucene are:

- `SpanTermQuery(Term term)`: Represents the building blocks of `SpanQuery`. The `SpanTermQuery` class is used for creating `SpanOrQuery`, `SpanNotQuery`, or `SpanNearQuery`.

- `SpanOrQuery(SpanQuery clauses)`: Can contain multiple `SpanQuery` clauses. We can use the `addClause(SpanQuery clause)` function to add more clauses to the `OR` span query.

- `SpanNotQuery(SpanQuery include, SpanQuery exclude)`: Constructs a `SpanNotQuery` matching spans from include that have no overlap with spans from exclude. The constructor also provides variations to include the distance between tokens or pre and post numbers of tokens.

- `SpanNearQuery(SpanQuery[] clauses, int slop, boolean inOrder)`: Constructs a `SpanNearQuery` class. Matches spans matching a span from each clause, with up to slop total unmatched positions between them. When `inOrder` is true, the spans from each clause must be ordered as in clauses.

Let us try and implement SWAN queries using Lucene `SpanQueries`. For this, we will have to index our documents in a fashion such that there is enough position gap between multiple sentences and paragraphs. Suppose we identify that in our complete document set, the maximum number of tokens that a sentence can have is 50 and that the maximum number of sentences that a paragraph can have is also 50. Therefore, during indexing of documents in the analysis phase, we will have to put a position gap of 50 tokens between sentences and 5000 between paragraphs. Refer to *Chapter 1, Solr Indexing Internals* for information on `PositionIncrementGap` and how to set it up.

For creating the `SwanQueries` class, we need to first define the lengths of the sentence and the paragraph with respect to the token positions in them:

```
static int MAX_PARAGRAPH_LENGTH = 5000;
static int MAX_SENTENCE_LENGTH = 500;
```

Next, we need to define the implementation for SAME, WITH, ADJ, and NEAR queries. For SAME, we define that the left and right clauses should be within the same paragraph irrespective of the order:

```
public static SpanQuery SAME(SpanQuery left,SpanQuery right) {
    return new SpanNearQuery(
       new SpanQuery[] { left, right }, MAX_PARAGRAPH_LENGTH, false);
}
```

For WITH, we need to define that the left and right clauses should be within the same sentence irrespective of the order in which they were mentioned:

```
public static SpanQuery WITH(SpanQuery left,SpanQuery right) {
    return new SpanNearQuery(
       new SpanQuery[] { left, right }, MAX_SENTENCE_LENGTH, false);
}
```

For ADJ, the left and right clauses should be next to each other and there should be a position difference of only 1 between them. Also, as order matters, the left clause should occur before the right clause:

```
public static SpanQuery ADJ(SpanQuery left,SpanQuery right) {
    return new SpanNearQuery(
       new SpanQuery[] { left, right }, 1, true);
}
```

For NEAR, the left and right clauses should be next to each other with a slop of 1, irrespective of the order. This means that the left clause can appear before the right clause and vice versa:

```
public static SpanQuery NEAR(SpanQuery left,SpanQuery right) {
    return new SpanNearQuery(
       new SpanQuery[] { left, right }, 1, false);
}
```

Creating a parboiled parser

Now that we have the implementation of SWAN queries, we need a parser to parse our syntax with respect to SWAN queries. We would need a parser generator such as *javacc - the Java compiler compiler*. A parser generator is a tool that reads a grammar specification and converts it into a Java program that can recognize matches for the specification. We will be creating a grammar specification that can be parsed by using JavaCC and be converted into a Java program. More information regarding the `javacc` class can be obtained from its official page: `https://javacc.java.net/`.

When dealing with a parser generator such as `javacc`, we have to create an external syntax definition file and then compile the grammar definitions to a sort of runnable Java code that can recognize matches for the definitions. This is somewhat complicated for a normal Java programmer. An easier way of implementing the parser would be to define the parsers directly inside the Java code. This is supported by the **parboiled** Java library and is commonly used as an alternative to `javacc`. A parboiled parser supports definition of **Parsing Expression Grammar** (PEG) parsers directly inside the Java source code. Since the parboiled parser does not require a separate syntax definition file, it is comparatively easy to build custom parsers using the parboiled one.

The PEG specification can include parser actions that perform arbitrary logic at any given point during the parsing process. A parboiled parser works in two phases. The first phase is rule construction where the parser builds a tree (or rather a directed graph) of parsing rules as specified in our code. The second phase is rule execution where the rules are run against a specific input text. The end result is the following information:

- A Boolean flag determining whether the input matched the root rule or not
- A list of potentially encountered parse errors
- One or more value object(s) constructed by your parser actions

We derive our custom parser class from `BaseParser`, the required base class of all parboiled for Java parsers, and define methods for returning `Rule` instances. These methods construct a rule instance from other rules, terminals, predefined primitives, and action expressions. A PEG parser is basically a set of rules that are composed of other rules and terminals, which are essentially characters or strings.

The primitive rules are defined as follows (where a and b denote other parsing rules):

- `Sequence(a,b)`: Creates a new rule that succeeds if the sub-rules a and b also succeed one after the other.

- `FirstOf(a,b)`: Creates a new rule that successively tries both the sub-rules a and b and succeeds when the first one of its sub-rules matches. If all sub-rules fail, this rule fails as well.

- `ZeroOrMore(a)`: Creates a new rule that tries repeated matches of its sub-rule **a** and always succeeds, even if the sub-rule doesn't match even once.

- `OneOrMore(a)`: Creates a new rule that tries repeated matches of its sub-rule a and succeeds if the sub-rule matches at least once. If the sub-rule does not match at least once, this rule fails.

- `Optional(a)`: Creates a new rule that tries a match on its sub-rule a and always succeeds, independently of the matching success of its sub-rule.

- `Test(a)`: Creates a new rule that tests the given sub-rule a against the current input position without actually matching any characters. It succeeds if the sub-rule succeeds, and fails if the sub-rule rails.

- `TestNot(a)`: Is the inverse of the `Test` rule. It creates a new rule that tests the given sub-rule a against the current input position without actually matching any characters. It succeeds if the sub-rule fails, and fails if the sub-rule succeeds.

In addition to the above primitives, the PEG parser also consists of the following elements:

- **Parser actions**: These are snippets of custom code that are executed at specific points during rule execution. Apart from inspecting the parser state, parser actions typically construct parser values and can actively influence the parsing process as semantic predicates.

- **The value stack**: During the rule execution phase, parser actions can make use of the value stack for organizing the construction of custom objects. The value stack is a simple stack construct that serves as temporary storage for custom objects.

- **The parse tree**: During the rule execution phase, parboiled parsers can optionally construct a parse tree, whose nodes correspond to the recognized rules. Each parse tree node contains a reference to the matcher of the rule it was constructed from, the matched input text (position), and the current element at the top of the value stack. The parse tree can be viewed as the record of what rules have matched a given input and is particularly useful during debugging.

- **The ParseRunner**: The `ParseRunner` class is responsible for supervising a parsing run and optionally applying additional logic, most importantly the handling of illegal input characters or parse errors.

More details about the Java parboiled library can be obtained from its wiki pages at:

`http://en.wikipedia.org/wiki/Parboiled_(Java).`

`http://www.parboiled.org.`

You can also refer to its official GitHub page at: `https://github.com/sirthias/parboiled/wiki.`

Let us use the parboiled library to create our SWAN parser. The parboiled library consists of the `parboiled-core` and `parboiled-java` JAR files that can be downloaded from the following URL: `https://github.com/sirthias/parboiled/downloads.`

Our class `SwanParser` extends `BaseParser` from parboiled that generates queries of type `SpanQuery` (from the Lucene API):

```
public class SwanParser extends BaseParser<SpanQuery>
```

We start by defining rules for input strings, OR, SAME, WITH, NEAR, and ADJ. These rules are defined as case-insensitive input strings followed by whitespace:

```
public Rule OR() {
    return Sequence(IgnoreCase("OR"), WhiteSpace());
}
public Rule SAME() {
    return Sequence(IgnoreCase("SAME"), WhiteSpace());
}
public Rule WITH() {
    return Sequence(IgnoreCase("WITH"), WhiteSpace());
}
public Rule NEAR() {
    return Sequence(IgnoreCase("NEAR"), WhiteSpace());
}
public Rule ADJ() {
    return Sequence(IgnoreCase("ADJ"), WhiteSpace());
}
```

We need to define rules for matching `Term`, `Char`, and `WhiteSpace` in the input string. A character is defined as any one of numbers, small or capital letters, and a dash (-) or an underscore (_):

```
public Rule Char() {
    return AnyOf("0123456789" +
      "abcdefghijklmnopqrstuvwxyz" +
      "ABCDEFGHIJKLMNOPQRSTUVWXYZ" +
      "-_"
    );
}
```

Whitespace is defined as any space (" "), tab ("\t"), or form feed character ("\f"):

```
public Rule WhiteSpace() {
    return OneOrMore(AnyOf(" \t\f"));
}
```

A term is defined as a sequence of one or more characters. We create a Lucene term query using the `Term` class and push it into the value stack:

```
public Rule Term() {
    return Sequence(
      OneOrMore(Char()),
        push(new SpanTermQuery(new Term(match())))
    );
}
```

We need to define the SAME expression as a sequence of WITH expression and ZeroOrMore of SAME rule, WITH expression. We also construct the SAME query by popping two elements from the value stack and push the SAME query into the value stack:

```
public Rule SameExpression() {
    return Sequence(
      WithExpression(),
      ZeroOrMore(
        Sequence(
          SAME(),
          WithExpression(),
          push(SwanQueries.SAME(pop(1), pop()))
        )
      )
    );
}
```

Similarly, the `WITH` expression is defined as a sequence of an `AdjNear` expression and `ZeroOrMore` of a sequence of the `WITH` rule along with the `AdjNear` expression. As before, we create a `WITH` query by popping two elements from the value stack and push the `WITH` query into the value stack:

```
public Rule WithExpression() {
    return Sequence(
      AdjNearExpression(),
      ZeroOrMore(
        Sequence(
          WITH(),
          AdjNearExpression(),
          push(SwanQueries.WITH(pop(1), pop()))
        )
      )
    );
}
```

Finally, we create the `AdjNear` expression to handle both `ADJ` and `NEAR` clauses. This would contain a sequence of `Term` followed by `ZeroOrMore` of whichever sequence occurs first from the following two sequences. The first sequence here is a `NEAR` rule followed by a term and a `NEAR` query constructed by popping two elements from the value stack. The second sequence is an `ADJ` rule followed by a term and an `ADJ` query constructed by popping two elements from the value stack. The expression will return a `Term` if none of the following sequences exist. Else, it will return whichever of the `NEAR` and `ADJ` sequences it finds first:

```
public Rule AdjNearExpression() {
    return Sequence(
      Term(),
      ZeroOrMore(FirstOf(
        Sequence(
          NEAR(),
          Term(),
          push(SwanQueries.NEAR(pop(1), pop()))
        ),
        Sequence(
          ADJ(),
          Term(),
          push(SwanQueries.ADJ(pop(1), pop()))
        )
      ))
    );
}
```

Next, we define the OR expression as a sequence of the SAME expression and ZeroOrMore of a sequence of expressions including OR, SAME, and SpanOrQuery, which is pushed into the stack. Here we pop the last two elements from the value stack, create a SpanOrQuery class, and push it into the value stack:

```
public Rule OrExpression() {
    return Sequence(
      SameExpression(),
      ZeroOrMore(
        Sequence(
          OR(),
          SameExpression(),
          push(new SpanOrQuery(pop(1), pop()))
        )
      )
    );
}
```

Finally, we create a rule for the Query() function that is a sequence of OR expressions followed by the End Of Expression (EOI):

```
public Rule Query() {
    return Sequence(OrExpression(),EOI);
}
```

In order to compile SwanParser.java, we would need the lucene-core, parboiled-core, and parboiled-java JAR files in our Java classpath.

Building a Solr plugin for SWAN queries

We will need to create a Solr plugin to incorporate the SWAN query parser that we created earlier. In order to create a Solr plugin for processing our custom query parser, we will need to extend the QParserPlugin class and override the createParser method to return an instance of type QParser. In order to plug in our Swan parser, we will have to create a SwanQParser class that extends the QParser class and override the parse method to return an object of type Query:

```
public class SwanQParser extends QParser {
  // Define the constructor
  public SwanQParser(String qstr, SolrParams localParams, SolrParams
  params, SolrQueryRequest req) {
    super(qstr, localParams, params, req);
  }
  // Override the parse method from QParser
```

```
    @Override
    public Query parse() throws SyntaxError {
      SwanParser parser = Parboiled.createParser(SwanParser.class);
      ParsingResult<?> result = new
      RecoveringParseRunner<SpanQuery>(parser.Query()).run(this.qstr);
       if (!result.parseErrors.isEmpty()){
         throw new SyntaxError(ErrorUtils.printParseError
         (result.parseErrors.get(0)));
      }
      SpanQuery query = (SpanQuery) result.parseTreeRoot.getValue();
      return query;
    }
  }
```

Once we have the `SwanQParser` class of type `QParser`, we will have to create the `SwanQParserPlugin` class, which extends the `QParserPlugin` class from Solr, and override the `createParser` method to return an object of type `SwanQParser`:

```
public class SwanQParserPlugin extends QParserPlugin {
  // Override the createParser method from QParserPlugin
  @Override
  public QParser createParser(String qstr, SolrParams localParams,
  SolrParams params, SolrQueryRequest req) {
    return new SwanQParser(qstr, localParams, params, req);
  }
}
```

In addition to the `parboiled` and `lucene` libraries (JAR files), we will need the `solr-core` and `solr-solrj` libraries in our Java classpath to compile the previously mentioned classes.

Integrating the SWAN plugin in Solr

Now that we have all the classes ready for creating our plugin, lets create a JAR file and include it in the `solrconfig.xml` file in order to integrate the SWAN plugin in Solr. Create the JAR file (`swan.jar`) and place it inside the library (`<solr_directory>/example/solr-webapp/webapp/WEB-INF/lib/`) folder. Also make the following change in the `solrconfig.xml` file:

```
<queryParser name="swan" class="com.plugin.swan.SwanQParserPlugin"/>
```

Note that all our classes were put inside the `com.plugin.swan` package. Restart Solr and try accessing the SWAN parser by specifying the `defType=swan` parameter in a Solr query. As shown in the following Solr query URL:

```
http://localhost:8983/solr/collection1/select?q=((galaxy ADJ samsung)
SAME note) AND (mobile OR tablet)&defType=swan
```

> We can also define a new handler `/swan` instead of `/select` for processing SWAN queries.

On accessing the above Solr query URL, we get a syntax error. To fix the dependency issues, include the parboiled and the ASM libraries into the Solr library path. Copy the `parboiled*` JAR files to the library folder. Also, download and copy the `asm-all-4.x.jar` file to the library folder.

> We are using ASM 4.2 and it can be downloaded from:
> `http://asm.ow2.org/download/index.html`.
> Code references: `https://gist.github.com/JnBrymn/`.

> If you are still getting a syntax exception, remember that we need to incorporate a position increment gap between multiple sentences and paragraphs within our index. We will need to define our analyzer to tokenize our input text in the required fashion for the SWAN queries to work.

Summary

We went through the internals of Solr and Lucene. We saw how a scorer works on an inverted index and how the DisMax parser works in finding and ranking a result set. We understood the algorithms that work within Lucene when we use the OR or AND clause in Solr. We saw how filters work during the scoring of documents within a result set and the importance and usage of the `minimum match` parameter.

In the second half of the chapter, we built our own query parser. We went through the concepts of the parboiled parser API and built a SWAN query parser using the API. We also understood what is required during indexing and search to integrate and use the SWAN query parser as a plugin in Solr. This also cleared our concepts of building a custom query parser plugin for Solr.

In the next chapter, we will be looking at the use of Solr in processing and handling big data problems.

4
Solr for Big Data

In the previous chapter, we learned about Solr internals and the creation of custom queries. We understood the algorithms behind the working of AND and OR clauses in Solr and the internals of the eDisMax parser. We implemented our own plugin in Solr for running a proximity search by using SWAN queries. We understood the internals of how filters work.

In this chapter, we will discuss how and why Solr is an appropriate choice for churning out analytical reports. We will understand the concept of big data and how Solr can be used to solve the problems that come along with running queries on big data. We will discuss different faceting concepts and see how distributed pivot faceting works.

The topics that we will cover in this chapter are:

- Introduction to big data
- Getting data points using facets
- Radius faceting for location-based data
- Data analysis using pivot faceting
- Introduction to graphical representation of analytical reports

Introduction to big data

Big data can simply be defined as data too large to be processed by a single machine. Let us say that we have 1 TB of data and the reports that need to be generated from it cannot be processed on a single machine in a time span acceptable to us. Let us take the example of click stream analysis. Internet companies such as Yahoo or Google keep an eye on the activity of the user by capturing each click that the user does on their website. Sometimes the complete page by page flow is also captured. Google, for example, captures the position from the top of a search result page for a search on a particular keyword or phrase. The amount of data generated and captured is huge and may be running into exabytes every day. This data needs to be processed on a day-to-day basis for analytical purposes. The analytical reports that are generated from this data are used to improve the experience of the user visiting the website.

Is it possible to process an exabyte of data? Of course it is, but the main concern is to process an exabyte of data every day to avoid creating a backlog. This would require huge processing power, generally distributed over a number of machines. A few factors that contribute to data being termed as big data are:

- **Volume**: Huge amounts of data, similar to the one we discussed earlier, are to be processed every day. This data is mostly unstructured making it difficult to process. Also, since the amount of data is huge, it needs to be collected using multiple machines.

- **Velocity**: Velocity can be defined as the amount of data being generated in a particular time span. In the example we saw earlier, we had a velocity of around one exabyte per day. If we are unable to process the data with the velocity it comes into the system, we will have a backlog that will keep on increasing and the analytical system will lose its purpose.

- **Variety**: Variety defines the format of data. Data can be an unstructured text document, financial transactions, e-mails, audio, video, and so on. The more variety the data has, the more difficult it is to process the data.

- **Veracity**: Complexity arises from the fact that the data is so huge and needs to be collected with such speed that a single machine cannot handle the task. We may need to deploy a number of machines and then collate the data and process it in a distributed fashion to generate the analytical reports required. The accuracy of analytical output depends on the veracity of the source data.

Now, how does Solr handle big data? Let us say that we are doing a click stream analysis of data, and since the amount of data is huge, we are gathering it from different machines and collating and processing it. We have the complete system setup so that we can handle the volume and velocity, and we are generating daily analytical reports that consist of certain data points. On a particular day, the analytics team wants to add a new data point and view analytical reports of all the past data with the added data point. What do we do? It is impossible to process past data to generate the new data point. If we go by the previous architecture, we will be setting up a huge number of machines to generate the new data point for all past data.

Would it make sense to parse the incoming data and store it so that reports can be generated on the fly? A new data point or a mix of multiple data points can be processed dynamically whenever needed. Instead of generating static reports, it would make sense to store the data and run queries to generate a report as and when required. A single Solr machine cannot handle such an amount of volume and velocity.

SolrCloud, which will be discussed in *Chapter 9*, *SolrCloud*, comes to our rescue here. It is the perfect tool for distributed data collection and processing. Using SolrCloud, we can have multiple Solr nodes where data can be fed into the system and processed by running queries. SolrCloud is horizontally scalable, which means that as data increases, all we need to do is add more machines to the cloud.

Let us look at some advanced faceting functionalities of Solr for generating the required reports.

Getting data points using facets

Let us refresh our memory about facets. Simply put, faceting refers to the method of categorizing data. A facet on a search result will contain categories and the number of documents in each category. The purpose of facets is to help the user narrow down his or her search result on the basis of some categories. Let us take an example to understand this better.

A search on mobile a phone would bring up a few of the following facets on the Amazon website:

- Facet for **Brand**: We can see a facet for **Brand** in the following screenshot:

Brand
- ☐ Samsung
- ☐ Apple
- ☐ Sony
- ☐ Nokia
- ☐ HTC
- ☐ LG
- ☐ Sanyo
- ☐ Motorola
- ☐ MOTCB
- ☐ Huhushop(TM)
- ☐ Virgin Mobile
- ☐ Unnecto
- ☐ BlackBerry
- ☐ Boost Mobile
- ☐ ZTE
- **+ See more**

The brand facet is purely intended to help the user shortlist his or her preferences. The count of cell phones for each brand is not displayed, although this information is readily available and can be used for display.

- **Facet for display size**: We can see the facet for display size in the following image:

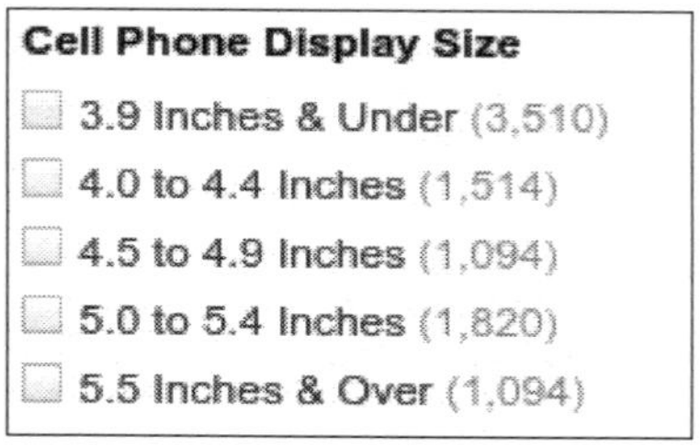

Cell Phone Display Size
- ☐ 3.9 Inches & Under (3,510)
- ☐ 4.0 to 4.4 Inches (1,514)
- ☐ 4.5 to 4.9 Inches (1,094)
- ☐ 5.0 to 5.4 Inches (1,820)
- ☐ 5.5 Inches & Over (1,094)

The display size category shows facets based on the range of display sizes. Phones having sizes of less than 3.9 inches are grouped together. Similarly, we can see the count of phones having display sizes in the range 4 to 4.4 inches, and so on.

- **Facet for internal memory**: We can see the facet for internal memory of mobile phones in the following image:

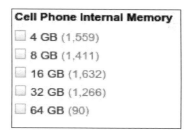

The facet for internal memory displays the number of cell phones having a particular size of internal memory. This categorization is based on the value of internal memory for each phone:

- **Facet for price and discount**: We can see the facet for **Price** and **Discount** in the following image:

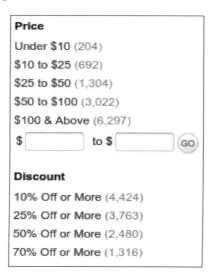

The facet for price is another example of range faceting where phones having prices less than $10 are grouped together. Similarly, phones costing between $10 and $25 are counted as a single category, and so on. Discount is another example of range faceting but in increasing order of discounts. Here phones having discounts of more than 10 percent are grouped together. However, this category also contains phones that have discounts of more than 25 percent.

All of the above facets can be built using three types of facet queries in Solr, field faceting, query faceting, and range faceting. Let us understand how they work.

Let us add some data into an empty Solr core. Upload the data from the `ch04data.csv` file provided as code with this chapter by running the following command inside the `<solr_folder>/example/exampledocs` folder:

```
java -Durl=http://localhost:8983/solr/collection1/update -Dtype=text/csv
-jar post.jar /path/to/ch04/Code/ch04data.csv
```

You can run a simple query to check whether the data has been loaded into the Solr core:

```
http://localhost:8983/solr/collection1/select/?q=*:*
```

Field faceting

Field faceting retrieves the count of all terms in a specific indexed field. Field faceting is done to categorize the data on the basis of values in a specific field. We have uploaded some data related to mobiles onto our Solr core. Let us categorize the data on the basis of the different brands of phones that we have in our index and see what we get.

Field faceting is simple; just add the following parameters to the `select` query:

```
&facet=true
&facet.field=brand_s
```

In order to facet on more than one field, add another field to the Solr query. Let us also categorize the indexes of mobile phones on the basis of their internal memory. Now the parameters in our query would be:

```
&facet=true
&facet.field=brand_s
&facet.field=memory_i
```

The complete Solr query is as follows:

```
http://localhost:8983/solr/collection1/
select/?q=*:*&facet=true&facet
.field=brand_s&facet.field=memory_i
```

The response can be seen in the following image:

```
      ▼<arr name="facet.field">
          <str>brand_s</str>
          <str>memory_i</str>
        </arr>
      </lst>
    </lst>
  ▶<result name="response" numFound="20" start="0">
  ▼<lst name="facet_counts">
      <lst name="facet_queries"/>
    ▼<lst name="facet_fields">
      ▼<lst name="brand_s">
          <int name="Nokia">5</int>
          <int name="Apple">4</int>
          <int name="Motorola">4</int>
          <int name="Samsung">4</int>
          <int name="HTC">3</int>
        </lst>
      ▼<lst name="memory_i">
          <int name="16">13</int>
          <int name="8">6</int>
          <int name="4">1</int>
        </lst>
      </lst>
    </lst>
```

How does this help in handling big data? When we have huge amounts of data, field faceting can be used to retrieve information regarding different fields in the index. For example, if we are dealing with the population in a country, we can have indexes on states and cities and facets on those states and cities. This will give us an analytical output on the population in those states and cities.

Query and range faceting

Query faceting or range faceting can be used to categorize data on the basis of a particular query or a set of queries. We can create a facet similar to the discount facet that we saw on the Amazon website using query faceting. The facet would categorize the data of mobile phones with discounts of greater than 5 percent, 10 percent, 15 percent, and 20 percent. The facet containing the count of mobile phones having discounts of greater than 10 percent will include phones with 15 and 20-percent discounts. To create this facet, we will be adding the following parameters in our Solr query:

```
&facet=true
&facet.query=discount_i:[5 TO *]
&facet.query=discount_i:[10 TO *]
&facet.query=discount_i:[15 TO *]
&facet.query=discount_i:[20 TO *]
```

The complete Solr query will be as follows:

```
http://localhost:8983/solr/collection1/
select/?q=*:*&facet=true&facet
.query=discount_i:[5 TO *]&facet.query=discount_i:[10 TO
*]&facet.query=discount_i:[15 TO *]&facet.query=discount_i:[20 TO *]
```

The output of the query will create the following facets:

```
▼<arr name="facet.query">
    <str>discount_i:[5 TO *]</str>
    <str>discount_i:[10 TO *]</str>
    <str>discount_i:[15 TO *]</str>
    <str>discount_i:[20 TO *]</str>
  </arr>
  <str name="q">*:*</str>
  </lst>
 </lst>
▶<result name="response" numFound="20" start="0">
▼<lst name="facet_counts">
 ▼<lst name="facet_queries">
    <int name="discount_i:[5 TO *]">19</int>
    <int name="discount_i:[10 TO *]">16</int>
    <int name="discount_i:[15 TO *]">8</int>
    <int name="discount_i:[20 TO *]">4</int>
  </lst>
```

When dealing with analytical data, we would need to create complex facets, which would be a combination of a query facet and a field facet. This would help us in getting different categories out of a single query and save us the overhead of running multiple queries. When dealing with big data, it is more important to create an efficient query, as owing to the size of the data, the time required for running a single query may be huge. Therefore, it is imperative to spend more time on creation of an efficient query to get as many facets as required from a single query.

Let us create a mixed facet of `price` and `brand` and `memory`, somewhat similar to the one we saw on the Amazon website. The `price` facet will contain the count of mobiles having prices in the ranges 0 to 100, 100 to 200, 200 to 300, and more than 300. We will also be getting facet counts for the brand and the internal memory of mobile phones.

The parameters that we will be adding to the Solr query would be:

```
&facet=true
&facet.query=price_i:[* TO 100]
&facet.query=price_i:[101 TO 200]
&facet.query=price_i:[201 TO 300]
&facet.query=price_i:[301 TO *]
&facet.field=brand_s
&facet.field=memory_i
```

The complete query that we would run on Solr to create this complex facet will be:

```
http://localhost:8983/solr/collection1/select/?q=*:*&facet=true&facet
.query=price_i:[* TO 100]&facet.query=price_i:[101 TO
200]&facet.query=price_i:[201 TO 300]&facet.query=price_i:[301 TO
*]&facet.field=brand_s&facet.field=memory_i
```

The output will contain the three facets that we wanted:

```
▼<lst name="facet_counts">
  ▼<lst name="facet_queries">
     <int name="price_i:[* TO 100]">3</int>
     <int name="price_i:[101 TO 200]">8</int>
     <int name="price_i:[201 TO 300]">4</int>
     <int name="price_i:[301 TO *]">5</int>
  </lst>
  ▼<lst name="facet_fields">
    ▼<lst name="brand_s">
       <int name="Nokia">5</int>
       <int name="Apple">4</int>
       <int name="Motorola">4</int>
       <int name="Samsung">4</int>
       <int name="HTC">3</int>
    </lst>
    ▼<lst name="memory_i">
       <int name="16">13</int>
       <int name="8">6</int>
       <int name="4">1</int>
    </lst>
  </lst>
</lst>
```

In the earlier example of population of a country, we can now create multiple facets such as average income, age, and gender in addition to the simple facets of city and state. We can create a complex Solr query that contains the query for faceting on a certain income range, or another query for faceting on age range, say 0 to 3 years, 3 to 12 years, 12 to 18 years, and so on. Once we obtain this data for the entire country, we can narrow down to state and city facets by adding filter queries to our query.

A filter query, if we remember, simply adds a restriction on the actual query to provide more targeted data. Filter queries are generally added by using the fq parameter in our Solr query. Therefore, to obtain the facet counts for a city, we will be adding a filter query fq=city_name in our Solr query, and this will generate statistical counts for a particular city.

The same fundamentals can be extended to click stream analysis, which we discussed earlier. We can create facets for urls, referrers, and even different features being accessed on each URL, provided we have captured the required data in our SolrCloud.

Radius faceting for location-based data

Location-based data can be represented in Solr using **latitudes** and **longitudes**. Applications can combine other data with location information to provide more insight into the data pertaining to a certain location. In analytics, location-based data is very important. Whether we are dealing with sales information, statistical information of any kind, or information pertaining to visits to a website, having a location in addition to the numbers that we already have provides an additional insight with a regional perspective.

We will delve into how geospatial searches happen in Solr in *Chapter 6, Solr for Spatial Search*. For the current chapter, let us understand the different types of location filters available with Solr.

For spatial filters, the following parameters are used in Solr:

- `d`: Radial distance in kilometers
- `pt`: Center point in the format of latitude and longitude
- `sfield`: Refers to a spatial indexed field

In order to run queries, we would need the default documents pushed into our running Solr instance. Simply run the following command in the `exampledocs` folder in your Solr installation to get these documents indexed in Solr:

`java -jar post.jar *.xml`

A query on the complete index will tell us that we now have around 52 records in our index:

`http://localhost:8983/solr/collection1/select/?q=*:*`

Different types of spatial filter queries can be defined as follows.

The geofilt filter

The geofilt filter allows us to retrieve results based on the geospatial distance from a given center point. That is, it creates a filter of a particular shape. For example, to find all documents within 5 km from a given `lat` / `lon` point, we could enter the value `&q=*:*&fq={!geofilt sfield=store}&pt=45.15,-93.85&d=5`.

This is shown in the following image:

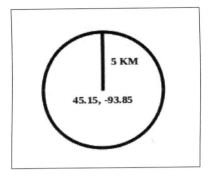

Let us execute the query we have formed on our Solr index. The complete query will be:

```
http://localhost:8983/solr/collection1/select/?q=*:*&fq={!geofilt%20s
field=store}&pt=45.15,-93.85&d=5
```

This gives us three records that are within 5 km from the specified `lat` / `lon` position (`45.15, -93.85`).

```
<str name="q">*:*</str>
<str name="pt">45.15,-93.85</str>
<str name="fq">{!geofilt sfield=store}</str>
</lst>
</lst>
▼<result name="response" numFound="3" start="0">
  ▼<doc>
    <str name="manu">Maxtor Corp.</str>
    <str name="store">45.17614,-93.87341</str>
  </doc>
  ▼<doc>
    <str name="manu">Belkin</str>
    <str name="store">45.18014,-93.87741</str>
  </doc>
  ▼<doc>
    <str name="manu">A-DATA Technology Inc.</str>
    <str name="store">45.18414,-93.88141</str>
  </doc>
</result>
```

The bounding box filter

The bounding box, or bbox filter is very similar to geofilt, except that the former uses the bounding box of the calculated circle, similar to the box shown in the following diagram. It takes the same parameters as geofilt, but the rectangular shape is faster to compute. Therefore, it's sometimes used as an alternative to geofilt when it's acceptable to return points outside of the radius.

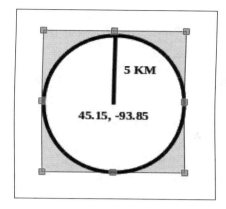

We can use the same query we ran earlier and ask for a bbox filter instead of a geofilt filter:

```
http://localhost:8983/solr/collection1/select/?q=*:*&fq={!bbox}&sfiel
d=store&pt=45.15,-93.85&d=5
```

We need to run the following query to apply a bbox filter:

```
        <str name="q">*:*</str>
        <str name="sfield">store</str>
        <str name="pt">45.15,-93.85</str>
        <str name="fq">{!bbox}</str>
      </lst>
    </lst>
  ▼<result name="response" numFound="5" start="0">
    ▼<doc>
        <str name="manu">Maxtor Corp.</str>
        <str name="store">45.17614,-93.87341</str>
      </doc>
    ▼<doc>
        <str name="manu">Belkin</str>
        <str name="store">45.18014,-93.87741</str>
      </doc>
    ▼<doc>
        <str name="manu">A-DATA Technology Inc.</str>
        <str name="store">45.18414,-93.88141</str>
      </doc>
    ▼<doc>
        <str name="manu">ViewSonic Corp.</str>
        <str name="store">45.18814,-93.88541</str>
      </doc>
    ▼<doc>
        <str name="manu">Canon Inc.</str>
        <str name="store">45.19214,-93.89941</str>
      </doc>
    </result>
```

The same query now returns five results instead of three. The last two results are outside the geofilt but inside the bbox filter.

The rectangle filter

Instead of using the bbox filter, we can also run the rectangle filter, which will fetch the same result if run for a square instead of a rectangle (since the bbox filter can be run for a square only and not for a rectangle). The query for executing the rectangular filter will be as follows:

```
http://localhost:8983/solr/collection1/select/?q=*:*&fq=store:[45,-94
TO 46,-93]
```

The following image shows the area that will be used for the rectangle filter:

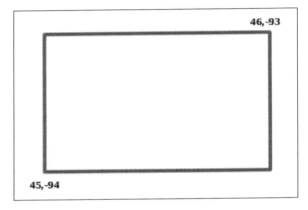

Distance function queries

Solr provides a set of function queries to calculate distance during querying:

- geodist: This takes three optional parameters (sfield, lat, lan) and can be used to sort results on the basis of distance. For example, to sort results by ascending distance, we would append the sort=geodist asc parameter to our previous geofilt query.

- dist: This is used to calculate the normal distance between two points on a plane surface.

- hsin: This is used to calculate the distance between two points on a sphere.

- sqedist: This is used to calculate the euclidean distance between two points.

Euclidean distance is used to measure the distance between two `lat` / `lon` coordinates more accurately. For more information, refer to the following wiki page: `http://en.wikipedia.org/wiki/Euclidean_distance`.

Radius faceting

Now that we have understood in brief the different distance filter queries and function queries that can be used with location information, we can use this information to filter our search results on the basis of the radial distance from a given location.

Let us say that we need to figure out how many people visit our website via mobile phones from different regions. For this, we capture the GPS coordinates of the mobile phone, and log and index the information into our SolrCloud.

Now in order to obtain the number of mobiles accessing our website at a particular time and from a particular region, we need to create range facets, mostly using the rectangular filter, and divide our target region into different sections. A sample facet query would be as follows:

```
facet=true&
facet.query=store:[45,-94 TO 46,-93]&
facet.query=store:[45,-93 TO 46,-92]&
facet.query=store:[46,-94 TO 47,-93]
```

If we have city names, we can facet by city and also add multiple geofilt filters to create multiple facets of regions inside the city that are of interest to us.

Another way to facet is by using the `frange` filter. With `frange`, we can create facets of concentric circular regions from a center point. The following query will create two facets from the center point (`45.15,-93.85`). The first facet will start from the center point and go up to a radius of 5 km. The second facet will start from 5.001 km from the center point and go up to 10 km:

```
http://localhost:8983/solr/select?q=*:*&sfield=store&pt=45.15,-
93.85&facet.query={!frange l=0 u=5}geodist()&facet.query={!frange
l=5.001 u=10}geodist()&facet=true
```

Analytics using location data is a very powerful tool in understanding and resolving issues that arise from location difference. Why sales do not happen well in a certain part of a city? Why is there a huge number of visits from a certain region spanning multiple cities to our website? The identification of such questions and their answers can be achieved only by indexing these data into SolrCloud and writing complex Solr queries with filters and facets. We can create facets by distance from certain store locations. We can use radius or range faceting from a store and figure out the number of sales from the different facets we have created. This can give us a deep insight into what can be done to improve the numbers that we are trying to achieve.

Data analysis using pivot faceting

As per the definition of pivoting in the Solr wiki, it is a summarization tool that lets you automatically sort, count, total, or average data stored in a table. Pivot faceting lets you create a summary table of the results from a query across numerous documents.

The output of pivot faceting can be referred to as decision trees. This means the output of pivot faceting is represented by a hierarchy of all sub-facets under a facet with counts both for individual facets and sub-facets. We can constrain the previous facet with a new sub-facet and get counts of the sub-sub-facets inside it. Let us see an example to understand pivot faceting.

Facet A has constraints as X,Y with counts M for X and N for Y. We could go ahead and constrain facet A by X and get a new sub-facet B with constraints W,Z and counts O for W and P for Z.

To understand better how pivot faceting works and hence how it could be helpful in analytics, let us see an example. Our index contains some mobile phones. Let us see the count of brands and the number of options having different memory capacities. The query will contain the following parameters for this faceting:

```
facet.pivot=brand_s,memory_i&
facet.pivot.mincount=1&
facet=true
```

In this snippet, note the following:

- The `facet.pivot` parameter defines the fields to use for the pivot. Multiple `facet.pivot` values will create multiple `facet_pivot` sections in the response.

- The `facet.pivot.mincount` parameter defines the minimum number of documents that need to match in order for the facet to be included in results. The default value is `1`.

The complete query would be as follows:

```
http://localhost:8983/solr/collection1/select?q=*:*&facet.pivot=brand
_s,memory_i&facet=true&facet.pivot.mincount=1
```

We can see that the output contains counts for all brands. Inside each brand, there are different memory options and their respective counts. A portion of the pivot faceting output is as follows. It shows two brands, Apple and Nokia, where Nokia has both 8 and 16 GB memory options but Apple has only a 16 GB memory option.

```
▼<lst name="facet_pivot">
  ▼<arr name="brand_s,memory_i">
    ▼<lst>
        <str name="field">brand_s</str>
        <str name="value">Nokia</str>
        <int name="count">5</int>
      ▼<arr name="pivot">
        ▼<lst>
            <str name="field">memory_i</str>
            <int name="value">16</int>
            <int name="count">3</int>
          </lst>
        ▼<lst>
            <str name="field">memory_i</str>
            <int name="value">8</int>
            <int name="count">2</int>
          </lst>
        </arr>
      </lst>
    ▼<lst>
        <str name="field">brand_s</str>
        <str name="value">Apple</str>
        <int name="count">4</int>
      ▼<arr name="pivot">
        ▼<lst>
            <str name="field">memory_i</str>
            <int name="value">16</int>
            <int name="count">4</int>
          </lst>
        </arr>
      </lst>
```

An interesting facet to watch over here is that of the price inside the discount percentage and brand inside memory options. The parameters to be added in our query would be the following:

```
facet.pivot=memory_i,brand_s&
facet.pivot=discount_i,price_i
```

The complete query would be as follows:

```
http://localhost:8983/solr/collection1/select?q=*:*&facet.pivot=memor
y_i,brand_s&facet.pivot=discount_i,price_i&facet=true&facet.pivot.min
count=1
```

We have created multiple `pivot` facets here. The first is of `brand` inside `memory`:

```
▼<lst>
    <str name="field">memory_i</str>
    <int name="value">8</int>
    <int name="count">6</int>
  ▼<arr name="pivot">
    ▼<lst>
        <str name="field">brand_s</str>
        <str name="value">Motorola</str>
        <int name="count">2</int>
      </lst>
    ▼<lst>
        <str name="field">brand_s</str>
        <str name="value">Nokia</str>
        <int name="count">2</int>
      </lst>
    ▼<lst>
        <str name="field">brand_s</str>
        <str name="value">HTC</str>
        <int name="count">1</int>
      </lst>
    ▼<lst>
        <str name="field">brand_s</str>
        <str name="value">Samsung</str>
        <int name="count">1</int>
      </lst>
    </arr>
  </lst>
▼<lst>
    <str name="field">memory_i</str>
    <int name="value">4</int>
    <int name="count">1</int>
  ▼<arr name="pivot">
    ▼<lst>
        <str name="field">brand_s</str>
        <str name="value">Samsung</str>
        <int name="count">1</int>
      </lst>
    </arr>
  </lst>
</arr>
```

Another `pivot` facet is that of `price` inside `discount` as shown in the following image:

```
▼<lst>
   <str name="field">discount_i</str>
   <int name="value">5</int>
   <int name="count">3</int>
 ▼<arr name="pivot">
   ▼<lst>
      <str name="field">price_i</str>
      <int name="value">110</int>
      <int name="count">1</int>
    </lst>
   ▼<lst>
      <str name="field">price_i</str>
      <int name="value">140</int>
      <int name="count">1</int>
    </lst>
   ▼<lst>
      <str name="field">price_i</str>
      <int name="value">190</int>
      <int name="count">1</int>
    </lst>
   </arr>
  </lst>
▼<lst>
   <str name="field">discount_i</str>
   <int name="value">25</int>
   <int name="count">2</int>
 ▼<arr name="pivot">
   ▼<lst>
      <str name="field">price_i</str>
      <int name="value">400</int>
      <int name="count">1</int>
    </lst>
   ▼<lst>
      <str name="field">price_i</str>
      <int name="value">450</int>
      <int name="count">1</int>
    </lst>
   </arr>
  </lst>
```

Pivot faceting can be used to generate summarization and decision tree–type analytical information out of big data, provided that we have the required data properly indexed into our SolrCloud. If we take the example of population analysis, we can create `pivot` facets on fields such as `age`, `gender`, and `income` and get a detailed location-wise summary.

Graphs for analytics

Once we know which queries to execute for getting the facets and hierarchical information, we need a graphical representation of the same. There are a few open source graph engines, mostly JavaScript based, that can be used for this. Most of these engines take JSON data and use it to display the graphs. Let us see some of the engines:

- **chart.js**: This is an HTML5 based graph engine. It can be downloaded from `http://www.chartjs.org`.

- **D3.js**: This is another JavaScript library that brings data to life using HTML and CSS. D3 can be used to generate an HTML table from an array of numbers or the same numbers can be used to draw an interactive bar chart. It is available for download at `http://d3js.org`.

- **Google charts**: This is another library provided by Google. It can be used to draw graphs based on data from Solr. Google charts provide a large range of graphs from simple line charts to complex hierarchical tree maps. Most of the charts are ready to use. Google charts can be downloaded from `https://developers.google.com/chart/`.

- **Highcharts**: This is the library that we will use here. It is one of the most used JavaScript graph libraries. Highcharts can be downloaded from `http://www.highcharts.com/`.

Getting started with Highcharts

In this section, we will download and run some samples from Highcharts. We will get familiar with how to give it data for creating graphs.

Let us download Highcharts from `http://www.highcharts.com/download`. We are using Highchart 4.0.4. Any version of Highcharts above this should work. Simply unzip the downloaded `Highcharts-4.*.*.zip` file and open the folder in your browser. When we open up the `index.htm` file in the browser, we will be able to see the samples of different types of charts:

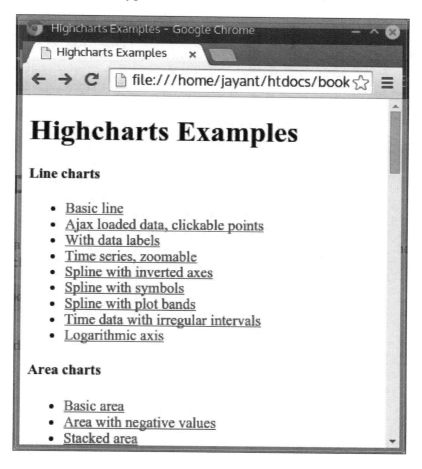

Go down to the **column and bar charts** section and click on **basic bar**. We will be able to see the bar chart as shown in the following image:

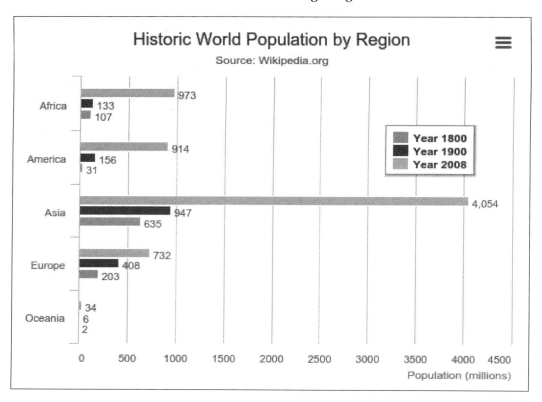

To check the code, open up the file `examples/bar-basic/index.htm` inside the folder where you had unzipped the `highchart.zip` file.

We can see that there is a `div` tag defined as follows called `container`:

```
<div id="container" style="min-width: 310px; max-width: 800px;
height: 400px; margin: 0 auto"></div>
```

Two JavaScripts have been included in the page:

```
<script src="../../js/highcharts.js"></script>
<script src="../../js/modules/exporting.js"></script>
```

The code for creating the graph is written in inline JavaScript. We have defined the `container` div tag for the chart. The chart type is `bar`, and `title` and `subtitle` for the chart have been provided. Next, we define the labels for the `X-Axis` and `Y-Axis` classes:

```
<script type="text/javascript">
$(function () {
    $('#container').highcharts({
        chart: {
            type: 'bar'
        },
        title: {
            text: 'Historic World Population by Region'
        },
        subtitle: {
            text: 'Source: Wikipedia.org'
        },
        xAxis: {
            categories: ['Africa', 'America', 'Asia', 'Europe',
'Oceania'],
            title: {
                text: null
            }
        },
        yAxis: {
            min: 0,
            title: {
                text: 'Population (millions)',
                align: 'high'
            },
            labels: {
                overflow: 'justify'
            }
        },
        tooltip: {
            valueSuffix: ' millions'
        },
        plotOptions: {
            bar: {
                dataLabels: {
                    enabled: true
                }
            }
        },
```

```
                legend: {
                    layout: 'vertical',
                    align: 'right',
                    verticalAlign: 'top',
                    x: -40,
                    y: 100,
                    floating: true,
                    borderWidth: 1,
                    backgroundColor: ((Highcharts.theme && Highcharts.theme.
        legendBackgroundColor) || '#FFFFFF'),
                    shadow: true
                },
                credits: {
                    enabled: false
                },
                series: [{
                    name: 'Year 1800',
                    data: [107, 31, 635, 203, 2]
                }, {
                    name: 'Year 1900',
                    data: [133, 156, 947, 408, 6]
                }, {
                    name: 'Year 2008',
                    data: [973, 914, 4054, 732, 34]
                }]
            });
        });
        </script>
```

The X-Axis class contains the name of regions and the Y-Axis class represents the population count per year. The series section provides data for X-Axis. Since there are five regions, each year in the series array contains five elements in the data sub-array.

Displaying Solr data using Highcharts

Now let us modify this Highchart to display data from Solr. Start a fresh instance of Solr and index all the xml and csv files from the exampledocs folder. You can use the following commands to index all the files in the exampledocs folder:

```
java -jar post.jar *.xml
java -Dtype=text/csv -jar post.jar *.csv
```

Now let us run a query that gives facets based on the `cat` field:

```
http://localhost:8983/solr/collection1/select/?q=*:*&facet=true&facet
.field=cat
```

The following are the facets obtained from the execution of the snippet:

```
▼<lst name="facet_fields">
  ▼<lst name="cat">
      <int name="electronics">12</int>
      <int name="book">10</int>
      <int name="currency">4</int>
      <int name="memory">3</int>
      <int name="connector">2</int>
      <int name="graphics card">2</int>
      <int name="hard drive">2</int>
      <int name="search">2</int>
      <int name="software">2</int>
      <int name="camera">1</int>
      <int name="copier">1</int>
      <int name="electronics and computer1">1</int>
      <int name="electronics and stuff2">1</int>
      <int name="multifunction printer">1</int>
      <int name="music">1</int>
      <int name="printer">1</int>
      <int name="scanner">1</int>
  </lst>
</lst>
```

Now let us write a simple PHP script to read facets from the preceding query and create the JSON required for the Highchart. The script created uses a PHP library for Solr known as **Solarium**. For advanced features of Apache Solr PHP integration, please refer to an earlier book on this topic, *Apache Solr PHP Integration, Packt Publishing*. Thus, we will not study the installation and integration details of Solr and PHP in depth.

To run the example code, we will need a web server, Apache, with PHP installed in it. We will have to install the Solarium library using composer and then open up the script on the browser to get the graph.

On a Linux or Ubuntu machine, use the following commands to get started with PHP and Solarium:

```
sudo apt-get install php5 apache2 libapache2-mod-php5
```

The web folder of Apache2 is located at the /var/www/html path.

Unzip the highcharts.zip file inside the html folder and put the code there.

To install Solarium using a composer, create the following composer.json file:

```
{
    "require": {
    "solarium/solarium": "3.2.0"
    }
}
```

Then run the following command:

```
composer install
```

This will download the composer library and install it in a folder vendor inside the /var/www/html folder. Now place facetGraph.php in the same folder.

On running the PHP code, we will get the following graph:

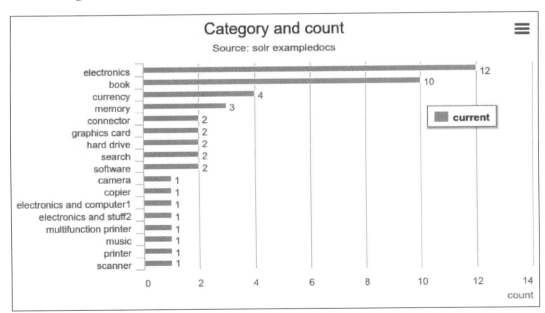

Now let us go through and understand the code.

We have defined our Solr connection parameters using the configuration variable and created a Solarium client:

```
$config = array(
   "endpoint" => array(
     "localhost" => array(
       "host"=>"127.0.0.1",
       "port"=>"8983",
       "path"=>"/solr",
       "core"=>"collection1",
     ),
   )
);
$client = new Solarium\Client($config);
```

We are creating our `select` query using the following code:

```
$query = $client->createSelect();
$query->setQuery('*:*');
```

We have created a facet for the `cat` field and named the facet as `category` for reference in our PHP code:

```
$facetset = $query->getFacetSet();
$facetset->createFacetField('category')->setField('cat');
```

Next, we execute the query and get the facets from the result set:

```
$resultSet = $client->select($query);
$facet_cat = $resultSet->getFacetSet()->getFacet('category');
```

In our JavaScript code required for generating the graph, we have defined the category names in the `x-Axis` class:

```
xAxis: {
            categories: [<?php foreach($facet_cat as $item => $count)
{ echo "'".$item."',"; } ?> ],
            title: {
                text: null
            }
          },
```

The category numbers in the `series` variable are defined as follows:

```
series: [{
        name: 'current',
            data: [<?php foreach($facet_cat as $item => $count) {
echo $count.","; } ?>]
        }]
```

The `highchart.js` files are referred to via the following lines in our code:

```
<script src="js/highcharts.js"></script>
<script src="js/modules/exporting.js"></script>
```

This shows that, using simple queries and JavaScript graph libraries, we can generate graphs required for analytics.

With SolrCloud, we can target terabytes of data—as it can be linearly scaled across multiple nodes or machines running Solr. We can create a data warehouse and use it to store massive amounts of data. We can feed the data to the system in real time and build graphs for analytics purposes. The graphs would then reflect the changes happening in real time and provide an insight into historical data.

Summary

In this chapter, we learnt how Solr can be used to churn out data for analytics purposes. We also understood big data and learnt how to use different faceting concepts, such as radius faceting and pivot faceting, for data analytics purposes. We saw some codes that can be used for generating graphs and discussed the different libraries available for this. We discussed that, with SolrCloud, we can build our own data warehouse and get graphs of not only historical data but also real-time data.

In the next chapter, we will learn about the problems that we normally face during the implementation of Solr on an e-commerce platform. We will also discuss how to debug such problems along with tweaks to further optimize the instance(s). Additionally, we will learn about semantic search and its implementation in e-commerce scenarios.

5
Solr in E-commerce

In this chapter, we will discuss in depth the problems faced during the implementation of Solr for search on an e-commerce website. We will look at the related problems and solutions and areas where optimizations may be necessary. We will also look at semantic search and how it can be implemented in an e-commerce scenario. The topics that will be covered in this chapter are listed as follows:

- Designing an e-commerce search
- Handling unclean data
- Handling variations (such as size and color) in the product
- Sorting
- Problems and solutions of flash sale searches
- Faceting with the option of multi-select
- Faceting with hierarchical taxonomy
- Faceting with size
- Implementing semantic search
- Optimizations that we can look into

Designing an e-commerce search

E-commerce search is special. For us, a Lucene search is a Boolean information retrieval model based on the vector space model. However, for an end user, or a customer, any search on an e-commerce website is supposed to be simple. A customer would not make a field-specific search but will focus on what he or she wants from the search.

Suppose a customer is looking out for a pink sweater. The search that will be conducted on the e-commerce website will be `pink sweater` instead of `+color:pink +type:sweater`—using the Solr query syntax. It is our search that will have to figure out how to provide results to the customer so that whatever is being searched for is available to the customer. The problem with e-commerce website searches is that most of the searches happen with the idea that the results are to be retrieved from bag of words or plain text documents. However, it is important for us to categorize and rank the results so that whatever is being searched for is present in the result set.

On a broad note, the following fields can be observed on an e-commerce website catering for clothes:

```
Category: Clothes
Brand: levis
Gender: Mens
Type: Jeans
Size: 34
Fitting: Regular
Occasion: Casual
Color: Blue
```

The following fields could be observed if the e-commerce website caters for electronics, especially mobiles:

```
Category: Mobile
Brand: Motorola
OS: Android
Screen size: 4
Camera: 5MP
Color: Black
```

What about the fields for electronics such as laptops?

```
Category: Laptop
Brand: Lenovo
Processor: intel i5
Screen size: 14 inch
Memory: 4GB
OS: Windows 8
Hard disk: 500 GB
Graphics Card: Nvidia
Graphics card memory: 2 GB DDR5
```

The point we are arriving at is that the scope of fields on any e-commerce website is huge. On the basis of the categories that we intend to serve through our website, we need to list down the fields for each category and then apply our mind to what needs to be tokenized. Suppose that the website we intend to create caters only for mobiles and laptops. Then, the number of fields are limited to the union of both of them. As we add more and more categories, we will need to add more and more fields specific to those categories. Dynamic fields come to our rescue as the number of fields on an e-commerce website increases.

Another important point is to decide which fields would be serving as facets, as we will have to keep a separate field for creating facets. Let us take an example of a website catering to the three categories we discussed earlier and design the schema for it.

Each product will have its unique ID, which is known as sku for the product. A **Stock Keeping Unit (SKU)** is a unique identifier for each product in e-commerce. It is recommended to use an SKU as the unique key in Solr as it is the unique key referencing each product in an e-commerce catalog. This would be an indexed, but not tokenized, field:

```
<field name="sku" type="lowercase" indexed="true" stored="true"
omitNorms="true"/>
```

In this case, the lowercase field type is defined as follows:

```
<fieldType name="lowercase" class="solr.TextField"
positionIncrementGap="100">
<analyzer>
<tokenizer class="solr.KeywordTokenizerFactory"/>
<filter class="solr.LowerCaseFilterFactory" />
</analyzer>
</fieldType>
```

Next, we define the category that is a string—again non-tokenized. Note that we have set multiValued as true, which is a provision for allowing a single product to belong to multiple categories:

```
<field name="cat" type="string" indexed="true" stored="true"
multiValued="true"/>
```

The `brand` and `product` name fields are whitespace tokenized and converted to lowercase:

```
<field name="name" type="wslc" indexed="true" stored="true"/>
<field name="brand" type="wslc" indexed="true" stored="true"/>

<fieldType name="wslc" class="solr.TextField"
positionIncrementGap="100">
<analyzer type="index">
<tokenizer class="solr.WhitespaceTokenizerFactory"/>
<filter class="solr.LowerCaseFilterFactory" />
</analyzer>
<analyzer type="query">
<tokenizer class="solr.WhitespaceTokenizerFactory"/>
<filter class="solr.SynonymFilterFactory" synonyms="synonyms.txt"
ignoreCase="true" expand="true"/>
<filter class="solr.StopFilterFactory" ignoreCase="true"
words="stopwords.txt" />
<filter class="solr.LowerCaseFilterFactory"/>
</analyzer>
</fieldType>
```

Notice that we have applied separate logic for indexing and search or querying on these fields and have also included `synonyms` and `stopwords` in our query logic. During indexing, the text is simply tokenized on whitespace and lowercased. However, during search, we are using stop words to remove unwanted tokens from the search query and synonyms to map certain words with similar meaning words, thus catering to more relevant results. If the user mistypes certain words, synonyms can be used to map common mistakes with relevant words in the index. They can also be used to map short names with full words. For example, `shirt` could be mapped to `t-shirt`, `polo`, and so on, and the search result for `shirt` will contain `t-shirts`, `polos`, and other variations of `t-shirts`. This would be a one-way mapping, which means that `t-shirts` and `polos` cannot be mapped back to shirts. Performing a reverse mapping will give irrelevant results.

Another common field across all these categories is `price`. This can be defined as follows:

```
<field name="price" type="float" indexed="true" stored="true"/>
```

Now that we have all the common fields defined, let's go ahead and define the category-specific fields.

For the `clothes` category, we would define the following fields:

```
<field name="clothes_gender" type="string" indexed="true"
stored="true"/>
<field name="clothes_type" type="string" indexed="true"
stored="true"/>
<field name="clothes_size" type="string" indexed="true"
stored="true"/>
<field name="clothes_fitting" type="string" indexed="true"
stored="true"/>
<field name="clothes_occassion" type="string" indexed="true"
stored="true"/>
<field name="clothes_color" type="string" indexed="true"
stored="true"/>
```

Similarly, we have to define fields for the categories `mobile` and `laptop`. We can also define these fields via a `dynamicField` tag. It is important to note that most of these fields would be used for faceting and in filter queries for narrowing down the results:

```
<dynamicField name="mobile_*" type="string" indexed="true"
stored="true" />
<dynamicField name="laptop_*" type="string" indexed="true"
stored="true" />
```

Using dynamic fields gives flexibility to the indexing script to add fields during the indexing process. In addition to all these fields, we will also have a `text` field that will be used to collect all data from different fields and provide that for search. We will also need a separate field to store the product description:

```
<field name="text" type="text_general" indexed="true" stored="false"
multiValued="true"/>
<field name="desc" type="text_general" indexed="true" stored="false"
/>
```

We will have to copy the required fields into the `text` field for generic search:

```
<copyField source="cat" dest="text"/>
<copyField source="name" dest="text"/>
<copyField source="brand" dest="text"/>
<copyField source="sku" dest="text"/>
<copyField source="clothes_color" dest="text"/>
<copyField source="clothes_type" dest="text"/>
```

This schema should be sufficient for our use case.

> We are copying only the `clothes_color` and `clothes_type` values in our `text` field for generic search, since we want to provide only color and type as a part of the generic search.

Let us see how we would perform a search for any particular query coming on our e-commerce website. Suppose a person searches for `iphone`. Now, the search engine is not aware that the person is searching for a mobile phone. The search will have to happen across multiple categories. Also, the search engine is not aware whether the search happened over a category or a brand or a product name. We will look at a solution for identifying and providing relevant results later in this chapter. Let us look at a generic solution for the query:

```
q=text:iphone cat:iphone^2 name:iphone^2
brand:iphone^2&facet=true&facet.mincount=1&facet.field=clothes_
gender&facet.field=clothes_type&facet.field=clothes_size&facet.
field=clothes_color&facet.field=brand&facet.field=mobile_os&facet.
field=mobile_screen_size&facet.field=laptop_processor&facet.
field=laptop_memory&facet.field=laptop_hard_disk&defType=edismax
```

The output from this query would contain results for `iphone`. As `iphone` is the `name` of a product, it will be boosted and results where the `name` field contains `iphone` will appear on top. In addition to this, we will be getting a lot of facets. As we have provided the parameter `facet.mincount=1`, only facets that contain at least one count will display in the result. All we need to do is loop through the facets that we got in the result and display them along with a checkbox.

Once the user clicks on the checkbox, we will have to rewrite our query with the filter query parameter. Suppose, in the preceding query, the user selects the screen size as 4. Then, the following filter query will be appended to our original Solr query:

```
fq=mobile_screen_size:4
```

This will narrow down the results and help the customer in getting closer to the product he or she is willing to search. As the customer selects more and more facets, we will keep on adding filter queries and the search will narrow down to what the customer wants.

Handling unclean data

What do we mean by unclean data? In the last section, we discussed a customer searching for `pink sweater`, where `pink` is the color and `sweater` is the type of clothing. However, the system or the search engine cannot interpret the input in this fashion. Therefore, in our e-commerce schema design earlier, we created a query that searched across all fields available in the index. We then created a separate `copyField` class to handle search across fields, such as `clothes_color`, that are not being searched in the default query.

Now, will our query give good results? What if there is a brand named pink? Then what would the results be like? First of all, we would not be sure whether pink is intended to be the color or the brand. Suppose we say that pink is intended to be the color, but we are also searching across brands and it will contain pink as the brand name. The results will be a mix of both clothes_color and brand. In our query, we are boosting brand, so what happens is we get sweaters from the pink brand in our output. However, the customer was looking for a sweater in pink color.

Now let's think from the user's point of view. It is not necessary that the user has the luxury of going through all the results and figuring out which pink sweater looks interesting. Moreover, the user may be browsing on a mobile, in which case, looping through the results page by page would become very tedious. Thus, we need high precision in our results. Our top results should match with what the user expects.

A way to handle this scenario is to not tokenize during the index time, but only during the search time. Therefore, exact fields such as brand and product name can be kept as it is. However, while searching across these fields, we would need to tokenize our query. Let us alter our schema to handle this scenario.

We had created a fieldType class named wslc to handle the fields brand and name. We will change the tokenizer during index time to keywordTokenizer and leave the tokenizer during query time as it is:

```
<fieldType name="wslc" class="solr.TextField"
positionIncrementGap="100">
  <analyzer type="index">
    <tokenizer class="solr.KeywordTokenizerFactory"/>
    <filter class="solr.LowerCaseFilterFactory" />
  </analyzer>
  <analyzer type="query">
    <tokenizer class="solr.WhitespaceTokenizerFactory"/>
    <filter class="solr.SynonymFilterFactory" synonyms="synonyms.txt"
    ignoreCase="true" expand="true"/>
    <filter class="solr.StopFilterFactory" ignoreCase="true"
    words="stopwords.txt" />
    <filter class="solr.LowerCaseFilterFactory"/>
  </analyzer>
</fieldType>
```

Also, let's change `fieldType` for `clothes_type` and `clothes_occassion` to `"wslc"` and include these fields in our Solr search query:

```
<field name="clothes_type" type="wslc" indexed="true" stored="true"/>
<field name="clothes_occassion" type="wslc" indexed="true"
stored="true"/>
```

We will also use the eDisMax parser, which we have seen in the earlier chapters. Our query for `pink sweater` will now be:

```
q=pink sweater&qf=text cat^2 name^2 brand^2 clothes_type^2 clothes_
color^2 clothes_occassion^2&pf=text cat^3 name^3 brand^3 clothes_
type^3 clothes_color^3 clothes_occassion^3&fl=*,score&defType=edi
smax&facet=true&facet.mincount=1&facet.field=clothes_gender&facet.
field=clothes_type&facet.field=clothes_size&facet.field=clothes_
color&facet.field=brand&facet.field=mobile_os&facet.field=mobile_
screen_size&facet.field=laptop_processor&facet.field=laptop_
memory&facet.field=laptop_hard_disk
```

We have given a higher boost to exact phrase matches in our query. Therefore, if a term is found as a phrase in any of the specified fields, the results will be a lot better. Also, now since we are tokenizing only during search and not during indexing, our results would be much better. Suppose we have a brand named `pink sweater` and it is picked up as a phrase and the document where the `brand=pink sweater` parameter is boosted higher. Next, documents where `clothes_color` is pink and `clothes_type` is `sweater` are boosted. Let us run a `debug` query and verify what we just said.

```
▼<lst name="debug">
  <str name="rawquerystring">pink sweater</str>
  <str name="querystring">pink sweater</str>
  ▼<str name="parsedquery">
    (+(DisjunctionMaxQuery((brand:pink^2.0 | clothes_color:pink^2.0 | cat:pink^2.0 |
    text:pink | clothes_type:pink^2.0 | clothes_occassion:pink^2.0 | name:pink^2.0))
    DisjunctionMaxQuery((brand:sweater^2.0 | clothes_color:sweater^2.0 |
    cat:sweater^2.0 | text:sweater | clothes_type:sweater^2.0 |
    clothes_occassion:sweater^2.0 | name:sweater^2.0)))
    DisjunctionMaxQuery((text:"pink sweater")) () DisjunctionMaxQuery((name:"pink
    sweater"^3.0)) DisjunctionMaxQuery((brand:"pink sweater"^3.0))
    DisjunctionMaxQuery((clothes_type:"pink sweater"^3.0)) ()
    DisjunctionMaxQuery((clothes_occassion:"pink sweater"^3.0)))/no_coord
  </str>
  ▼<str name="parsedquery_toString">
    +((brand:pink^2.0 | clothes_color:pink^2.0 | cat:pink^2.0 | text:pink |
    clothes_type:pink^2.0 | clothes_occassion:pink^2.0 | name:pink^2.0)
    (brand:sweater^2.0 | clothes_color:sweater^2.0 | cat:sweater^2.0 | text:sweater |
    clothes_type:sweater^2.0 | clothes_occassion:sweater^2.0 | name:sweater^2.0))
    (text:"pink sweater") () (name:"pink sweater"^3.0) (brand:"pink sweater"^3.0)
    (clothes_type:"pink sweater"^3.0) () (clothes_occassion:"pink sweater"^3.0)
  </str>
```

Query: pink sweater

Now even if we give multiple words in our search query, the results should be a lot better. A search for `tommy hilfiger green sweater` should give very precise results. Cases where results are not available are handled by the default search `text` field. In case there are no results that match our search query, there would be some results due to the copying of fields into `text` and the index time tokenization that happens over there.

As we go further in depth in this chapter, we will see more and more ways of indexing and searching data in an e-commerce website.

Handling variations in the product

Now that we have somewhat better search results for our e-commerce site, let us look at handling variations. What do we mean by variations? Let us take our earlier example of `tommy hilfiger green sweater`. For the sake of simplicity, let's say that it comes in three sizes—small, medium, and large. Do we intend to show all three sizes in our search results as individual products? That would be a waste of the display area. If we take the example of a mobile screen, even if our top result is exactly the `green sweater` we are looking at, in this scenario, it will have three products on the first screen. Instead, we could have shown some other results that may have been of interest to our customer.

Let us push in the sample data for clothes with the schema given in this chapter. Replace the `schema.xml` file in the default Solr installation with that shared in this chapter and run the following command to push the `data_clothes.csv` file into the Solr index:

```
java -Dtype=text/csv -jar solr/example/exampledocs/post.jar data_clothes.csv
```

The query we created earlier can be modified for `tommy hilfiger green sweater` as follows:

```
http://localhost:8983/solr/collection1/select?q=tommy%20hilfiger%20green%20sweater&qf=text%20cat^2%20name^2%20brand^2%20clothes_type^2%20clothes_color^2%20clothes_occassion^2&pf=text%20cat^3%20name^3%20brand^3%20clothes_type^3%20clothes_color^3%20clothes_occassion^3&fl=name,brand,price,clothes_color,clothes_size,score&defType=edismax&facet=true&facet.mincount=1&facet.field=clothes_gender&facet.field=clothes_type&facet.field=clothes_size&facet.field=clothes_color&facet.field=brand&facet.field=mobile_os&facet.field=mobile_screen_size&facet.field=laptop_processor&facet.field=laptop_memory&facet.field=laptop_hard_disk
```

On running this query, we are getting the following output:

```
-<result name="response" numFound="6" start="0" maxScore="0.13487813">
 -<doc>
     <str name="name">tommy hilfiger sweater</str>
     <str name="brand">tommy hilfiger</str>
     <float name="price">150.0</float>
     <str name="clothes_size">medium</str>
     <str name="clothes_color">green</str>
     <float name="score">0.13487813</float>
  </doc>
 -<doc>
     <str name="name">tommy hilfiger sweater</str>
     <str name="brand">tommy hilfiger</str>
     <float name="price">150.0</float>
     <str name="clothes_size">large</str>
     <str name="clothes_color">green</str>
     <float name="score">0.13487813</float>
  </doc>
 -<doc>
     <str name="name">tommy hilfiger sweater</str>
     <str name="brand">tommy hilfiger</str>
     <float name="price">150.0</float>
     <str name="clothes_size">small</str>
     <str name="clothes_color">green</str>
     <float name="score">0.13487813</float>
  </doc>
 -<doc>
     <str name="name">tommy hilfiger sweater</str>
     <str name="brand">tommy hilfiger</str>
     <float name="price">170.0</float>
     <str name="clothes_size">medium</str>
     <str name="clothes_color">red</str>
     <float name="score">0.041787125</float>
  </doc>
```

Running query : "tommy hilfiger green sweater"

We can see that the first three results are exactly the same—they even have the same score. They only differ in size. Therefore, what is required is that the results that have variations in clothes_color and clothes_size be grouped together. However, which grouping field do we select out of the two? Should we group by color so that all greens are shown together, or should we group by size so that all medium sizes are shown together? It depends on the input the user has already selected. If the user has not selected any of color or size, it would make sense to group by color, so that different sizes of the same color come together. On the other hand, if the user has already selected a size, we would need to add a filter query on clothes_size to get the desired output.

In our previous query, grouping by `clothes_color` will give the following output:

```xml
<lst name="grouped">
  <lst name="clothes_color">
    <int name="matches">5</int>
    <arr name="groups">
      <lst>
        <str name="groupValue">green</str>
        <result name="doclist" numFound="3" start="0"
        maxScore="0.43155915">
          <doc>
            <str name="name">tommy hilfiger sweater</str>
            <str name="brand">tommy hilfiger</str>
            <float name="price">150.0</float>
            <str name="clothes_size">medium</str>
            <str name="clothes_color">green</str>
            <float name="score">0.43155915</float>
          </doc>
        </result>
      </lst>
      <lst>
        <str name="groupValue">red</str>
        <result name="doclist" numFound="1" start="0"
        maxScore="0.1737936">
          <doc>
            <str name="name">tommy hilfiger sweater</str>
            <str name="brand">tommy hilfiger</str>
            <float name="price">150.0</float>
            <str name="clothes_size">medium</str>
            <str name="clothes_color">red</str>
            <float name="score">0.1737936</float>
          </doc>
        </result>
```

Results grouped by color

The Solr query will contain the following extra parameters to group by the field `clothes_color`:

```
group=true&group.field=clothes_color
```

Once the user selects the size he or she is interested in, say `medium`, grouping by `clothes_color` after applying the `clothes_size` filter query will give the following output:

```xml
-<lst name="grouped">
  -<lst name="clothes_color">
    <int name="matches">3</int>
    -<arr name="groups">
      -<lst>
        <str name="groupValue">green</str>
        -<result name="doclist" numFound="1" start="0" maxScore="0.13487813">
          -<doc>
            <str name="name">tommy hilfiger sweater</str>
            <str name="brand">tommy hilfiger</str>
            <float name="price">150.0</float>
            <str name="clothes_size">medium</str>
            <str name="clothes_color">green</str>
            <float name="score">0.13487813</float>
          </doc>
        </result>
      </lst>
      -<lst>
        <str name="groupValue">red</str>
        -<result name="doclist" numFound="1" start="0" maxScore="0.041787125">
          -<doc>
```

We will add the following filter query to our earlier Solr query:

```
fq=clothes_size:medium
```

The same fundamentals can be used to handle variations across multiple products and categories. This feature in e-commerce is known as field collapsing. As in the previous scenario, we have given priority to color over size for any product variation. We will have to give priority to a certain aspect of the product variation. Grouping would happen on the basis of that aspect. Remaining aspects would appear as facets and will be used to filter out the results.

Sorting

In addition to search, we also need to provide sorting options on an e-commerce website. By default, the search results are ordered by the relevancy score that has been computed on the basis of the boosting we have provided. However, there would still be requirements to sort the search results by other factors such as `price`, `discount`, or `latest products`. Sorting by already known fields is simple. All we need to do is add the sorting criteria behind our Solr search query:

```
sort=price asc
```

Alternatively, add the following sorting code:

```
sort=price desc
```

The intelligence that needs to be built into the system here is sorting by relevance after `price`. This is to take care of scenarios where the ordered results may contain irrelevant results in the top when, say, sorted by price in the ascending order. Therefore, we would be modifying our query to include the score while sorting:

```
sort=price asc,score desc
```

Now, the top results would be better. Another intelligence that needs to be taken care of is to exclude or de-boost results that are *"out of stock"*. For this, we will have to include inventory information in our index. We can say that we include the inventory information as the availability of a particular product, so a new Boolean field named `'instock'` can be added to the index, which contains the availability of the product:

```
<field name="instock" type="boolean" indexed="true" stored="true"/>
```

To exclude the products that are out of stock, we will need to simply add a filter query:

```
fq=instock:true
```

This filter query will ensure that the results that we get from our Solr index will contain only those products that are in stock. However, what if the search result contains only `"out of stock"` products? In that case, the search will return zero results. To fix this, we need to display out of stock products after the products that are in stock. For this, we can run multiple queries. The first query runs with the above filter query such that the results contain only `instock` products. Then, we run the same query again after replacing the filter query parameter to get products that are *"out of stock"*:

```
fq=instock:false
```

De-boosting of *"out of stock"* products is another way of achieving the same result, but with a single query. Let us understand this with the help of an example. Run the following query on the Solr index. Notice the `sort` and `boost` parameters passed in the query:

```
q=iphone&qf=text%20cat^2%20name^2%20brand^2%20clothes_type^2%20
clothes_color^2%20clothes_occassion^2&pf=text%20cat^3%20name^3%20
brand^3%20clothes_type^3%20clothes_color^3%20clothes_occassion^3&f
l=name,brand,price,instock,score&defType=edismax&facet=true&facet.
mincount=1&facet.field=clothes_gender&facet.field=clothes_type&facet.
field=clothes_size&facet.field=clothes_color&facet.field=brand&facet.
field=mobile_os&facet.field=mobile_screen_size&facet.field=laptop_
processor&facet.field=laptop_memory&facet.field=laptop_hard_
disk&sort=score%20desc,price%20asc&boost=if(instock,10,0.1)
```

We want the cheapest `iphone` on top, but also want to de-boost all *"out of stock"* iPhones. The boost parameter over here provides a multiplicative factor to the relevance score. It states that if `instock` is `true`, multiply the relevance score by **10**. Else, multiply the relevance score by **0.1**. Therefore, products that are in stock are boosted, while products that are *"not in stock"* are de-boosted. Also, here instead of sorting by `price` directly, we have first sorted by `score`, and then by `price`. The results are very impressive:

```
<result name="response" numFound="5" start="0" maxScore="4.218697">
  <doc>
    <str name="name">iphone 4s</str>
    <float name="price">230.0</float>
    <bool name="instock">true</bool>
    <float name="score">4.218697</float>
  </doc>
  <doc>
    <str name="name">iphone 5c</str>
    <float name="price">450.0</float>
    <bool name="instock">true</bool>
    <float name="score">4.218697</float>
  </doc>
  <doc>
    <str name="name">iphone 5</str>
    <float name="price">500.0</float>
    <bool name="instock">true</bool>
    <float name="score">4.218697</float>
  </doc>
  <doc>
    <str name="name">iphone 5s</str>
    <float name="price">550.0</float>
    <bool name="instock">true</bool>
    <float name="score">4.218697</float>
  </doc>
  <doc>
    <str name="name">iphone 4</str>
    <float name="price">200.0</float>
    <bool name="instock">false</bool>
    <float name="score">0.04218697</float>
```

Relevance scoring – results sorted by availability

We can see that the cheapest of all iphones comes at last because it is out of stock. Remaining `iphones` are sorted by `price` in the ascending order.

Problems and solutions of flash sale searches

The major problem that flash sale sites face is the sudden and large amount of traffic. Generally, people are notified in advance about the time of the sale, so at that exact moment, a large number of customers hit the site to purchase the objects on sale. Therefore, we see a sudden spike in traffic and low traffic when there is no flash sale happening.

Another problem is that, as soon as a product is sold out, it should be moved to the bottom of the search result. We have already seen how this situation can be handled in the previous section. However, this requires very frequent updates to the Solr index. Ideally, as soon as a sale happens, the inventory status should be updated in the index. This is a general problem, but with flash sale sites, the problem becomes more acute. This is because at the time when the sale opens, there is a rush for a certain product. Moreover, the site can lose customers if inventory is not properly tracked and reported during flash sale time.

Thus, when we combine both the scenarios, we have a site that has a sudden spike in traffic, and we also need to keep the inventory status updated in the index to prevent over-selling of the product. Solr NRT indexing would help a lot in this scenario. A soft commit at certain durations could be used to reflect the changes in the index. To implement NRT in our index, we need to take care of two things in our `solrconfig.xml` file.

 A soft commit is much faster since it only makes index changes visible and does not `fsync` index files or write a new index descriptor to disk.

We need to ensure that the `DirectoryFactory` directive used for creating the Solr index is `NRTCachingDirectoryFactory` class:

```
<directoryFactory name="DirectoryFactory"
class="${solr.directoryFactory:solr.NRTCachingDirectoryFactory}">
```

We need to ensure the time duration for soft commits. This is handled via the `autoSoftCommit` directive:

```
<autoSoftCommit>
<maxTime>30000</maxTime>
</autoSoftCommit>
```

This indicates that, every 30 seconds (30,000 milliseconds), changes in the Solr index will become available irrespective of whether they have been written to disk or not. An `autoCommit` directive specifies the duration when the index will be written to disk. It is important to note that, in the case of a system failure, if the changes that are available via soft commit are not written to disk, the transaction log will be lost. If the soft commit has been written to the transaction log, it will be replayed when the Solr server restarts. If no hard commit has been made, the transaction log can contain a lot of documents that can result in a considerable Solr server startup time.

The third problem is that a product on sale should be searchable only after the exact sale time of the product. For example, if a product is supposed to go on sale at 2 pm in the afternoon, it should be in the index before 2 pm but should be searchable only after 2 pm.

In order to handle this scenario, we need to include time-sensitive data in our search index. To do this, we need to add two additional fields in the Solr index that define the start and end time of the sale for that particular product:

```
<field name="sale_start" type="date" indexed="true" stored="true"/>
<field name="sale_end" type="date" indexed="true" stored="true"/>
```

Once this information is stored in the index, all we need to do is add another filter query to get the time sensitive products as a part of our search result. The filter query will be:

```
fq=+sale_start:[* TO NOW]+sale_end:[NOW+1HOUR TO *]
```

However, this filter query is very inefficient because NOW calculates the time every time the query is run. Therefore, filter query caching does not happen. A better way to do this would be to round off the time to the nearest hour or minute to cache the filter query for that duration. Thus, our filter query would become:

```
fq=+sale_start:[* TO NOW/HOUR]+sale_end:[NOW/HOUR+1HOUR TO *]
```

Now, as soon as the end time for the sale goes by, the product automatically goes offline.

Faceting with the option of multi-select

Facets are extracted from the search result. Once a customer selects an option from the facet, we create a filter query that is typically an AND logic. For example, on searching for a particular item, say `tommy hilfiger`, we would be getting results that will have facets for size and color. It was previously assumed that the customer would select a single option from both the facets. Say the selections are `medium` for size and `green` for color. The filter query would be:

```
fq=clothes_size:medium&fq=clothes_color:green
```

This will be appended to our search query:

```
q=tommy%20hilfiger&qf=text%20cat^2%20name^2%20brand^2%20clothes_
type^2%20clothes_color^2%20clothes_occassion^2&pf=text%20cat^3%20
name^3%20brand^3%20clothes_type^3%20clothes_color^3%20clothes_
occassion^3&fl=name,clothes_size,clothes_color,score&defType=edis
max&facet=true&facet.mincount=1&facet.field=clothes_gender&facet.
field=clothes_type&facet.field=clothes_size&facet.field=clothes_
color&facet.field=brand&facet.field=mobile_os&facet.field=mobile_
screen_size&facet.field=laptop_processor&facet.field=laptop_
memory&facet.field=laptop_hard_disk&fq=clothes_size:medium&fq=clothes_
color:green
```

What happens if the customer intends to select multiple options in facets? In this case, suppose the customer is interested in both `medium` and `large` sizes and also in `green` and `red` colors. To handle this, we will have to use OR between multiple options in our filter query for a particular field. The filter query in this case will be:

```
fq=clothes_size:medium clothes_size:large&fq=clothes_color:red
clothes_color:green
```

The complete query will be:

```
q=tommy%20hilfiger&qf=text%20cat^2%20name^2%20brand^2%20clothes_
type^2%20clothes_color^2%20clothes_occassion^2&pf=text%20cat^3%20
name^3%20brand^3%20clothes_type^3%20clothes_color^3%20clothes_
occassion^3&fl=name,clothes_size,clothes_color,score&defType=edis
max&facet=true&facet.mincount=1&facet.field=clothes_gender&facet.
field=clothes_type&facet.field=clothes_size&facet.field=clothes_
color&facet.field=brand&facet.field=mobile_os&facet.field=mobile_
screen_size&facet.field=laptop_processor&facet.field=laptop_
memory&facet.field=laptop_hard_disk&fq=clothes_size:mediumclothes_
size:large&fq=clothes_color:redclothes_color:green
```

The filter query is interpreted as follows:

```
- <arr name="fq">
    <str>clothes_size:medium clothes_size:large</str>
    <str>clothes_color:red clothes_color:green</str>
  </arr>
  <str name="defType">edismax</str>
```

Filter query for the multi-select option

The results would be as follows:

```xml
<result name="response" numFound="4" start="0" maxScore="0.41651493">
  <doc>
    <str name="name">tommy hilfiger sweater</str>
    <str name="clothes_size">medium</str>
    <str name="clothes_color">green</str>
    <float name="score">0.41651493</float>
  </doc>
  <doc>
    <str name="name">tommy hilfiger sweater</str>
    <str name="clothes_size">large</str>
    <str name="clothes_color">green</str>
    <float name="score">0.41651493</float>
  </doc>
  <doc>
    <str name="name">tommy hilfiger sweater</str>
    <str name="clothes_size">medium</str>
    <str name="clothes_color">red</str>
    <float name="score">0.41651493</float>
  </doc>
  <doc>
    <str name="name">tommy hilfiger sweater</str>
    <str name="clothes_size">large</str>
    <str name="clothes_color">red</str>
    <float name="score">0.41651493</float>
  </doc>
</result>
```

Multi-select search result

Another problem that plagues faceting on an e-commerce site is known as disappearing facets. To show only facets that are relevant to the search result, we set the `facet.mincount` parameter to 1. This ensures that only facets that contain certain values are shown. What if further filter queries reduce the facet count to 0 and make it disappear from the facets?

Let us take an example to understand the problem.

A search for `tommy hilfiger` gives us facets in *size* and *color*:

```
- <lst name="facet_fields">
  - <lst name="clothes_size">
      <int name="large">2</int>
      <int name="medium">2</int>
      <int name="small">1</int>
    </lst>
  - <lst name="clothes_color">
      <int name="green">3</int>
      <int name="red">2</int>
    </lst>
```

Facets for "tommy hilfiger" search

When we apply a filter query for `size=small`, we intend to have an output specifying that there are no sweaters in `red` matching the size we have selected:

```
size: small -> 1, medium -> 0, large -> 0
color: red -> 0, green -> 1
```

However, since the `facet.mincount=1` parameter, the output is:

```
size: small -> 1
color: green -> 1
```

```
▼<lst name="clothes_size">
    <int name="small">1</int>
  </lst>
▼<lst name="clothes_color">
    <int name="green">1</int>
  </lst>
```

Disappearing facets

The way to handle this is to tag filter queries and exclude them from facets. The filter query can be tagged as follows:

```
fq={!tag=size_fq}clothes_size:small
```

The tagged filter query can be excluded from the facet using the following syntax:

```
facet.field={!ex=size_fq}clothes_size
```

In order to handle the disappearing facet scenario, we have created multiple facets on the same field—one facet bearing the exact count from the result set taking into consideration the filter queries and another facet that excludes all filter queries.

We have modified the preceding query to handle this scenario, and simplified the query to focus exactly on the modifications that we have implemented:

```
q=tommy%20hilfiger&qf=text%20cat^2%20name^2%20brand^2%20clothes_
type^2%20clothes_color^2%20clothes_occassion^2&pf=text%20cat^3%20
name^3%20brand^3%20clothes_type^3%20clothes_color^3%20clothes_
occassion^3&fl=name,clothes_size,clothes_color,score&defType=edi
smax&facet=true&facet.mincount=1&facet.field=clothes_size&facet.
field=clothes_color&facet.field={!ex=size_fq,color_fq key=all_size_
facets}clothes_size&facet.field={!ex=size_fq,color_fq key=all_color_
facets}clothes_color&fq={!tag=size_fq}clothes_size:small
```

Here, we have created multiple facets on both `clothes_size` and `clothes_color` fields, one in which filter queries are excluded and another in which they are not. Also, the filter queries are tagged as `size_fq`. The facets in which filter queries are excluded are tagged as `all_size_facets` and `all_color_facets`. The following is the output from the query:

```
▼<arr name="facet.field">
  <str>clothes_size</str>
  <str>clothes_color</str>
  ▼<str>
    {!ex=size_fq,color_fq key=all_size_facets}clothes_size
  </str>
  ▼<str>
    {!ex=size_fq,color_fq key=all_color_facets}clothes_color
  </str>
  </arr>
  <str name="fq">{!tag=size_fq}clothes_size:small</str>
  <str name="defType">edismax</str>
  </lst>
</lst>
▶<result name="response" numFound="1" start="0" maxScore="0.4165
▼<lst name="facet_counts">
  <lst name="facet_queries"/>
  ▼<lst name="facet_fields">
    ▼<lst name="clothes_size">
      <int name="small">1</int>
    </lst>
    ▼<lst name="clothes_color">
      <int name="green">1</int>
    </lst>
    ▼<lst name="all_size_facets">
      <int name="large">2</int>
      <int name="medium">2</int>
      <int name="small">1</int>
    </lst>
    ▼<lst name="all_color_facets">
      <int name="green">3</int>
      <int name="red">2</int>
    </lst>
    </lst>
```

Both missing facets and all results facets seen here

Our program has to take care of merging both the facets for **size** and **color** and create the appropriate output. For example, the output can contain the facet counts from the `all_clothes_color` tag. Except for `green`, all others could be disabled (instead of displaying `0`).

Faceting with hierarchical taxonomy

You will have come across e-commerce sites that show facets in a hierarchy. Let's take a look at www.amazon.com and check how hierarchy is handled there. A search for `"shoes"` provides the following hierarchy:

```
Department Shoes -> Men -> Outdoor -> Hiking & Trekking -> Hiking
Boots
```

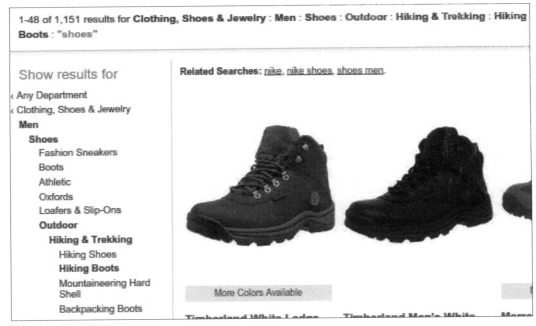

Hierarchical facets on www.amazon.com

How is this hierarchy built into Solr and how do searches happen on it?

In earlier versions of Solr, this used to be handled by a tokenizer known as `solr. PathHierarchyTokenizerFactory`. Each document would contain the complete path or hierarchy leading to the document, and searches would show multiple facets for a single document.

For example, the `shoes` hierarchy we saw earlier can be indexed as:

```
doc #1 : /dept_shoes/men/outdoor/hiking_trekking/hiking_boots
doc #2 : /dept_shoes/men/work/formals/
```

The `PathHierarchyTokenizerFactory` class will break this field, say, into the following tokens:

```
doc #1 : /dept_shoes, /dept_shoes/men, /dept_shoes/men/outdoor,
/dept_shoes/men/outdoor/hiking_trekking,
/dept_shoes/men/outdoor/hiking_trekking/hiking_boots
doc #2 : /dept_shoes, /dept_shoes/men, /dept_shoes/men/work,
/dept_shoes/men/work/formals
```

The initial query would contain the `facet.field` value as `hierarchy`:

```
facet.field="hierarchy"&facet.mincount=1
```

The `facet.prefix` parameter can be used to drill down into the query:

```
facet.prefix="/dept_shoes/men/outdoor"
```

This will list down sub-facets of outdoor-mens-shoes:

Here we have to take care of creating the hierarchy during indexing, which can be a tedious task.

A better way to handle this in the new Solr 4.x version is by using pivot facets. Pivot facets are implemented by splitting the hierarchical information or *bread crumbs* across multiple fields, with one field for each level of the hierarchy. For the earlier example, the fields for pivot faceting would be:

```
doc #1 => hr_l0:dept_shoes, hr_l1:men, hr_l2:outdoor,
hr_l3:hiking_trekking, hr_l4:hiking_boots
doc #2 => hr_l0:dept_shoes, hr_l1:men, hr_l2:work, hr_l3:formals
```

The initial query for creating the facet pivots would be:

```
facet.pivot=hr_l0,hr_l1,hr_l2,hr_l3,hr_l4
```

To implement this in our index, we will need to add a dynamic field of type `string` to our `schema.xml` file:

```
<dynamicField name="hr_*" type="string" indexed="true"
stored="true" />
```

Let us index the `data_shoes.csv` file and then run pivot faceting and see the results:

```
java -Dtype=text/csv -jar solr/example/exampledocs/post.jar data_shoes.
csv
```

```
q=shoes&qf=text%20cat^2%20name^2%20brand^2%20clothes_type^2%20clothes_
color^2%20clothes_occassion^2&pf=text%20cat^3%20name^3%20brand^3%20
clothes_type^3%20clothes_color^3%20clothes_occassion^3&fl=*,score&face
t=true&facet.pivot=hr_10,hr_11,hr_12,hr_13,hr_14
```

On implementing pivot faceting using this query, we should be getting the
following output:

```
▼<arr name="hr_10,hr_11,hr_12,hr_13,hr_14">
  ▼<lst>
    <str name="field">hr_10</str>
    <str name="value">dept_shoes</str>
    <int name="count">7</int>
    ▼<arr name="pivot">
      ▼<lst>
        <str name="field">hr_11</str>
        <str name="value">mens</str>
        <int name="count">7</int>
        ▼<arr name="pivot">
          ▼<lst>
            <str name="field">hr_12</str>
            <str name="value">outdoor</str>
            <int name="count">5</int>
            ▼<arr name="pivot">
              ▼<lst>
                <str name="field">hr_13</str>
                <str name="value">hiking</str>
                <int name="count">3</int>
                ▼<arr name="pivot">
                  ▼<lst>
                    <str name="field">hr_14</str>
                    <str name="value">boots</str>
                    <int name="count">2</int>
                  </lst>
                  ▼<lst>
                    <str name="field">hr_14</str>
                    <str name="value">shoes</str>
                    <int name="count">1</int>
                  </lst>
                </arr>
              </lst>
              ▼<lst>
                <str name="field">hr_13</str>
                <str name="value">running</str>
                <int name="count">2</int>
                ▼<arr name="pivot">
                  ▼<lst>
                    <str name="field">hr_14</str>
                    <str name="value">sports shoes</str>
                    <int name="count">2</int>
                  </lst>
                </arr>
              </lst>
            </arr>
          </lst>
        </arr>
      </lst>
      ▼<lst>
        <str name="field">hr_12</str>
        <str name="value">work</str>
        <int name="count">2</int>
        ▼<arr name="pivot">
          ▼<lst>
            <str name="field">hr_13</str>
            <str name="value">formals</str>
            <int name="count">2</int>
            ▼<arr name="pivot">
```

Pivot faceting output

To drill down, all we need to do is add the respective field and value as a filter query in our Solr search query.

Faceting with size

The problem with faceting with size is that the ordering by size is not directly visible. Let us take the following sizes:

```
XS, S, M, L, XL, XXL
```

These sizes would be listed in the alphabetical order as follows:

```
M, L, S, XL, XS, XXL
```

To handle such ordering scenarios in size for different apparel, we could encode a size tag into the size facet label. Therefore, the size ordering would be somewhat as follows:

```
[00002]XS
[00003]S
[00004]M
[00005]L
[00006]XL
[00007]XXL
```

This will ensure that the facets we get from Solr are ordered in the way we want them to be ordered.

Implementing semantic search

Semantic search is when the search engine understands what the customer is searching for and provides results that are based on this understanding. Therefore, a search for the term shoes should display only items that are of type shoes instead of items with a description *goes well with black shoes*. We could argue that since we are boosting on the fields category, type, brand, color, and size, our results should match with what the customer is looking or searching for. However, this might not be the case. Let us take a more appropriate example to understand this situation.

Suppose a customer is searching for blue jeans where blue is intended to be the color and jeans is the type of apparel. What if there is a brand of products called blue jeans? The results coming from the search would not be as expected by the customer. As all the fields are being boosted by the same boost factor, the results will be a mix of the intended blue colored jeans and the products from the brand called blue jeans.

Now, how do we handle such a scenario? How would the search engine decide what products to show? We saw the same problem earlier with `pink sweater` and tried to solve it by proper boosting of fields. In this scenario, `brand`, `type`, and `color` are boosted by the same boost factor. The result is bound to be a mix of what is intended and what is not intended.

Semantic search could come to our rescue. We need the search engine to understand the meaning of `blue jeans`. Once the search engine understands that `blue` is the `color` and `jeans` is the `type` of clothing, it can boost the `color` and `type` fields only giving us exactly what we want.

The downside over here is that we have to take a call. We need to understand that `blue jeans` is a mix of `color` and `type` instead of `brand` or the other way around. The results that are returned will be heavily dependent on our call. The ideal way would be to give importance to different fields on the basis of the searches our site receives. Suppose that our site receives a lot of brand searches. We would then intend to make the search engine understand that `blue jeans` is a brand instead of `type` and `color`. On the other hand, if we analyze the searches happening on the site and find that the searches are mostly happening on `type` and `color`, we would have to make the search engine interpret `blue jeans` as `type` and `color`.

Let us try to implement the same.

To make the search engine understand the meaning of the terms, we need a dictionary that maps the terms to their meanings. This dictionary can be a separate index having just two fields, words and meanings. Let us create a separate core in our Solr installation that stores our dictionary:

```
cd<solr_installation>/example/solr
mkdir -p dictionary/data
mkdir -p dictionary/conf
cp -r collection1/conf/* dictionary/conf
```

Define the Solr core in `solr.xml` file in the `<solr_installation>/example/solr` directory by adding the following snippet to the `solr.xml` file:

```
<solr sharedLib="lib">
<cores adminPath="/admin/cores">
<core name="collection1" instanceDir="/collection1">
<property name="dataDir" value="/collection1/data" />
</core>
<core name="dictionary" instanceDir="/dictionary">
<property name="dataDir" value="/dictionary/data" />
</core>
</cores>
</solr>
```

The format of the `solr.xml` file will be changed in Solr 5.0. An optional parameter `coreRootDirectory` will be used to specify the directory from where the cores for the current Solr will be auto-discovered. The new format will be as follows:

```
<solr>
  <str name="adminHandler"
>${adminHandler:org.apache.solr.handler.admin.CoreAdminHandler}<
/str>
    <int name="coreLoadThreads">${coreLoadThreads:3}</int>
    <str name="coreRootDirectory">${coreRootDirectory:}</str>
    <str name="managementPath">${managementPath:}</str>
    <str name="sharedLib">${sharedLib:}</str>
    <str name="shareSchema">${shareSchema:false}</str>
</solr>
```

Also, as of Solr 5.0, the core discovery process will involve keeping a `core.properties` file in each Solr core folder. The format of the `core.properties` file will be as follows:

```
name=core1
shard=${shard:}
collection=${collection:core1}
config=${solrconfig:solrconfig.xml}
schema=${schema:schema.xml}
coreNodeName=${coreNodeName:}
```

Solr parses all the directories inside the directory defined in `coreRootDirectory` parameter (which defaults to the Solr home), and if a `core.properties` file is found in any directory, the directory is considered to be a Solr core. Also, `instanceDir` is the directory in which the `core.properties` file was found. We can also have an empty `core.properties` file. In this case, the data directory will be in a directory called `data` directly below. The name of the core is assumed to be the name of the folder in which the `core.properties` file was discovered.

The Solr schema would contain only two fields, `key` and `value`. In this case, `key` would contain the field names and `value` would contain the bag of words that identify the field name in `key`:

```
<field name="key" type="lowercase" indexed="true" stored="true"
required="true" />
<field name="value" type="wslc" indexed="true" stored="true"
multiValued="true" />
```

Also, the `key` field needs to be marked as unique, as the `key` contains fields that are unique:

```
<uniqueKey>key</uniqueKey>
```

Also, we will need to change the default search field to `value` in the `solrconfig.xml` file for the `dictionary` core. For the request handler named `/select`, make the following change:

```
<str name="df">value</str>
```

Once the schema is defined, we need to restart Solr to see the new core on our Solr interface.

collection1	Core	
dictionary	startTime:	2 minutes ago
	instanceDir:	/home/jayant/installed/solr-4.7.2/example/solr/dictionary/
	dataDir:	/home/jayant/installed/solr-4.7.2/example/solr/dictionary/data/

New core in Solr

In order to populate the `dictionary` index, we will need to upload the `data_dictionary.csv` file onto our index. The following command performs this function. Windows users can use the Solr admin interface to upload the CSV file:

```
curl "http://localhost:8983/solr/dictionary/update/csv?commit=true&f.value.split=true" --data-binary @data_dictionary.csv -H 'Content-type:application/csv; charset=utf-8'
```

In order to check the dictionary index, just run a query q=*:*:

```
http://localhost:8983/solr/dictionary/select/?q=*:*
```

```
▼<result name="response" numFound="5" start="0">
  ▼<doc>
    <str name="key">clothes_type</str>
    ▼<arr name="value">
      <str>sweater</str>
      <str>jeans</str>
      <str>shirt</str>
      <str>pant</str>
    </arr>
    <long name="_version_">1467589856796344320</long>
  </doc>
  ▼<doc>
    <str name="key">brand</str>
    ▼<arr name="value">
      <str>tommy hilfiger</str>
      <str>levis</str>
      <str>lee</str>
      <str>wrangler</str>
    </arr>
    <long name="_version_">1467589856816267264</long>
  </doc>
  ▼<doc>
    <str name="key">clothes_size</str>
    ▼<arr name="value">
      <str>medium</str>
      <str>large</str>
      <str>extra large</str>
      <str>small</str>
    </arr>
    <long name="_version_">1467589856817315840</long>
  </doc>
```

Query on the dictionary index

We can see each key has multiple strings as its values. For example, brand is defined by values tommy hilfiger, levis, lee, and wrangler.

Now that we have the dictionary index, we can query our input string and figure out what the customer is looking for. Let us input our search query blue jeans against the index and see the output:

```
http://localhost:8983/solr/dictionary/select/?q=blue%20jeans
```

```
        <str name="q">blue jeans</str>
      </lst>
    </lst>
  ▼<result name="response" numFound="2" start="0">
    ▼<doc>
        <str name="key">clothes_type</str>
      ▼<arr name="value">
          <str>sweater</str>
          <str>jeans</str>
          <str>shirt</str>
          <str>pant</str>
        </arr>
        <long name="_version_">1478098383777300480</long>
      </doc>
    ▼<doc>
        <str name="key">clothes_color</str>
      ▼<arr name="value">
          <str>red</str>
          <str>blue</str>
          <str>green</str>
          <str>black</str>
          <str>pink</str>
          <str>yellow</str>
        </arr>
        <long name="_version_">1478098383801417728</long>
      </doc>
  </result>
```

Query on the dictionary index

We can see that the output contains keys `clothes_type` and `clothes_color`. Now using this information, we will need to create our actual search query. In this case, the boost will be higher on these two fields than that on the remaining fields. Our query would now become:

```
q=blue%20jeans&qf=text%20cat^2%20name^2%20brand^2%20clothes_type^4%20
clothes_color^4%20clothes_occassion^2&pf=text%20cat^3%20name^3%20
brand^3%20clothes_type^5%20clothes_color^5%20clothes_occassion^3&fl=na
me,brand,clothes_type,clothes_color,score
```

We have two pairs of jeans in our index, one is `blue` and the other is `black` in color. The black pair is identified by the brand `blue jeans`. Earlier, if we had not incorporated dynamic boosting, the brand `blue jeans` would have been boosted higher as it is part of **pf** in the query. Now that we have identified that the customer is searching for `clothes_type` and `clothes_color` fields, we increase the boost for these fields in both `qf` and `pf`. Therefore, even though the keywords `blue` and `jeans` occur separately in fields `clothes_type` and `clothes_color`, we get them above the item where `brand` is `blue jeans`.

```
▼<lst name="params">
  ▼<str name="pf">
      text cat^3 name^3 brand^3 clothes_type^5 clothes_color^5 clothes_occassion^3
  </str>
    <str name="fl">name,brand,clothes_type,clothes_color,score</str>
    <str name="q">blue jeans</str>
  ▼<str name="qf">
      text cat^2 name^2 brand^2 clothes_type^4 clothes_color^4 clothes_occassion^2
  </str>
  </lst>
</lst>
<result name="response" numFound="2" start="0" maxScore="2.5137613">
▼<doc>
    <str name="name">wrangler jeans</str>
    <str name="brand">wrangler</str>
    <str name="clothes_type">jeans</str>
    <str name="clothes_color">blue</str>
    <float name="score">2.5137613</float>
  </doc>
▼<doc>
    <str name="name">skinny fit black jeans</str>
    <str name="brand">blue jeans</str>
    <str name="clothes_type">jeans</str>
    <str name="clothes_color">black</str>
    <float name="score">2.3705869</float>
  </doc>
</result>
```

Search with dynamic boosting

This is one way of implementing semantic search. Note that we are performing two searches over here, the first identifies the input fields of the customer's interest and the second is our actual search where the boosting happens dynamically on the basis of the results of the first search.

Optimizations

Performing two searches in Solr for every search on the website would not be optimal. However, we need to identify the fields before performing the search. Another easier way to do this is to incorporate the dictionary in the product catalog index itself.

For this, we will have to create fields in our index matching the dictionary key fields. Then during indexing, we need to populate the key fields with words that match the product. Let us take an example to understand this. In our case, let us say that we are dealing with three fields in our dictionary, `clothes_type`, `clothes_color`, and `brand`. We would create three new fields in our product index, `key_clothes_type`, `key_clothes_color`, and `key_brand`. These fields would contain product-specific information that matches with our dictionary.

For the product, `wrangler jeans`, the information in these fields would be:

```
key_clothes_type : jeans
key_clothes_color : blue
key_brand : wrangler
```

For the next product, `skinny fit black jeans`, the information would be:

```
key_clothes_type : jeans
key_clothes_color : black
key_brand :
```

Here `key_brand` would be empty as we do not identify `blue jeans` as a brand in our dictionary.

Now the search would contain higher boosts to these fields to give more importance to the dictionary. A sample query would be:

```
q=blue%20jeans&qf=text%20cat^2%20name^2%20brand^2%20clothes_type^2%20
clothes_color^2%20clothes_occassion^2&key_clothes_type^4&key_clothes_
color^4&key_brand^4&pf=text%20cat^3%20name^3%20brand^3%20clothes_
type^3%20clothes_color^3%20clothes_occassion^3&key_clothes_type^5&key_
clothes_color^5&key_brand^5&fl=name,brand,clothes_type,clothes_
color,score
```

This will give us results that would be comparable to the somewhat clean implementation we described earlier and would be much faster as we are doing a single search instead of two searches. The only problem over here is with the creation of an index where we will have to figure out which words to populate our product dictionary fields with, as it will be an intersection between the field values of the product and the dictionary values for that field.

Summary

In this chapter, we studied in depth the implementation of Solr in an e-commerce scenario. We saw how to design an e-commerce index in Solr. We discussed the problems faced in e-commerce while implementing a search. We saw different ways of sorting and faceting the products. We also saw multi-select and hierarchical faceting. We had a look at the concept of semantic search and some optimizations that could be used while implementing the same.

In the next chapter, we will look at best practices and ideas for using Solr for a spatial or geospatial search.

6
Solr for Spatial Search

In the previous chapter, we discussed in depth the problems faced during the implementation of Solr for search operations on an e-commerce website. We saw solutions to the problems and areas where optimizations may be necessary. We also took a look at semantic search and how it can be implemented in an e-commerce scenario.

In this chapter, we will explore Solr with respect to spatial search. We will look at different indexing techniques and study query types that are specific to spatial data. We will also learn different scenario-based filtering and searching techniques for geospatial data.

The topics that we will cover in this chapter are:

- Features of spatial search
- Lucene 4 spatial module
- Indexing for spatial search
- Search and filtering on spatial index
- Distance sort and relevance boost
- Advanced concepts
    - Quadtrees
    - Geohash

Features of spatial search

With Solr, we can combine location-based data with normal text data in our index. This is termed spatial search or geospatial search.

Earlier versions of Solr (Solr 3.x) provided the following features for spatial search:

- Representation of spatial data as latitude and longitude in Solr
- Filtering by `geofilt` and bound box filters
- Use of the `geodist` function to calculate distance
- Distance-based faceting and boosting of results

With Solr 4, the following new features have been introduced in Solr:

- **Support for new shapes**: Polygon, LineString, and other new shapes are supported as indexed and query shapes in Solr 4. Shapes other than points, rectangles, and circles are supported via the **Java Topology Suite (JTS)**, an optional dependency that we will discuss later.

- **Indexing multi-valued fields**: This is critical for storing the results of automatic place extraction from text using natural language processing techniques, since a variable number of locations will be found for a single record.

- **Indexing both point and non-point shapes**: Non-point shapes are essentially pixelated to a configured resolution per shape. By default, that resolution is defined by a percentage of the overall shape size, and it applies to query shapes as well. If the extremely high precision of shape edges needs to be retained for accurate indexing, then this solution probably won't scale too well during indexing because of large indexes and slow indexing. On the other hand, query shapes generally scale well to the maximum configured precision regardless of shape size.

- **Solr 4 now supports rectangles with user-specifiable corners**: As discussed earlier, Solr 3 spatial only supports the bounding box of a circle.

- **Multi-valued distance sorting and score boosting**: It is an unoptimized implementation as it uses large amounts of RAM.

- **Configurable precision**: This is possible in Solr 4, which can vary as per shape at query time and during sorting at index time. This is mainly used for enhancing performance.

- **Fast filtering**: The code outperforms the **LatLonType** of Solr 3 at single-valued indexed points. Also, Solr 3 LatLonType at times requires all the points to be in memory, while the new spatial module here doesn't.
- **Support for Well-known Text (WKT) via JTS**: WKT: This is arguably the most widely supported textual format for shapes.

Let us look at an example of storing and searching locations in Solr. We will need two fields in our Solr `schema.xml` file. A field of `fieldType solr.LatLonType` named location is used along with another dynamic field named `dynamicField_coordinate` of type `tdouble` as a field suffix in the previous field to index the data points:

```
<!-- A specialized field for geospatial search. If indexed, this
fieldType must not be multivalued. -->
    <fieldType name="location" class="solr.LatLonType"
subFieldSuffix="_coordinate"/>
<!-- Type used to index the lat and lon components for the "location"
FieldType -->
    <dynamicField name="*_coordinate"  type="tdouble" indexed="true"
stored="false" />
```

We will have to define the field named `store` of type `location`, which will implement the geospatial index for the location:

```
<field name="store" type="location" indexed="true" stored="true"/>
```

Let us index a few locations into Solr and see how geospatial search works. Go into the `exampledocs` folder inside the Solr installation and run the following command to index the `location.csv` file provided with this chapter:

```
java -Dtype=text/csv -jar post.jar location.csv
```

Now let us see which stores are near our location. On Google Maps, we can see that our location is `28.643059, 77.368885`. Therefore, the query to figure out stores within 10 km from our location will be:

```
http://localhost:8983/solr/collection1/select/?q=*:*&fq={!geofilt
pt=28.643059,77.368885 sfield=store d=10}
```

We can see that our query consists of a filter query that contains the geofilt filter that in turn looks for stores within `d=10` kilometers from location `pt`. We can see that there are three stores nearby in `Noida`, `Ghaziabad`, and `East Delhi`, as per the tags associated with the latitude / longitude points.

The output of our query is shown in the following image:

```
▼<str name="fq">
    {!geofilt pt=28.643059,77.368885 sfield=store d=10}
  </str>
 </lst>
</lst>
▼<result name="response" numFound="3" start="0">
  ▼<doc>
     <str name="id">LXXX1</str>
     <str name="name">Noida</str>
     <str name="store">28.570485,77.324713</str>
     <long name="_version_">1489890679893000192</long>
   </doc>
  ▼<doc>
     <str name="id">LXXX2</str>
     <str name="name">Ghaziabad</str>
     <str name="store">28.642211,77.373445</str>
     <long name="_version_">1489890679896145920</long>
   </doc>
  ▼<doc>
     <str name="id">LXXX3</str>
     <str name="name">East Delhi</str>
     <str name="store">28.620588,77.311854</str>
     <long name="_version_">1489890679897194496</long>
   </doc>
</result>
```

Stores within 10 km from our location point

In order to find more stores, we will have to change distance d from 10 to say 30:

```
http://localhost:8983/solr/collection1/select/?q=*:*&fq={!geofilt
pt=28.643059,77.368885 sfield=store d=30}
```

This will give us stores in Rohini and Paschim vihar as well, which are far from the current location.

The output of this query is shown in the following image:

```
▼<str name="fq">
   {!geofilt pt=28.643059,77.368885 sfield=store d=30}
   </str>
 </lst>
</lst>
▼<result name="response" numFound="5" start="0">
 ▼<doc>
   <str name="id">LXXX1</str>
   <str name="name">Noida</str>
   <str name="store">28.570485,77.324713</str>
   <long name="_version_">1489890679893000192</long>
 </doc>
 ▼<doc>
   <str name="id">LXXX2</str>
   <str name="name">Ghaziabad</str>
   <str name="store">28.642211,77.373445</str>
   <long name="_version_">1489890679896145920</long>
 </doc>
 ▼<doc>
   <str name="id">LXXX3</str>
   <str name="name">East Delhi</str>
   <str name="store">28.620588,77.311854</str>
   <long name="_version_">1489890679897194496</long>
 </doc>
 ▼<doc>
   <str name="id">LXXX4</str>
   <str name="name">Rohini</str>
   <str name="store">28.721514,77.109313</str>
   <long name="_version_">1489890679899291648</long>
 </doc>
 ▼<doc>
   <str name="id">LXXX6</str>
   <str name="name">Paschim vihar</str>
   <str name="store">28.671499,77.097522</str>
   <long name="_version_">1489890679902437376</long>
 </doc>
</result>
```

Java Topology Suite

The JTS is an API for modeling and manipulating a two-dimensional linear geometry. It provides numerous geometric predicates and functions. It complies with the standards and provides a complete, robust, and consistent implementation of algorithms that are intended to be used to process linear geometry on a two-dimensional plane. It is fast and meant for production use.

Well-known Text

WKT is a text mark-up language for representing vector geometry objects on a map, spatial reference systems of spatial objects, and transformations between spatial reference systems. The following geometric objects can be represented using WKT:

- Points and multi-points
- Line Segment (LineString) and multi-line segment
- Triangle, polygon, and multi-polygon
- Geometry
- CircularString
- Curve, MultiCurve, and CompoundCurve
- CurvePolygon
- Surface, multi-surface, and polyhedron
- Triangulated irregular network
- GeometryCollection

The Spatial4j library

Spatial4j is an open source Java library that is basically intended for general-purpose spatial or geospatial requirements. Its primary responsibilities are wrapped up at three levels:

- Providing shapes that function well with Euclidean and spherical surface models
- Calculating distance and applying other mathematical operations
- Reading shapes from WKT strings

The primary strength of Spatial4j is its collection of shapes that possess the following set of capabilities:

- Calculation of the latitude / longitude bounding box
- Computation of the area of different shapes
- Figuring out if a shape contains a given point
- Computation of relationships such as CONTAINS, WITHIN, DISJOINT, INTERSECTS, and so on for a rectangle

Lucene 4 spatial module

Solr 4 contains three field types for spatial search: LatLonType (or its non-geodetic twin **PointType**), **SpatialRecursivePrefixTreeFieldType** (**RPT** for short), and **BBoxField** (to be introduced in Solr 4.10 onward). LatLonType has been there since Lucene 3. RPT offers more features than LatLonType and offers fast filter performance. LatLonType is more appropriate for efficient distance sorting and boosting. With Solr, we can use both the fields simultaneously — LatLonType for sorting or boosting and RPT for filtering. BBoxField is used for indexing bounding boxes, querying by a box, specifying search predicates such as `Intersects`, `Within`, `Contains`, `Disjoint`, or `Equals`, and relevancy sorting or boosting of properties such as **overlapRatio**.

We have already seen the LatLonType field, which we used to define the location of our store in the earlier examples. Let us explore RPT and have a look at BBoxField.

SpatialRecursivePrefixTreeFieldType

RPT available in Solr 4 is used to implement the `RecursivePrefixTree` search strategy. `RecursivePrefixTreeStrategy` is grid- or prefix tree–based class that implements recursive descent algorithms. It is considered as the most mature strategy till date that has been tested well.

It has the following advantages over the `LatLonType` field:

- Can be used to query by polygons and other complex shapes, in addition to circles and rectangles

- Has support for multi-valued indexed fields

- Ability to index non-point shapes such as polygons as well as point shapes

- Has support for rectangles with user-specified corners that can cross the dateline

- Has support for unoptimized multi-valued distance sorting and score boosting

- Supports the WKT shape syntax, which is required for specifying polygons and other complex shapes

- Incorporates the basic features of the `LatLonType` field and enables the use of `geofilt`, `bbox`, and `geodist` query filters with RPT

We can use the RPT field in our Solr by configuring a field in our `schema.xml` file of type `solr.SpatialRecursivePrefixTreeFieldType`. Our `schema.xml` file contains the following code for the RPT field:

```
<fieldType name="location_rpt" class =
"solr.SpatialRecursivePrefixTreeFieldType"
        spatialContextFactory =
"com.spatial4j.core.context.jts.JtsSpatialContextFactory"
        autoIndex="true"
        geo="true"
        distErrPct="0.025"
        maxDistErr="0.000009"
        units="degrees" />
```

We can change the type of the field named `store` from `location` to `location_rpt` and make it multi-valued:

```
<field name="store" type="location_rpt" indexed="true" stored="true"
multiValued="true" />
```

Now restart Solr.

If you get an error `java.lang.ClassNotFoundException: com.vividsolutions.jts.geom.CoordinateSequenceFactory`, please download the JTS library (`jts-1.13.jar`) from `http://sourceforge.net/projects/jts-topo-suite/`.

Now, put it in the `<solr folder>/example/solr-webapp/webapp/WEB-INF/lib` path.

Let us understand the options available for the `SpatialRecursivePrefixTreeFieldType` field type in our `schema.xml` file:

- `name`: This is the name of the field type that we specified as `location_rpt`.

- `class`: This should be `solr.SpatialRecursivePrefixTreeFieldType` as we have declared.

- `spatialContextFactory`: It is specified as `com.spatial4j.core.context.jts.JtsSpatialContextFactory` only when there is a requirement to implement polygons or linestrings. The JAR file `jts-1.13.jar` that we put in our `lib` folder (as mentioned in notes above) is used if this is specified. This context factory has its own options, which can be found if we go through the Java docs for the same. One option that we enabled in our declaration is `autoIndex="true"`, which provides a major performance boost for polygons.

- `units`: This is a mandatory parameter and currently accepts the only value as degrees. How the `maxDistErr` attribute, the radius of a circle, or any other absolute distances are interpreted depends upon this parameter. One degree measures to approximately 111.2 km, which is based on the value we compute as the average radius of Earth.

- `geo`: This parameter specifies whether the mathematical model is based on a sphere, or on Euclidean or Cartesian geometry. It is set to `true` for us, so latitude and longitude coordinates will be used and the mathematical model will generally be a sphere. If set to `false`, the coordinates will be generic X and Y on a two-dimensional plane having Euclidean or Cartesian geometry.

- `WorldBounds`: It sets the valid numerical ranges of x and y coordinates in the `minX minY maxX maxY` format. In case `geo="true"`, the value of this parameter is assumed to be `-180 -90 180 90`; else, it needs to be specified exclusively.

- `distCalculator`: Defines the distance calculation algorithm. If `geo=true`, the `haversine` value is the default. If `geo=false`, the `cartesian` value will be the default. Other possible values are `lawOfCosines`, `vincentySphere`, and `cartesian^2`.

The `PrefixTree` based field visualizes the indexed coordinates as a grid. Each grid cell is further fragmented as another set of grid cells that falls under the next level, thus forming a hierarchy with different levels. The largest set of cells fall under level 1, the next set of fragmented cells in level 2, and so on. Here are some configuration options related to `prefixTree`:

- `prefixTree`: Defines the spatial grid implementation. Since a `PrefixTree` (such as `RecursivePrefixTree`) maps the world as a grid, each grid cell is decomposed to another set of grid cells at the next level. If `geo=false`, then the default prefix tree is `geohash`; otherwise, it's `quad`. Geohash has 32 children at each level, and quad has 4. Geohash cannot be used for `geo=false` as it's strictly geospatial.

- `distErrPct`: Defines the default precision of non-point shapes for both the index and the query as a fraction between `0.0` (fully precise) and `0.5`. The closer this number is to zero, the more accurate is the shape. We have defined it as `0.025` allowing small amounts of inaccuracy in our shape. More precise indexed shapes use more disk space and take longer to index. Bigger `distErrPct` values will make querying faster but less accurate.

- `maxDistErr`: Defines the highest level of detail required for indexed data. The default value is 1 m, a little less than `0.000009` degrees. This setting is used internally to compute an appropriate `maxLevels` value.

- `maxLevels`: Sets the maximum grid depth for indexed data. It is usually more intuitive to compute an appropriate `maxLevels` by specifying `maxDistErr`.

We will need to clear our index and re-index the `location.csv` and `*.xml` files.

 The data inside the Solr index for a collection can be entirely deleted using the following Solr queries:

```
http://localhost:8983/solr/collection1/update?stream.
body=<delete/><query>*:*</query></delete>
http://localhost:8983/solr/collection1/update?stream.
body=<commit/>
```

We will study some queries employing predicates such as `Intersects`, `isWithin`, and others on the store field (of type RPT), which we create later in this chapter.

BBoxField (to be introduced in Solr 4.10)

The BBoxField field type can be used to index a single rectangle or bounding box per document field. It supports searching via a bounding box and most spatial search predicates. It has enhanced relevancy modes based on the overlap or area between the search rectangle and the indexed rectangle.

To define it in our schema, we have to first declare a `fieldType` of class `solr.BBoxField` having `numberType` as defined by a separate `fieldType` having the class `solr.TrieDoubleField`:

```
<fieldType name="bbox" class="solr.BBoxField" geo="true"
units="degrees" numberType="_bbox_coord" />
<fieldType name="_bbox_coord" class="solr.TrieDoubleField"
precisionStep="8" docValues="true" stored="false"/>
```

Now we define a field of type `bbox`:

```
<field name="bbox" type="bbox" />
```

Since this feature is available in Solr 4.10 onward, we will not delve into the implementation.

Indexing for spatial search

Now that we know the features supported by Solr for spatial search, let us see how indexing should be done for spatial search. We will need to index the coordinates for point, circle, rectangle, and other spatial representations in Solr as documents before we execute a search for them. Every geographical point is represented as latitude and longitude with the format `lat,lon`.

We saw points being indexed in the last section in our `location.csv` file. They are indexed in the lat,lon format:

```
<field name="store">28.570485,77.324713</field>
```

The points can be indexed in the lat-lon format by omitting the comma:

```
<field name="store">28.570485 77.324713</field>
```

We saw that Solr also supports different geometrical shapes such as rectangle, circle, and polygon. Let us learn how to index these.

In order to index a rectangle, we need the two points that form the starting and the ending points of the rectangle. Consider a two-dimensional coordinate system with X and Y axes. The said two points represent the maximum and minimum values of X and Y coordinates, as shown in the following figure:

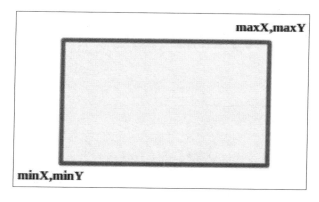

```
<doc>
<field name="id">CXXX1</field>
<field name="name">rectangle</field>
<field name="store">28.57 77.32 29.67 78.41</field>
</doc>
```

In order to index documents directly from the Solr admin interface, go to the documents section inside the collection. This will lead you to the following URL: http://localhost:8983/solr/#/collection1/documents.

Select the **Document Type** as XML and write the XML document(s) in the given text box. Now, click on **Submit Document**, as shown in the following image:

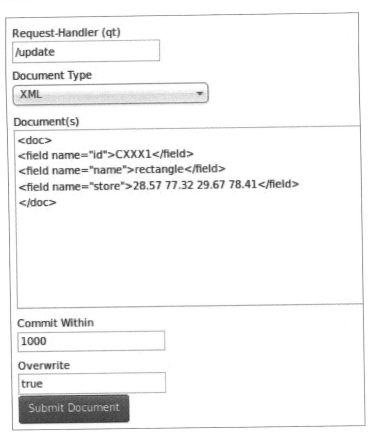

A circle is also specified in the following format:

```
<doc>
<field name="id">CXXX2</field>
<field name="name">circle</field>
<field name="store">Circle(28.57,77.32 d=0.051)</field>
</doc>
```

The first point is in the lat,lon format, and the point represents the center of a circle. Further, d represents the distance radius in degrees. In order to convert the radius from degree to a desired unit, such as kilometers or miles, we need to use the following conversion formula:

```
degreeInDesiredUnit = degrees * radiusOfEarthInDesiredUnit
```

In the given case, note the following:

- `degreeInDesiredUnit`: This parameter represents the unit we wish to convert degree to, such as kilometers or miles

- `degrees`: This parameter represents the radius in degrees (that is, the value we specify for the d parameter)

- `radiusOfEarthInDesiredUnit`: This parameter represents the radius of Earth in the desired unit

Refer to the following example for better understanding:

```
Degree (in Kilometers) = d * 111.1951
Degree (in Miles) = d * 69.09341
```

As per standard WKT specifications, we can index polygons as follows:

```
<doc>
<field name="id">CXXX3</field>
<field name="name">polygon</field>
<field name="store">POLYGON((20 50, 18 60, 24 68, 26 62, 30 55, 20
50))</field>
</doc>
```

The double parentheses are a part of the WKT specification.

Execute the following Solr query to index these documents:

```
http://localhost:8983/solr/collection1/select/?q=*:*&fq=name:circle
polygon rectangle&fl=store
```

The shapes that we have indexed are shown in the following image:

```
      <str name="fq">name:circle polygon rectangle</str>
    </lst>
  </lst>
▼<result name="response" numFound="3" start="0">
  ▼<doc>
    ▼<arr name="store">
      <str>28.57 77.32 29.67 78.41</str>
    </arr>
  </doc>
  ▼<doc>
    ▼<arr name="store">
      ▼<str>
        POLYGON((20 50, 18 60, 24 68, 26 62, 30 55, 20 50))
      </str>
    </arr>
  </doc>
  ▼<doc>
    ▼<arr name="store">
      <str>Circle(28.57,77.32 d=0.051)</str>
    </arr>
  </doc>
</result>
```

Searching and filtering on a spatial index

Spatial fields in a Solr index can be searched and filtered using the {!geofilt} and {!bbox} query filters. These filters were introduced and are available in Solr 4.2 onward. We saw a working example of geofilt earlier in this chapter. Let us go through some other queries that can be executed on a spatial index in Solr.

The bbox query

The working of a bbox filter is similar to that of geofilt, except that the former uses the bounding box of a calculated circle. The query remains the same, except that we use the {!bbox} filter instead of the {!geofilt} filter. To convert the earlier query to bbox from geofilt, we run the following query:

```
http://localhost:8983/solr/collection1/select/?q=*:*&fq={!bbox
pt=28.643059,77.368885 sfield=store d=10}
```

The output in our case would remain the same as that in the figure – *Stores within 10 km from our location point* – shown earlier in this chapter, but the search now includes the grayed-out area, as shown in the following image. If there were any store locations in the grayed-out area, the earlier search using the {!geofilt} filter would not return them in the result, while the {!bbox} filter would do so.

The following figure shows the area covered by the bbox query:

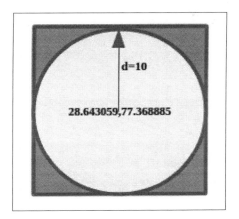

In order to understand the execution of the query, let us index the default documents available with Solr into our index. In the exampledocs folder, run the following command:

```
java -jar post.jar *.xml
```

This will index the default documents in Solr that carry the store locations. Now execute the following query:

```
http://localhost:8983/solr/collection1/select/?fl=name,store&q=*:*&fq
={!geofilt}&sfield=store&pt=45.15,-93.85&d=5
```

This will give out 3 stores that are within 5 km of the point 45.15,-93.85.

The execution of the previous query in Solr yields the following output:

```
      <str name="sfield">store</str>
      <str name="pt">45.15,-93.85</str>
      <str name="fq">{!geofilt}</str>
    </lst>
  </lst>
▼<result name="response" numFound="3" start="0">
  ▼<doc>
      <str name="store">45.17614,-93.87341</str>
    </doc>
  ▼<doc>
      <str name="store">45.18014,-93.87741</str>
    </doc>
  ▼<doc>
      <str name="store">45.18414,-93.88141</str>
    </doc>
  </result>
```

Here we are using the `geofilt` filter. If we convert this to the `bbox` filter, we will be getting five store locations in our output. The Solr query would be:

```
http://localhost:8983/solr/collection1/select/?fl=store&q=*:*&fq={!bb
ox}&sfield=store&pt=45.15,-93.85&d=5
```

The output will be as shown in the following figure:

```
      <str name="sfield">store</str>
      <str name="pt">45.15,-93.85</str>
      <str name="fq">{!bbox}</str>
    </lst>
  </lst>
▼<result name="response" numFound="5" start="0">
  ▼<doc>
      <str name="store">45.17614,-93.87341</str>
    </doc>
  ▼<doc>
      <str name="store">45.18014,-93.87741</str>
    </doc>
  ▼<doc>
      <str name="store">45.18414,-93.88141</str>
    </doc>
  ▼<doc>
      <str name="store">45.18814,-93.88541</str>
    </doc>
  ▼<doc>
      <str name="store">45.19214,-93.89941</str>
    </doc>
  </result>
```

Since this search is executed within the bounding box of a circle, the area thus covered is always a square. Therefore, the bbox filter cannot be used to search a rectangle. To search a rectangle, we can use the following range query:

```
http://localhost:8983/solr/collection1/select/?fl=store&q=*:*&fq=stor
e:[45.15,-93.9 TO 45.2,-93.88]
```

This search ranges from the lower left point at 45.15,-93.9 to the top right point at 45.2,-93.88 forming a rectangle. The query in the following image shows the results of this search:

```
▼<lst name="params">
    <str name="fl">store</str>
    <str name="q">*:*</str>
    <str name="fq">store:[45.15,-93.9 TO 45.2,-93.88]</str>
  </lst>
</lst>
▼<result name="response" numFound="3" start="0">
  ▼<doc>
      <str name="store">45.18414,-93.88141</str>
    </doc>
  ▼<doc>
      <str name="store">45.18814,-93.88541</str>
    </doc>
  ▼<doc>
      <str name="store">45.19214,-93.89941</str>
    </doc>
</result>
```

Filters such as geofilt, bbox, and geodist use certain spatial search–specific parameters.

These parameters are as follows:

d: It denotes the distance and is measured in kilometers.

pt: It represents a specific point in the latitude / longitude coordinate format.

sfield: It specifies a spatial field and is of location field type by default.

An unconventional Solr query parser known as the field-query style approach has been introduced in Solr 4.0. This syntax is used for a spatial predicate that excludes Intersects, or to use WKT formatted shapes (for example, a polygon), or to add some precision tuning options. Let us see some examples:

```
fq=store:"Intersects(28 77 29 78)"
```

The complete query will be:

```
http://localhost:8983/solr/collection1/select/?q=*:*&fq=store:"Inters
ects(28 77 29 78)"
```

This query looks for any store that intersects the rectangle formed by the specified coordinates. We can see that the rectangle with the ID CXXX1 is the output of our query, as shown in the following image:

```
        <str name="fq">store:"Intersects(28 77 29 78)"</str>
      </lst>
    </lst>
  ▼<result name="response" numFound="1" start="0">
    ▼<doc>
        <str name="id">CXXX1</str>
        <str name="name">rectangle</str>
      ▼<arr name="store">
          <str>28.57 77.32 29.67 78.41</str>
        </arr>
        <long name="_version_">1490271757473415168</long>
      </doc>
    </result>
```

Suppose that we are located at the location specified by (28.642815,77.368413) and we want to inspect a circle having a radius of 20 km with reference to our location, for any store that intersects this circle.

First, we will have to convert 20 km into degrees using the formula introduced in the previous section:

```
Degree d = 20 / 111.1951
         = 0.1798
```

Now our query using the Intersects predicate will be:

```
http://localhost:8983/solr/collection1/select/?q=*:*&fq=store:"Inters
ects(Circle(28.642815,77.368413 d=0.1798))"&fl=store,name
```

We can see that the result indicates three stores. Also, the circle that we indexed earlier intersects the circle specified in the query.

The following image shows the output obtained from the execution of the previous query:

```xml
          ▼<str name="fq">
             store:"Intersects(Circle(28.642815,77.368413 d=0.1798))"
           </str>
         </lst>
      </lst>
   ▼<result name="response" numFound="4" start="0">
     ▼<doc>
         <str name="name">Noida</str>
       ▼<arr name="store">
          <str>28.570485,77.324713</str>
         </arr>
       </doc>
     ▼<doc>
         <str name="name">Ghaziabad</str>
       ▼<arr name="store">
          <str>28.642211,77.373445</str>
         </arr>
       </doc>
     ▼<doc>
         <str name="name">East Delhi</str>
       ▼<arr name="store">
          <str>28.620588,77.311854</str>
         </arr>
       </doc>
     ▼<doc>
         <str name="name">circle</str>
       ▼<arr name="store">
          <str>Circle(28.57,77.32 d=0.051)</str>
         </arr>
       </doc>
    </result>
```

Now let us see an example of the `IsWithin` predicate:

```
fq=store:"IsWithin(POLYGON((19 49, 17 61, 25 70, 27 62, 31 55, 19
49))) distErrPct=0"
```

We are trying to determine whether there is anything in the polygon specified earlier for which the Solr query will be:

```
http://localhost:8983/solr/collection1/select/?q=*:*&fq=store:"IsWith
in(POLYGON((19 49, 17 61, 25 70, 27 62, 31 55, 19 49)))
distErrPct=0"&fl=store,name
```

The result from our query shows the polygon that we had indexed earlier.

The output from the previous query is shown in the following image:

```
▼<str name="fq">
    store:"IsWithin(POLYGON((19 49, 17 61, 25 70, 27 62, 31 55, 19
    49))) distErrPct=0"
  </str>
 </lst>
</lst>
▼<result name="response" numFound="1" start="0">
 ▼<doc>
    <str name="name">polygon</str>
   ▼<arr name="store">
     ▼<str>
        POLYGON((20 50, 18 60, 24 68, 26 62, 30 55, 20 50))
       </str>
     </arr>
    </doc>
  </result>
```

This example shows the implementation of WKT with a tuning option. The spatial chunk of the query is placed as a subquery in the full Solr query that resembles a Lucene phrase query. The query starts with spatial predicates such as Intersects and IsWithin followed by either WKT or some other shape format that is enclosed in parentheses.

The distErrPct class defines the precision option for the query shape. Its default value is 0.025 (2.5%). We have set distErrPct as 0, which makes the query shape as accurate as that of a grid. We may also specify the distErr option if we want to explicitly set the precision for the shape for which we know the accuracy in exact terms instead of the relative terms.

Solr 4.3 introduces additional predicates such as isWithin, Contains, and isDisjointTo. The predicates Intersects or isDisjointTo work fine for only indexed points. Also, isWithin and Contains predicates are useful for searching indexed non-point shapes. In addition, isWithin is used to search for indexed shapes that are within the query shape, while Contains searches for indexed shapes that contain the query shape.

Distance sort and relevancy boost

During spatial search, it may be required to sort the search results on the basis of their distance from a specific geographical location (the lat-lon coordinate). With Solr 4.0, the spatial queries seen earlier are capable of returning a distance-based score for sorting and boosting.

Let us see an example wherein spatial filtering and sorting are applied and the distance is returned as the score simultaneously. Our query will be:

```
http://localhost:8983/solr/collection1/select/?fl=*,score&sort=score
asc&q={!geofilt score=distance sfield=store pt=28.642815,77.368413
d=20}
```

The query output from Solr shows four results along with their scores. Our results are sorted in ascending order on score, which represents the distance as per our query. Hence, the results that are closest to our location appear on top.

The execution of the previous query yields the following output:

```
  ▼<str name="q">
      {!geofilt score=distance sfield=store pt=28.642815,77.368413
      d=20}
    </str>
  </lst>
</lst>
▼<result name="response" numFound="4" start="0" maxScore="180.0">
  ▼<doc>
    <str name="name">Ghaziabad</str>
    ▼<arr name="store">
      <str>28.642211,77.373445</str>
    </arr>
    <float name="score">0.0044576833</float>
  </doc>
  ▼<doc>
    <str name="name">East Delhi</str>
    ▼<arr name="store">
      <str>28.620588,77.311854</str>
    </arr>
    <float name="score">0.054391615</float>
  </doc>
  ▼<doc>
    <str name="name">Noida</str>
    ▼<arr name="store">
      <str>28.570485,77.324713</str>
    </arr>
    <float name="score">0.08187561</float>
  </doc>
```

In order to add user keywords to the previous Solr query, we will have to add an additional `fq` parameter probably with the `{!edismax}` filter. Moreover, we have used `score=distance` as the local parameter, which sets the distance to degrees relative to the center of the shape. If we don't use this parameter or set it to `none` value, all documents will hold the score `1.0`.

In order to perform relevance boosting, we can use the `recipDistance` option. This option applies the reciprocal function in such a way that distance 0 achieves a score of 1 and gradually decreases as the distance increases till the score reaches 0.1 and closer to 0 for even higher distances.

Let us modify our preceding query such that it sorts the results in the same way as done for the previous query, but does not implement the spatial filter. The following will be the modified query:

```
fl=*,score&sort=score asc&q={!geofilt score=distance filter=false
sfield=store pt=28.642815,77.368413 d=20}
```

The only change here is the option `filter=false`. This will give us all the documents in our index sorted by distance in an ascending order. If we execute this query on our index, we will get around 45 results (all documents in the index), even if they lie outside the query circle. In this case, the d option doesn't make sense as the sorting is limited to the center of the shape. However, it is still necessary to define the shape (in our case, circular) for this query. If a document doesn't have any point in the spatial field, the distance used will be equal to 0.

Let us also look at some functions provided by Solr for calculating the distance between vectors in an n-dimensional space.

`dist` is a function provided by Solr and can be used to calculate the distance between two vectors or points. The function definition is as follows:

```
dist(power, vector 1 coordinates, vector 2 coordinates)
```

Note the following:

- `power`: This parameter takes the values 0, 1, 2, and `infinite`. The values 1 and 2 are important and denote the Manhattan (taxicab) distance and Euclidean distance, respectively.
- `vector 1` and `vector 2` coordinates: These coordinates depend on the space in which calculations are to be done. For a two-dimensional space, vectors 1 and 2 can be (x,y) and (z,w), respectively. For a three-dimensional space, the values of vectors 1 and 2 can be (x,y,z) and (a,b,c), respectively.

Let us study some examples for calling the `dist` function in Solr:

- `dist(1,x,y,a,b)`: This function calculates the Manhattan distance between two points `(a,b)` and `(x,y)` for each document in the search result
- `dist(2,x,y,a,b)`: This function calculates the Euclidean distance between two points `(a,b)` and `(x,y)` for each document in the search result
- `dist(2,x,y,z,a,b,c)`: This function calculates the Euclidean distance between `(x,y,z)` and `(a,b,c)` for each document

In the previous examples, each letter `(x,y,z,a,b,c)` is a field name in the indexed document.

The `dist` function can be used for sorting by distance in our query. For example, the following query is intended for sorting results on the basis of the Euclidean distance between points `(a,b)` and `(x,y)` in the descending order:

```
http://localhost:8983/solr/collection1/select?q=*:*&sort=dist(2,a,b,x
,y) desc
```

The `dist` function is a very expensive operation.

`sqedist` is another function provided by Solr that calculates the Euclidean distance but does not evaluate the square root of this value, thus saving additional processing time required for the `dist` function. This function is used for applications that require the Euclidean distance for scoring purposes (for example). Nevertheless, `sqedist` does not need the actual distance and can use the squared Euclidean distance. The `sqedist` function does not take the power as the first argument. The power is set at 2 for Euclidean distance calculation. The `sqedist` function, in fact, calculates the distance between two vectors. The function is defined as follows:

```
sqedist(vector 1 coordinates, vector 2 coordinates)
```

For a two-dimensional space with points `(x,y)` and `(a,b)`, the function call will be:

```
sqedist(x,y,a,b)
```

Advanced concepts

As discussed earlier, RPT is based on a model where the world is divided into grid squares or cells. This is done recursively to get almost any amount of accuracy required. Each cell is indexed in Lucene with a byte string that has the parent cell's byte string as a prefix. Therefore, it is named `PrefixTree`. The `PrefixTreeStrategy` class for indexing and search uses a `SpatialPrefixTree` abstraction that decides how to divide the world into grid squares and what the byte encoding looks like to represent each grid square. It has two implementations, namely **geohash** and **quadtrees**. Let us look at both implementations in detail.

Quadtree

A quadtree is a simple and effective spatial indexing technique wherein each of the nodes represents a bounding box covering the parts of the space that has been indexed. Each node is either a leaf-node that contains one or more indexed points with no child, or an internal node with four children, one for each quadrant. The index structure of a quadtree is shown in the following image:

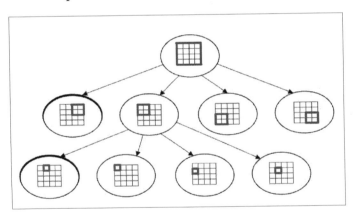

Indexing data

Data can be inserted into a quadtree as follows:

1. Start with the root that determines the quadrant the point in question occupies.
2. Go deeper into the tree till you find a leaf node.
3. Add the point to the list of points in that node.

4. While performing the preceding steps, if you come across a scenario wherein this list exceeds a pre-defined maximum allowed element count, proceed to the next step; else, it can be ignored.

5. Split the node further and push the points into the appropriate sub-nodes

Searching data

A search on the indexed quadtree involves the following steps:

1. Investigate each child node starting from the root and check whether it intersects the area it is being queried.

2. If the point intersects the area, dig deeper into that child node until a leaf node is found.

3. Once you encounter a leaf node, investigate each entry to see whether it intersects the query area. If so, return the leaf node.

A quadtree follows a **Trie** structure (http://en.wikipedia.org/wiki/Trie) as the values of the nodes are independent of the data that are being inserted. Thus, each of our nodes can be assigned a unique number. We simply assign a binary code to each of the quadrants (00 for top left, 10 for top right, and so on), and the node number of its ancestor gets concatenated in the case of a multi-level tree. For instance, in the preceding diagram, the bottom right node would be numbered as 00 11.

In geohash, which we will discuss next, each cell is divided into 32 smaller cells. On the other hand, in a quadtree, each cell is divided into four smaller cells in a 2x2 grid. So, with each additional level, there will be 32/2 = 16 times as many cells as those in the previous level for geohash. For a quadtree, the factor is 4/2 = 2 times. Therefore, there are fewer hierarchical levels in geohash than in a quadtree, which has certain performance gain during search.

Geohash

Geohash is a system for encoding geographical coordinates into a single field as a string. There is a web service geohash.org that provides a geocode class, which is based on the latitude and longitude of any location. Geocode is represented as a hierarchy of spatial data that subdivides the overall space into a grid. Let us first understand how geohash.org works before looking at the indexing- and search-related features provided by Solr for geohash.

Let us go to `geohash.org` and enter our location (`28.642815,77.368413`), which points to **Swarna Jayanti Park**, **Indirapuram**, **Ghaziabad**, India, in the search bar. After executing the search, we zoom in to see the exact location on the map. The output would be as displayed in the following image:

The hash generated for our latitude and longitude coordinates is `ttp4bw3bqxwn`. This hash is unique and can be used with `geohash.org` to refer to our lat-lon coordinate.

There are some basics required for using a geohash such as:

- Naming geohashes
- Geohash format
- Google map tools to generate geohash using Google Maps
- Quering geohash

These details can be obtained from the following URL:
`http://geohash.org/site/tips.html`.

Let us also get a brief idea on how a point is indexed in geohash's `SpatialPrefixTree` grid. The geohash that we generated, `ttp4bw3bqxwn`, is a 12 character string. This is indexed in Solr and the underlying Lucene as 12 terms, as follows:

```
t, tt, ttp, ttp4, ttp4b, ttp4bw, ttp4bw3, ttp4bw3b, ttp4bw3bq,
ttp4bw3bqx, ttp4bw3bqxw, ttp4bw3bqxwn
```

These 12 characters lead to an accurate point inside **Swarn Jayanti Park, Indirapuram**. Now, change the last digit of the longitude coordinate from 3 to 4. The lat-lon coordinate now becomes `28.642815-77.368414`, and in the geohash, only the last character changed from `n` to `y`.

The new geohash is now `ttp4bw3bqxwy`, which is inside **Swarn Jayanti Park**, **Indirapuram, Ghaziabad**, as shown in the following image:

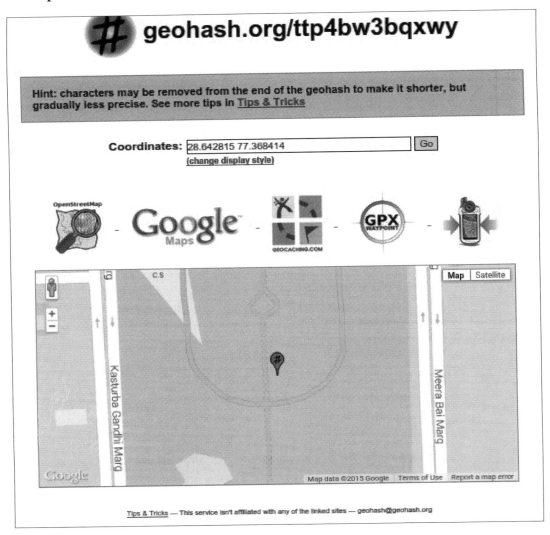

This shows us the concept of how the geohash is being indexed as 12 terms. A search on the first 11 characters would lead to a location that is defined by a 1 m grid. The accuracy of our search in this case would be 1 m. If we reduce the search characters further, our accuracy will decrease.

In order to index the geohash into our index, we need to define a `fieldType` class, namely `solr.GeoHashField`:

```
<fieldtype name="geohash" class="solr.GeoHashField"/>
```

Also, we need to define a field for indexing or storage:

```
<field name="store_hash" type="geohash" indexed="true"
stored="true"/>
```

Further operations such as indexing and querying are similar to those available with RPT, which we saw earlier.

Summary

In this chapter, we learnt how Solr can be used for geospatial search. We understood the features provided by the Solr 4 spatial module and saw how indexing and search can be executed with Solr. We discussed different types of geofilters available with Solr and performed sorting and boosting using distance as the relevancy score. We also saw some advanced concepts of geospatial operations such as quadtrees and geohash.

In the next chapter, we will learn about the problems that we normally face during the implementation of Solr in an advertising system. We will also discuss how to debug such a problem along with tweaks to further optimize the instance(s).

7
Using Solr in an Advertising System

In this chapter, we will discuss in depth the problems faced during the implementation of Solr in an advertising system. An advertising system generates ads related to the content a user is currently viewing on his or her browser. These contextual ads need to be displayed quickly and need to be relevant for the user so that the user is prompted to click on them. We will look at Solr as a platform to provide solutions to the issues related to this aspect. We will delve into performance optimizations and then proceed with making Solr work with Redis. The topics that will be covered in this chapter are:

- Ad system functionalities
- Ad distribution system architecture
- Ad distribution system requirements
- Performance improvements
- Merging Solr with Redis

Ad system functionalities

An ad system is based on the concept of provision of contextual ads (or documents in Solr terms) that are related to either the searched keyword or the document being viewed. Ads can also be generated or searched on the basis of the user's profile information and browsing history. The positioning and placement of an ad must match with the space available on the web page. On the basis of these functionalities, advertisements can be broadly divided into the following categories:

- Ads based on keywords searched — referred to as a listing ad

- Ads based on the placement and positioning available on the web page
- Ads based on the user's browsing history and his or her profile — also known as user-targeted ads

To understand how an ad system works, we need to understand the functionalities it provides. On the back end or the admin side, the ad system should provide the following functionalities:

- The definition of ad placement or the position where the ad would be able to fit on a web page, in terms of not only the size of the ad but also its visibility, say the top of the page or bottom right corner of the page.
- **Sales interface**: This is an interface where all sales are recorded with respect to the client and payment or billing information.
- **Creative management**: This is an interface to manage the creatives (images, flash files, or any content related to the ad) required to create an ad. It should also contain an approval mechanism for finalized creatives.
- **Reporting**: This is a very broad topic and includes interfaces for reporting both the performance of the ad and the billing or usage statistics. It should contain and track statistics for CPM / CPC / CPA of the ads. For people who are new to the ad system, **CPM** stands for **Cost Per Mile** (1 mile = 1000 impressions). CPM is generally used for premium ads by premium publishers as ad publishers get paid for every impression. **CPC** stands for **Cost Per Click**, where the publisher gets paid only when the user clicks on the ad. **CPA** stands for **Cost Per Aquision** where the publisher gets paid only if the ad resulted in a sale.
- **Merchant tool**: This is used by merchants to upload their requirements and track reports related to their ads as well as to check their billing information.
- **Campaign management**: This is required to define a campaign. A campaign in an ad system generally refers to the ad or ads to be shown for a certain duration or with a capping of CPM, CPC, or CPA.
- **Budget**: This can be used to place a cap on the bill generated with respect to a client or an inventory.
- **Bidding**: This is generally used to compete for the visibility and placement of an ad. There are various algorithms available to calculate the value of an ad. Merchants can also use the merchant tool to increase the CPM, CPC, or CPA of an ad to increase its visibility.
- **Targeting media**: This defines the keywords and URLs or category of websites where the ad would be displayed. For example, we can say that a particular ad should be displayed only on e-commerce websites.

In addition to the ad management system, we need an ad distribution system, which would display the ad based on the placement of ad, keyword matching to define the context of the ad. In addition, the ad distribution system needs to take care of the behavioral and demographic information related to the user.

The advertising system should also be capable of identifying the type of device on which the ad is to be displayed. It could be a laptop, mobile, or tablet. We could also build big-data analytics into the advertising system in order to identify behavioral patterns. The system should be able to connect to other affiliate networks.

Architecture of an ad distribution system

Now that we have a brief overview of the functionalities provided by an advertising system, we can look at the architecture of the advertising system and understand where Solr fits in the picture.

The system would receive parameters such as placement of the ad, keywords related to the ad, and the type of ad to be displayed. On the basis of these parameters, the system will identify the ad to be displayed. Most of the data required for ad display is stored as a browser cookie on an end user's system. This cookie can contain tracking and targeting information. This cookie information is sent over to the ad distribution network and is used for identifying the ad to be displayed and also for gathering the tracking and behavioral information.

The ad system generally works on JSON, HTML, and JavaScript frameworks on the frontend. JavaScript is used on the client side and is placed on the web page on which the ad is to be displayed. JavaScript handles all the communication between the ad distribution network and the browser on which the ad is to be displayed. Data is generally shared between the ad distribution network and the JavaScript client on the browser in the JSON format.

On the backend, the ad distribution system requires searching, filtering, sorting, and logging of data. This is where Solr comes into the picture. Ad distribution systems are high-performance and high-availability systems. Each web page can contain multiple ads, and there are various web pages on multiple sites on which ads are to be displayed. Hence, the number of requests per second for an ad distribution network will be much higher than the total number of page views on all the sites that cater to ads from this ad distribution network. Also, 100 percent availability is required, as downtime not only leads to loss of revenue but it also brings down the credibility of the ad distribution system.

Logs are collected and analyzed to improve profitability. There are various technologies used on the back end, from databases such as MySQL and Mongo and caching systems such as Redis, to web servers such as Nginx or Apache and of course Solr for search. A demo system architecture for an ad distribution system is shown in the following screenshot:

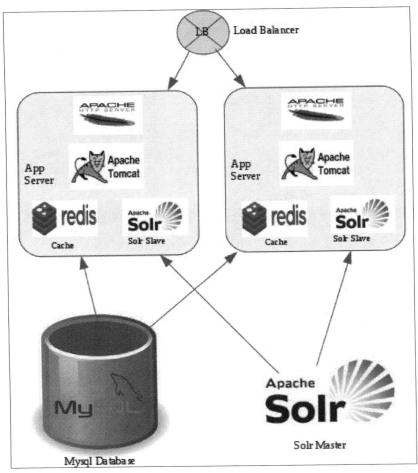

Ad distribution system architecture

We can see that there is a load balancer that, on receiving requests, distributes them to back-end web servers. Here we are using **Apache** as the web or HTTP server. The HTTP server forwards requests to the **Apache Tomcat** application server, which contains the business logic. The application server interacts with the **redis** cache to get cached information. If it does not find the required information in the cache, it uses the **MySQL** database to fetch the information and caches this information on the **redis** server. If the request is related to targeting or search, the application server checks **redis** for the cache and gets information from **Solr Slave**, if that information is not found in the **redis** cache. The indexing happens on the **Solr Master**, which can be scheduled at certain intervals, and the updated index is replicated onto **Solr Slave**.

We have high availability of web, application, caching, and Solr servers. The database master and the Solr indexing server can be organized in a master-master arrangement to achieve high availability at that level. The aim here should be to achieve a *no single point of failure* scenario.

We have included the Solr slave, Redis cache, and the application on the web server itself. Therefore, each server acts as an independent node behind the load balancer. This reduces the internal network bandwidth and simplifies the number of moving parts. However, if a single server cannot host all the parts required for the application, it is recommended to move or spread them out and balance the load between internal hosts using a load balancer. In such a scenario, we would have a cluster of Redis slaves behind a load balancer, a cluster of Solr slaves, and so on.

We may consider replacing the Apache web server with the event-driven Nginx web server, which will be able to handle more requests. The Nginx server is a lightweight event-based server, unlike the Apache web server, and it can handle more connections. The Solr master-slave architecture can be replaced with SolrCloud, which provides better indexing performance and higher availability of Solr slaves. This will be discussed in *Chapter 9, SolrCloud*. Currently, in order to update the Solr schema, the following process needs to be followed:

1. Stop replication between the master and slave servers.

2. Remove one or more web or application servers from the load balancer disabling all requests on that server.

3. Update the Solr schema on the master server.

4. Replicate it onto the Solr slaves that have been removed from the load balancer and that do not serve any requests.

5. Update the application on the machines that have been removed from the load balancer.

6. Put the updated machines back into the load balancer and remove all the other machines from the load balancer.

7. Replicate the Solr slave on the remaining machines that are out of the load balancer.

8. Update the application on the remaining machines.

9. Put the remaining machines back into the load balancer after Solr replication is complete.

Use of SolrCloud simplifies the entire process of updating the schema as this approach does not require such extensive planning and manual intervention. SolrCloud uses a centralized configuration system known as ZooKeeper, which acts as a referral point for schema updates. We will be discussing the same in *Chapter 9, SolrCloud*.

Requirements of an ad distribution system

Now that we have studied the system architecture of an ad distribution network and the various components, let us look at the requirements of an ad distribution system from the viewpoint of performance. Of course, performance is of primary importance. We saw that there are multiple ways in which an ad publisher generates revenue from an ad network. CTR is the most preferred way of measuring the performance of an ad and hence that of the ad network.

CTR stands for **Click Through Rate**. It is defined as the division of the number of clicks made on an advertisement by the total number of times the advertisement was served (impressions).

In order to deliver a good CTR, the ad being displayed needs to be close to the context of the page currently being viewed by the user. In order to derive the context, we need to run a search with the title and metadata on the page and identify the ads related to that page. Let us create a sample Solr schema for an ad distribution network.

Schema for a listing ad

The schema for a listing ad can contain the following fields:

```
<field name="adid" type="lowercase" indexed="true" stored="true"
required="true" omitNorms="true"/>
<field name="keywords" type="wslc" indexed="true" stored="true"/>
<field name="category" type="wslc" indexed="true" stored="true"/>
<field name="position" type="string" indexed="true" stored="true"
multiValued="true"/>
<field name="size" type="string" indexed="true" stored="true"/>
```

We have the field name as adid, which is a unique ID associated with an advertisement. We have the keywords field related to adid. The keywords herein are whitespace tokenized and appear in lowercase. category is another field that specifies the category of ads. It can be used to categorize an ad to be displayed on an e-commerce website, a blog, or some other specific website. position specifies the position in which the ad is to be displayed, and size specifies the size of the ad in pixels.

Our query for fetching an ad will be based solely on the keyword. The JavaScript client will pass the category, position, and size parameters related to an ad on the website. It will also pass the page title and metadata on the page. Our search for an ad would be based on the value in the keywords field. We will be performing an OR match between the content on the page (title and metadata) against the keywords for that advertisement.

A simple filtering query on the category, position, and size parameters should return the ads that can be displayed on the page. In addition, there are certain parameters that we discussed earlier such as the campaign, the start and stop dates, and the number of *impressions* or *budget* related to the ad. All these parameters would also need to be added into the schema and queried during the fetching of the ad:

```
<field name="startdt" type="date" indexed="true" stored="false" />
<field name="enddt" type="date" indexed="true" stored="false" />
<field name="campainid" type="int" indexed="true" stored="true"/>
<field name="impressions" type="int" indexed="true" stored="true"/>
```

Note that if we store the number of impressions to be served in the Solr index, then we will have to continually update the index as soon as an impression is served. This increases both reads and writes on the Solr index and the system is required to be more real time.

Changes in impressions should be immediately reflected in the Solr index. Only then would the Solr query be able to fetch the ads that need to be displayed. If an ad has served its budged impressions, it should not be served further. This can happen only if the impressions served are updated immediately into the ad index. The NRT indexing feature based on soft commits (discussed in *Chapter 5, Solr in E-commerce*) in Solr and SolrCloud can be used to achieve this.

Schema for targeted ads

A targeted ad is based on a user's browsing history and profile information. How can we get the user's browsing history or profile information? We need to drop cookies into the user's browser when he or she visits a certain site. The merchant who provides ads to the ad publisher also drops cookies into the user's browser. Let us look at an example scenario to understand this system.

Suppose a user is browsing www.amazon.com for certain products, say t-shirts. Each of the user's actions results in the addition or update of cookies on his or her browser. Therefore, if the user views some t-shirts, there would be a cookie on his browser containing information on that product. The advertising system provides the merchant with a piece of code that is used to drop the cookie. The merchant may also register with the ad network and ask for certain CTR / CPM plans. Such an ad distribution system would have tie-ups with ad publishers or websites where the ads are to be displayed. The ad system would provide a JavaScript code to the ad publisher system to be added to the page on which the ad is to be displayed.

Suppose the user now goes to some other website, say www.hindustantimes.com, which is a content and news website. Given that the ad distribution system has a tie-up with www.hindustantimes.com, there is a JavaScript code on the www.hindustantimes.com home page that fetches ads from our ad distribution system. This JavaScript code will read all cookies on the user's browser and pass them to the ad distribution system. The ad distribution system now knows that the user was earlier viewing certain t-shirts on www.amazon.com. Using this information, ads offering t-shirts earlier seen by the user are displayed on the user's browser.

It is also possible to capture the user's profile information, such as age, sex, online shopping preferences, and location, and use it to display targeted ads to the user. These types of targeted ads have gained a lot of popularity as they are close to the user's interest.

A sample Solr schema for the ad network for targeted ads would contain the following fields in addition to the fields meant for listing ads:

```
<field name="merchant" type="string" indexed="true" stored="true" />
<field name="pincode" type="int" indexed="true" stored="true" />
```

These fields specify the merchant and the user location as part of the user profile.

When searching for an ad to be displayed to a particular user, the search query also incorporates cookie information regarding the merchant and the user. The products to be displayed for a particular merchant are picked up from the user's cookie.

Performance improvements

We learnt in the previous section that the ad distribution system needs to be very fast and capable of handling a large number of requests as compared to a website. In addition, the system should be always available, with the least possible downtime (none if possible). The ads have to be relevant so that merchants obtain the desired response. Let us look at a few parameters that will improve Solr's performance by optimally using the inbuilt caching mechanism.

An index searcher, which is used to process and serve search queries, is always associated with a Solr cache. As long as an index searcher is valid, the associated cache also remains valid. When a new index searcher is opened after a commit, the old index searcher keeps on serving requests until the new index searcher is warmed up. Once the new index searcher is ready, it will start serving all the new search requests. The old index searcher will be closed after it has served all the remaining search requests. When a new index searcher is opened, its cache is auto-warmed using the data from the cache of an old index searcher. The caching implementations in Solr are **LRUCache (Least Recently Used)**, **FastLRUCache**, and **LFUCache (Least Frequently Used)**.

fieldCache

Lucene, the search engine inside Solr, has an inbuilt caching mechanism for a field known as **fieldCache**. Field cache contains field names as keys and a map of document ids corresponding to field values as values in the map. Field cache is primarily used for faceting purposes. This does not have any configuration options and cannot be managed by Solr. We can use the `newSearcher` and `firstSearch` event listeners in Solr to explicitly warm the field cache. Both the events are defined in the `solrconfig.xml` file:

```
<listener event="newSearcher" class="solr.QuerySenderListener">
  <arr name="queries">
```

```
          <lst> <str name="q">anything</str> <str name="sort">impressions
          desc, enddt asc</str> </lst>
       </arr>
    </listener>
    <listener event="firstSearcher" class="solr.QuerySenderListener">
      <arr name="queries">
        <!-- seed common sort fields -->
        <lst> <str name="q">anything</str> <str name="sort">impressions
        desc, enddt asc</str> </lst> </lst>
        <!-- seed common facets and filter queries -->
        <lst> <str name="q">anything</str>
              <str name="facet.field">merchant</str>
              <str name="fq">size:200px50px</str>
        </lst>
      </arr>
    </listener>
```

We can see the performance of the **fieldCache** from the statistics page in Solr:

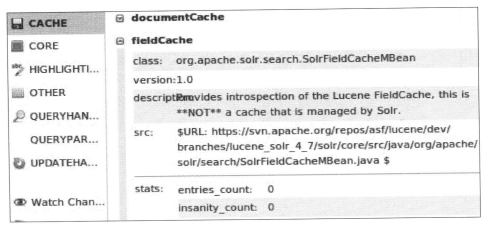

fieldCache Statistics

entries_count defines the total number of items in fieldCache, and **insanity_count** defines the number of insane instances. Insane indicates that something is wrong with the working of fieldCache. It is not critical and may not require an immediate fix.

fieldValueCache

It is similar to FieldCache in Lucene, but it is inside Solr and supports multiple values per item. This cache is mainly used for faceting. The keys are field names and the values contain large data structures that map docId parameters to values. The following screenshot shows an output from the Solr statistics page for **fieldValueCache**:

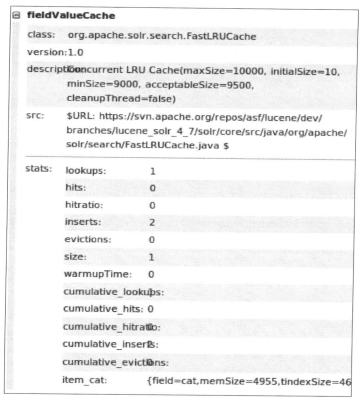

fieldValueCache statistics

documentCache

It stores Lucene documents that have been previously fetched from the disk. The size of the document cache should be greater than the estimated (max no of results) * (max concurrent queries) value for this cache for it to be used effectively. If these criteria are met, Solr may not need to fetch documents from disk, except for the first time (when not in cache). The following code snippet shows how documentCache is configured in the solrConfig.xml file:

```
<!-- Document Cache

        Caches Lucene Document objects (the stored fields for each
        document). Since Lucene internal document ids are transient,
        this cache will not be autowarmed.
    -->
<documentCache class="solr.LRUCache"
                size="102400"
                initialSize="1024"
                autowarmCount="0"/>
```

The document cache should not be auto-warmed, as the document IDs and fields within a document may change when a document is re-indexed. Memory usage can be high for this cache, and the usage depends on the number of fields stored in the documents in the index. The higher the number of stored fields, the more will be the memory usage.

The statistics for the usage of **documentCache** is shown on the Solr admin stats interface:

documentCache

class:	org.apache.solr.search.LRUCache
version:	1.0
description:	LRU Cache(maxSize=512, initialSize=512)
src:	$URL: https://svn.apache.org/repos/asf/lucene/dev/branches/lucene_solr_4_7/solr/core/src/java/org/apache/solr/search/LRUCache.java $

stats:		
	lookups:	15
	hits:	7
	hitratio:	0.47
	inserts:	11
	evictions:	0
	size:	11
	warmupTime:	0
	cumulative_lookups:	15
	cumulative_hits:	7
	cumulative_hitratio:	0.47
	cumulative_inserts:	8
	cumulative_evictions:	0

documentCache statistics

Solr has a concept of lazy loading of fields that can be enabled by the
enableLazyFieldLoading parameter.

```
<enableLazyFieldLoading>true</enableLazyFieldLoading>
```

When lazy loading is enabled, only fields specified in the fl parameter in the query
are obtained from the index and stored in DocumentCache. Other fields are marked
as LOAD_LAZY. When there is a cache hit on that document at a later date, the fields
that are already present in the document are returned directly, while the fields that
are marked as LOAD_LAZY are loaded from the index. The document object is updated
with data for fields that were earlier marked as LOAD_LAZY. In this case as well,
we notice an increase in memory usage without any increase in the number of
cached documents.

filterCache

A filter cache is mainly used for caching the results of filter queries. It stores a set of
document IDs that match with a filter query. The filter cache can be used for faceting
in some cases. The filterCache class is configured in the solrconfig.xml file with
the following configuration options:

```
<filterCache class="solr.FastLRUCache"
              size="409600"
              initialSize="40690"
              autowarmCount="4096"/>
```

The filterCache class can also be used for sorting results by enabling the following
parameter in the solrconfig.xml file:

```
<useFilterForSortedQuery>true</useFilterForSortedQuery>
```

The following screenshot shows an output from the Solr admin statistics page that shows the usage of the **filterCache** class:

filterCache

class:	org.apache.solr.search.FastLRUCache
version:	1.0
description	Concurrent LRU Cache(maxSize=512, initialSize=512, minSize=460, acceptableSize=486, cleanupThread=false)
src:	$URL: https://svn.apache.org/repos/asf/lucene/dev/branches/lucene_solr_4_7/solr/core/src/java/org/apache/solr/search/FastLRUCache.java $

stats:		
	lookups:	19
	hits:	12
	hitratio:	0.63
	inserts:	9
	evictions:	0
	size:	9
	warmupTime:	0
	cumulative_lookups:	19
	cumulative_hits:	12
	cumulative_hitratio:	0.63
	cumulative_inserts:	9
	cumulative_evictions:	0

filterCache usage statistics

Passing the parameter {!cache=false} will prevent the filter cache from being used in that query. The following is a sample filter query that does not use a filter:

```
fq={!cache=false}inStock=true
```

queryResultCache

The queryResultCache class is used to prevent repeated searches on the index. The cache stores the ordered set of document IDs for a particular query. It is defined in the solrconfig.xml file by the queryResultCache parameter:

```
<queryResultCache class="solr.LRUCache"
                  size="512"
                  initialSize="512"
                  autowarmCount="0"/>
```

The statistics on the Solr admin page can be referred to in order to judge the performance of the cache.

queryResultCache

class:	org.apache.solr.search.LRUCache
version:	1.0
description:	LRU Cache(maxSize=512, initialSize=512)
src:	$URL: https://svn.apache.org/repos/asf/lucene/dev/branches/lucene_solr_4_7/ solr/core/src/java/org/apache/solr/search/LRUCache.java $

stats:		
	lookups:	4
	hits:	2
	hitratio:	0.5
	inserts:	3
	evictions:	0
	size:	3
	warmupTime:	0
	cumulative_lookups:	4
	cumulative_hits:	2
	cumulative_hitratio:	0.5
	cumulative_inserts:	2
	cumulative_evictions:	0

queryResultCache usage statistics

The usage statistics for different caches is almost the same. We have the `size` statistic that specifies the number of objects in the cache. The `inserts` statistic tells us about the number of inserts that were made into the cache. When the `size` is full, `inserts` will happen but `size` will not increase. Instead `evictions` will happen where the least recently used object will be removed from the cache memory. We have the `lookups` parameter that specifies the number of times the cache was queried, and the `hits` parameter specifies the number of times the cache query provided results. The higher the `hit ratio`, the better is the cache performance.

Query cache can also be ignored for a particular request using cache local parameter.

Refer to the following usage example:

```
q={!cache=false}*:*
```

Application cache

In addition to the caches provided by Solr and Lucene, most advertising applications have their own local cache. This cache can be used to reduce the search time to less than 1 millisecond. Remember that we require a fast search in order to achieve the CPM / CPC target.

The application will also need to handle cache invalidation and refresh whenever any updates happen in the index.

Garbage collection

Java performs **Garbage Collection (GC)** at certain intervals to clean up unused objects from the memory. During full garbage collection, Solr or any Java application comes to a standstill. Depending on the amount of heap memory allocated, the pause time can go up to 1 second or higher for large heaps. The aim here is to avoid full GC and work on concurrent GC. There are certain parameters in Java or Tomcat that can be used for concurrent garbage collection.

These parameters can be added to the Tomcat environment variables to enable better garbage collection:

```
FULL_GC_OPTS="-XX:+UseConcMarkSweepGC -XX:+UseParNewGC
-XX:+SurvivorRatio=8 -XX:MaxTenuringThreshold=32
-XX:TargetSurvivorRatio=90"
```

 For other servers such as Jetty or Resin, please refer to the respective guides on how to add these variables to the environments.

For more information on the variables passed to the Tomcat environment, refer to the following description:

- `UseConcMarkSweepGC`: This acts as a concurrent collector. The related GC algorithm attempts to do most of the garbage collection work in the background without stopping application threads while it works. However, there are phases where it has to stop application threads, but these phases are attempted to be kept to a minimum.

- `UseParNewGC`: This function uses a parallel version of the young-generation copying collector alongside the default collector. It minimizes pauses by using all available CPUs in parallel.

- `SurvivorRatio`: This class serves to increase the survivor spaces in order to keep survivors alive longer.

- `MaxTenuringThreshold`: This class serves to prevent objects from being copied to the tenured space too early.

- `TargetSurvivorRatio`: This class serves to increase the maximum percentage of available survivor space.

We need to tune the parameters as per our requirements. With upgrades, the **Java Virtual Machine (JVM)** will have much better ways of handling garbage collection, which will have to be looked into.

Merging Solr with Redis

Solr indexing involves huge costs. Therefore, handling of real-time data is expensive. Every time a new piece of information comes into the system, it has to be indexed to be available for search. Another way of handling this is to break the Solr index into two parts, stable and unstable. The stable part of the index is contained inside Solr, while the unstable part can be handled by a plugin by extracting information from Redis. The unstable part of the index, which is now inside Redis, can handle real-time additions and deletions through an external script, which is reflected in the search results.

Redis is an advanced key value store that can be used to store documents containing keys and values in the memory. It offers advantages over Memcache, as it syncs the data onto disk and provides replication and clustering facilities. In addition to the storage of normal key values, it provides facilities to store data structures such as *strings*, *hashes*, *lists*, *sets*, and *sorted sets*. It also has a publisher-subscriber functionality built into the server.

In an advertising system, the Solr index can be used for searches based on the keyword, placement, and user profile or behavioral information. The data inside Redis can be used for filtering and sorting and contains the following information:

- Status of the ad, whether active or not
- Ad price and rank, which affects the CTR
- Ad contents, such as image path, link, or text to be displayed

The data inside Redis can be small or large depending on the type of advertisements. If an advertisement contains large images and text, it can bloat. However, since this data is outside Solr, it would not affect the search performance.

Since, we are creating a plugin for sorting and filtering using Redis, we need to decide where to place it. Solr provides two entry points for a plugin, `ResponseWriter` and `SearchComponent`.

- `ResponseWriter`: This class is used for sending responses and is unsuitable for filtering and sorting of data.

- `SearchComponent`: This class is easy to implement and configure and contains a `QueryComponent` class that can be easily modified. The `QueryComponent` class is the base for default searching.

We have learnt in *Chapter 3, Solr Internals and Custom Queries* how to write a query parser plugin. We first create a `RedisQParserPlugin` class, which extends the `QParserPlugin` class, and then override the `createParser` function:

```
public class RedisQParserPlugin extends QParserPlugin {

    @Override
    public QParser createParser
        (String qstr, SolrParams localParams, SolrParams params,
        SolrQueryRequest req) {
      return new QParser(qstr, localParams, params, req) {
      @Override
      public Query parse() throws SyntaxError {
        logger.info("Redis Post-filter invoked");
        return new RedisPostFilter();
      }
    };
  }
}
```

Inside the `parse` function, we are calling `RedisPostFilter`, which does all the hard work.

The `PostFilter` interface provides a mechanism for filtering documents after they have already gone through the main query and other filters.

The `RedisPostFilter` class extends the `ExtendedQueryBase` class and implements the `PostFilter` interface. The APIs for `PostFilter` and `ExtendedQueryBase` can be accessed from the following URLs:

http://lucene.apache.org/solr/4_7_0/solr-core/org/apache/solr/search/PostFilter.html

http://lucene.apache.org/solr/4_7_0/solr-core/org/apache/solr/search/ExtendedQueryBase.html

Let us also go through the code for the `PostFilter`:

```
public RedisPostFilter() {
    setCache(false);
    Jedis redisClient = new Jedis("localhost", 6379);
```

In the constructor, we have disabled caching and are connecting to the Redis server on `localhost` port 6379. The post filter over here just filters the ads on the basis of their status, as `active` (online) or `inactive` (offline):

```
redisClient.select(1);
onlineAds = redisClient.smembers("myList");
this.adsList = new HashSet<BytesRef>(onlineAds.size());
for (String ad : onlineAds) {
  this.adsList.add(new BytesRef(ad.getBytes()));
}
```

After connecting to the Redis server, we select a table (or index in terms of Redis) and get a list of all online ads from the Redis server. The same is added to the `adsList` set in the object.

Next, we define a function `isValid`, which checks whether the ad is valid or not:

```
public boolean isValid(String adId) throws IOException {
    return this.onlineAds.contains(adId);
}
```

We construct a `delegatingCollector` class, which is run after the main query and all filters but before any sorting or grouping collectors:

```
public DelegatingCollector getFilterCollector(final IndexSearcher
indexSearcher) {
    return new DelegatingCollector() {
```

We override two functions, `setNextReader` and `collect`, which gets the IDs from `FieldCache` (the search results on the index) and returns them to the parent's result `Collector`, respectively:

```
@Override
public void setNextReader(AtomicReaderContext context) throws
IOException {
  this.docBase = context.docBase;
  this.store = FieldCache.DEFAULT.getTerms(context.reader(),
  "id", false);
  super.setNextReader(context);
}
@Override
public void collect(int docId) throws IOException {
  String id = context.reader().document(docId).get("id");
  if (isValid(id)) {
    super.collect(docId);
  }
}
```

Inside the `RedisPostFilter` parameter, we override the `getCache` and `getCost` functions:

```
@Override
public int getCost() {
    return Math.max(super.getCost(), 100);
}
```

The `getCost` function returns a value that is greater than `100`:

```
@Override
public boolean getCache() {
    return false;
}
```

The `getCache` function is required to be `false` for caching to be disabled, and `getCost` is required to be greater than 100. Only then would the post filter interface be used for filtering.

`equals` and `hashCode` are two methods that are overridden from the `org.apache.lucene.search.Query` abstract class. This extends the functionality of the Lucene search query.

In order to compile the code, we will need to use the following JAR files in our class path to handle the dependencies:

* `jedis-1.5.0.jar`
* `log4j-1.2.16.jar`
* `lucene-core-4.8.1.jar`
* `solr-core-4.8.1.jar`
* `slf4j-log4j12-1.6.6.jar`
* `slf4j-api-1.6.6.jar`
* `solr-solrj-4.8.1.jar`

Once compiled, we can create a JAR file using the following command:

```
$ jar -cvf redis.jar packt/*
```

We will see the following output on the screen:

```
added manifest
adding: packt/search/(in = 0) (out= 0)(stored 0%)
adding: packt/search/RedisQParserPlugin$1.class(in = 1335) (out= 568)
(deflated 57%)
adding: packt/search/RedisQParserPlugin.class(in = 1179) (out= 524)
(deflated 55%)
adding: packt/search/RedisPostFilter.class(in = 2720) (out= 1497)
(deflated 44%)
adding: packt/search/RedisPostFilter$1.class(in = 2135) (out= 986)
(deflated 53%)
```

In order to load the plugin, copy redis.jar and jedis-1.5.0.jar to the <solr_installation_dir>/example/lib folder and specify the library path in the solrconfig.xml file:

```
<lib dir="../../lib/" regex="redis\.jar" />
<lib dir="../../lib/" regex="jedis-1\.5\.0\.jar" />
```

We will need to define the implementation class in the solrconfig.xml file. This is an important glue to hook in the Redis post-filter implementation:

```
<queryParser name="redis" class="packt.search.RedisQParserPlugin" />
```

On starting Solr, we can see that the specified JAR files are loaded:

```
3110 [coreLoadExecutor-4-thread-2] INFO  org.apache.solr.core.
SolrResourceLoader  - Adding 'file:/home/jayant/installed/solr-4.7.2/
example/lib/redis.jar' to classloader
```

Now restart the Solr server and check whether Redis is working on the localhost port 6379:

Redis server working

In order to call the filter, we will have to pass fq={!redis} to our Solr query:

```
http://localhost:8983/solr/collection1/select?q=*:*&fq={!redis}
```

The calls to `RedisPostFilter` can be seen in the Solr logs, as shown in the following image:

```
3; packt.search.RedisQParserPlugin$1; Redis Post-filter invoked
4; org.apache.solr.core.SolrCore; [collection1] webapp=/solr pat
5; packt.search.RedisQParserPlugin$1; Redis Post-filter invoked
7; packt.search.RedisPostFilter$1; count 1
; packt.search.RedisPostFilter$1; count 2
2; packt.search.RedisPostFilter$1; count 3
4; packt.search.RedisPostFilter$1; count 4
3; packt.search.RedisPostFilter$1; count 5
; org.apache.solr.core.SolrCore; [collection1] webapp=/solr pat
```

This plugin can be used to filter the ads on the basis of their status. Updates regarding the status of ads can be made into the Redis database through an external script. The actual implementation inside Solr can differ depending on the logic that you want to implement in the post filter.

Summary

In this chapter, we understood how an advertising network works. We went through the implementation of Solr for a large-scale ad distribution network. We saw the problems plaguing such an implementation in an advertising network and the solutions to these problems. We also saw the architecture of a large-scale Solr system. We saw the cache optimization options in Solr. We also built a plugin that interacts with Redis to aid the real-time update of the status of ads.

In the next chapter, we will explore a framework known as AJAX Solr, which can be used to execute queries on Solr directly from the client browser without the need for any application.

8

AJAX Solr

In the previous chapter, we learnt how Solr can be used in an advertising system. We understood the working of an advertising system, its architecture, and the complexities involved in the implementation of the system. We also discussed some performance improvements in Solr with respect to the advertising system. In addition, we wrote a custom plugin for Solr intended for the integration of Solr with Redis (the key value memory store).

In this chapter, we will explore an advanced package known as AJAX Solr. We will first look at the architecture of AJAX Solr and then see how different functionalities of Solr such as pagination, search result faceting, customization of search results, and tag cloud can be performed using AJAX Solr. We will cover the following topics:

- The purpose of AJAX Solr
- The AJAX Solr architecture
- Working with AJAX Solr
- Performance tuning

AJAX is a JavaScript library that can be used to create interfaces in Apache Solr. It does not require any JavaScript framework to work, but needs an AJAX implementation to communicate with Solr. Therefore, it can be used in conjunction with JavaScript libraries and frameworks such as jQuery and Angular.js, which support AJAX. Earlier a JavaScript library called **SolrJS** was developed as a Solr JavaScript client. AJAX Solr is a fork of this library and has evolved as a JavaScript client for Solr.

The purpose of AJAX Solr

AJAX Solr is a Solr client developed using JavaScript. AJAX Solr facilitates interesting visualizations of a result set that includes widgets to display tag clouds of facets, filtering of results by date fields, and plotting of maps based on country code information. AJAX Solr can be integrated with any web application enabling the Solr-related operations to be performed directly on the Apache Solr interface, without the necessity to incorporate any language in between.

Ideally, any request on the Internet is received by a web application residing on the server, and Solr-related operations are forwarded to the Solr server for processing. This is shown in the following diagram. The request originating from the browser travels over the Internet to the web application residing on the web server. The web server then creates a Solr request and performs the required operation on the Solr server.

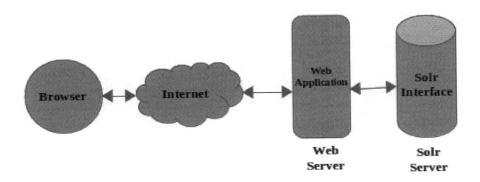

With AJAX Solr, the intermediary web application can be removed from the picture, allowing the JavaScript application on the user's browser to communicate directly with Solr servers. This is shown in the following diagram. We can now add a visually appealing AJAX view of the search results without any impact on the web application.

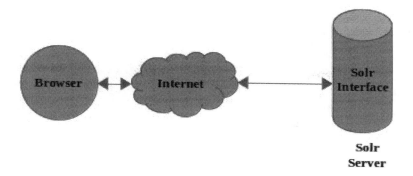

**Solr
Server**

While working with AJAX Solr, operations to be performed in Solr, such as Solr queries, are processed on the web browser using JavaScript. This reduces processing on the web application and its complexity.

The primary features of AJAX Solr are as follows:

- A dynamic and interactive GUI
- A faster GUI
- An enhanced hit highlighter
- Modernized standards
- Cost-effectiveness
- A widget framework

The AJAX Solr architecture

AJAX Solr follows the **Model-View-Controller** (**MVC**) pattern. The components of AJAX Solr are:

- **ParameterStore**: This is the model of an MVC framework. This class stores the Solr parameters and hence the state of the application.
- **Manager**: This acts as the controller in the MVC framework. It talks to the ParameterStore class and sends requests to the Solr server and delegates the response received to the widgets for rendering.
- **Widgets**: Widgets act as views rendering the interface.

AJAX Solr library can be downloaded from `https://github.com` using the Git client and the following command:

`git clone https://github.com/evolvingweb/ajax-solr.git`

You will need to install the Git client on your machine to execute this command. For Linux users, Git can be installed using the following command:

`sudo apt-get install git`

Windows users can download Git from the following URL and install it on their machines: `http://git-scm.com/downloads`.

This will create a folder called `ajax-solr` with the following sub-folders:

- `core`: This sub-folder includes all the managers, parameter stores, and abstract widgets
- `managers`: This sub-folder includes all the framework-specific managers
- `widgets`: This sub-folder includes all framework-specific widgets
- `examples`: This sub-folder includes working examples

AJAX Solr is built with extensibility in mind. Therefore, we can take an existing class and extend its functionality by writing a new class that inherits the existing class. AJAX Solr classes reside in the `AjaxSolr` namespace. In order to extend any class, we can simply write:

```
AjaxSolr.ChildClass = AjaxSolr.ParentClass.extend({
   /* our code */
});
```

The architecture of the components of AJAX Solr can be understood from the following image:

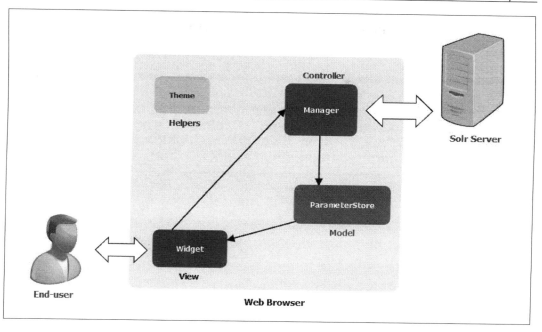

Let us understand the components of AJAX Solr.

In order to use AJAX Solr, we will need to include the following JavaScript libraries on our web page:

```
<script type="text/javascript" src="ajax-
solr/core/Core.js"></script>
<script type="text/javascript" src="ajax-
solr/core/AbstractManager.js"></script>
<script type="text/javascript" src="ajax-
solr/managers/Manager.jquery.js"></script>
<script type="text/javascript" src="ajax-
solr/core/Parameter.js"></script>
<script type="text/javascript" src="ajax-
solr/core/ParameterStore.js"></script>
```

Also, we will need an AJAX library for which we can download jQuery from: http://jquery.com/download/.

We also include jQuery the library in our web page:

```
<script type="text/javascript" src="jquery-
1.11.2.min.js"></script>
```

The Manager controller

The Manager controller performs a two-way communication with our Solr server. It accepts `solrUrl` or `proxyUrl` as its parameter. `SolrUrl` is used when Manager communicates with Solr directly. `ProxyUrl` is used when it interacts with Solr through a proxy. Ideally, we would not like to expose our Solr server to the Internet, so we can put it behind a proxy server and specify `ProxyUrl` in the Manager. The proxy server can also be configured to prevent **Denial of Service (DoS)** attacks and ensure the number of records in the result set is at a maximum (by restricting the row parameter).

The `solrUrl` parameter should hold the absolute URL of the Solr application and can be represented using the following code snippet:

```
Manager = new AjaxSolr.Manager({
  solrUrl: "http://127.0.0.1:8983/solr/"
});
```

In our case, the Solr server is on the local machine, so we have specified the local machine's IP address.

In the implementation of the `solrUrl` parameter, AJAX Solr uses the `select` servlet by default. If you want to change the default value of the servlet parameter, you need to pass the servlet parameter to `Manager` at the time of initialization, as shown in the following code snippet:

```
Manager = new AjaxSolr.Manager({
  solrUrl: 'http://127.0.0.1:8983/solr/',
  servlet: 'readonly'
});
```

The `Manager` life cycle can be represented using the following image that shows how the different components of AJAX Solr interact with each other.

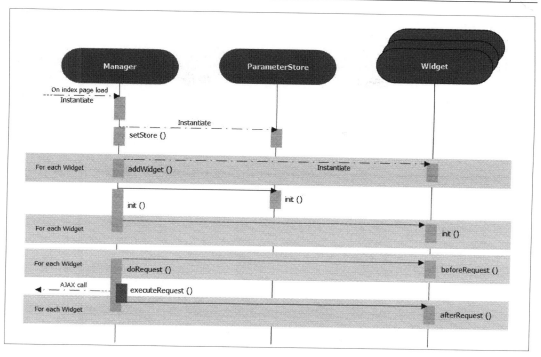

The `ParameterStore` object can be attached to `Manager` by the `setStore` method, as shown in the following snippet:

```
Manager.setStore(new AjaxSolr.ParameterStore());
```

Similarly, the widgets to be used for display can be attached to `Manager` by using the `addWidget` method, as shown in the following snippet:

```
Manager.addWidget(new AjaxSolr.AbstractWidget({
    id: 'identifier',
    target: '#css-selector'
}));
```

Once `parameterStore` and `widgets` are attached to `Manager`, we can call the `init` method of the `Manager` to initialize AJAX Solr. This in turn calls the `init` methods of the attached components, `ParameterStore` and `widgets`.

```
Manager.init();
```

Once `Manager` is initialized, we can call the `doRequest()` method to send the first request to Solr:

```
Manager.doRequest();
```

If any widget wishes to perform an action prior to sending the request to Solr (for instance, displaying `throbber` gif image), `doRequest` triggers the `beforeRequest` method of each of the widgets. The `throbber` may include activities such as content download, computation of some values, or interaction with an external device. Then, the `executeRequest` abstract method is called that actually sends the request to Solr. The AJAX implementation of Solr is JavaScript framework agnostic. Any framework supporting AJAX implementation can be used to send the AJAX request to Solr. This is handled by the `Manager.jquery.js` file, which resides in the `managers` folder inside the `ajax-solr` library. This implements the `executeRequest` method using jQuery. As soon as the Manager receives a response from Solr, it captures the JSON response in its response property. It then triggers the `afterRequest` method of each widget so that the response property is investigated by the widgets and rendered to the interface accordingly.

The ParameterStore model

The `parameterStore` model is used to store Solr parameters. It defines functions for fetching, setting, and removing Solr parameters. Some Solr parameters, such as `facet.field` and `fq`, may be specified multiple times. Other parameters, such as `q` and `start`, may be specified only once. There is the `isMultiple` method, which returns `true` if the parameter can be specified multiple times.

There is a list of functions that operate on Solr parameters, and their behavior is based on whether a specific parameter needs to be used multiple times or just once. These functions can be categorized as follows:

- **Available parameters**: Parameters that are directly available for us to use
- **Exposed parameters**: Consists of parameters that are exposed by AJAX Solr for the end users to play around with

Let us understand these categories.

Available parameters

Solr parameters are represented as `Parameter` objects. The `Parameter` class defines the following attributes and functions for its usage:

- `val`: This attribute gets and sets the parameter value
- `local`: This attribute gets and sets local parameters
- `remove`: This attribute removes the local parameters
- `string`: This attribute returns the parameter as a query string key-value pair

- `parseString`: This attribute parses the query string key-value pair back into a parameter
- `valueString`: This attribute returns the parameter value as a query string-safe value
- `parseValueString`: This attribute parses the query string-safe value back into a parameter value

The following is a list of parameters that are available for use:

- `CoreQueryParameters` (`https://wiki.apache.org/solr/CoreQueryParameters`)
- `CommonQueryParameters` (`https://wiki.apache.org/solr/CommonQueryParameters`)
- `HighlightingParameters` (`https://wiki.apache.org/solr/HighlightingParameters`)
- `SimpleFacetParameters` (`https://wiki.apache.org/solr/SimpleFacetParameters`)
- `TermsComponent` (`https://wiki.apache.org/solr/TermsComponent`)
- `TermVectorComponent` (`https://wiki.apache.org/solr/TermVectorComponent`)
- `SpellCheckComponent` (`https://wiki.apache.org/solr/SpellCheckComponent`)
- `StatsComponent` (`https://wiki.apache.org/solr/StatsComponent`)
- `LocalParams` (`https://wiki.apache.org/solr/LocalParams`)
- `MoreLikeThis` (`https://wiki.apache.org/solr/MoreLikeThis`)

Exposed parameters

With exposed parameters, widgets allow end users to alter the Solr parameters. This means that, if an end user modifies the value of a parameter, the application reacts to the change that has been triggered by the end user. It is important to save the respective states in case the end user performs a bookmark trigger or wants to move across the states using the browser navigation button. Though we can implement our custom storage method by extending `ParameterStore` (discussed in the *Extending the ParameterStore class* section of this chapter), the easiest way is using the `ParameterHashStore` class that stores the parameters in the URL hash.

Using the ParameterHashStore class

The `ParameterHashStore` class stores Solr parameters in the URL hash. To use `ParameterHashStore`, add its JavaScript file, which is available inside the core folder of the `ajax-solr` library:

```
<script type="text/javascript" src="ajax-
solr/core/ParameterHashStore.js"></script>
```

Before calling the `Manager.init()` function, create a new object out of `ParameterHashStore` and set it as a store for the Manager using the following code:

```
Manager.setStore(new AjaxSolr.ParameterHashStore());
```

Also, the following code lists the Solr parameters that your widget will expose and allow the user to set or change as this store's property.

```
Manager.store.exposed = [ 'fq', 'q', 'start' ];
```

Using these two lines, we can use `ParameterHashStore` in our implementation of AJAX Solr.

Extending the ParameterStore class

The `init` method of `Manager` calls the `init` abstract method of `ParameterStore`. When extending the `ParameterStore` class, it is important to implement its `init` method so that any one-time initializations are handled using this `init` method. Also, the parameters that we want our widgets to allow the users to use directly or indirectly in the exposed property. The method `exposedString` can be used to retrieve these parameters as a query string.

The `Manager` class calls the `save` abstract method in its `doRequest` method. This also means that the save method is triggered once before each request is sent to Solr. The save method should be capable of storing the values of the exposed parameters such that the end user is able to bookmark and move between states. The `ParameterHashStore` class implements the `save` method in order to store the state in the URL hash.

Another method, `storedString`, returns the current state of the application as a string. It is implemented by `ParameterHashStore` in order to return the URL hash.

If we want to implement our own storage method instead of using `ParameterHashStore`, we need to implement only two abstract methods, `save` and `storedString`. We can also implement the load method, which by default resets the exposed parameters by calling the `exposedReset` method. It also calls the `parseString` method on the string returned by `storedString` thereby recreating the parameter object.

Widgets

The purpose of widgets is to inspect the JSON response retrieved from Solr by `Manager` and update the interface accordingly. `AbstractWidget` is the base class from which all widgets are inherited. Each widget accepts two parameters:

- `id`: A mandatory identifier that identifies the widget
- `target`: An optional parameter that is normally the CSS selector for the HTML element that the widget updates upon each Solr request

The `AbstractWidget` base class exposes three abstract methods:

- `init`: Triggered by the `init` method of `Manager` to perform one-time initializations
- `beforeRequest`: Triggered by the `doRequest` method of `Manager` prior to the request being sent to Solr
- `afterRequest`: Called by the `handleResponse` method of `Manager` after receiving a response from Solr

AJAX Solr defines a set of abstract widgets that we can use to write our own widgets. In order to benefit from the functions that are contained in these widgets, we just need to write a new widget that inherits one of the following widgets:

- `AbstractFacetWidget`: It is applied to the new widgets that intend to manipulate the `fq` parameter and has been discussed in the *Adding facets* section of this chapter
- `AbstractSpatialWidget`: It is applied to the widgets that manipulate the Spatial Solr local parameters
- `AbstractSpellcheckWidget`: It helps us write widgets that deal with the spell-check data in the Solr response
- `PagerWidget`: It applies to the widgets that are intended for performing pagination activities and have been discussed in the *Adding pagination* section of this chapter
- `AbstractTextWidget`: It helps us write widgets that manipulate the `q` parameter

Working with AJAX Solr

Now that we have seen the architecture and components of AJAX Solr, let us go ahead and see how to implement it. We will download the default **reuters** index and build some features on top of it.

The reuters index is included as a part of code of this chapter. It can also be downloaded from http://public.slashpoundbang.com.s3.amazonaws.com/ data-solr-4-index.zip.

Start with a fresh installation of Solr. Unzip the downloaded index and replace the data folder inside the <solr_installation>/example/solr/collection1 folder.

If the data folder does not exist, start Solr using the following command inside the <solr_installation>/example folder:

```
java -jar start.jar
```

Once Solr is running, simply shut it down using Ctrl-C on the Command Prompt.

This will create the data folder and the related configuration files inside the <solr_ installation>/example/solr/collection1 folder.

We will also need to add and modify certain fields in our Solr schema. Open up the schema.xml file inside the <solr_installation>/example/solr/collection1/ conf folder and add the following lines to it:

```
<field name="places" type="string" indexed="true" stored="true"
multiValued="true" omitNorms="true" termVectors="true" />
<field name="countryCodes" type="string" indexed="true" stored="true"
multiValued="true" omitNorms="true" termVectors="true" />
<field name="topics" type="string" indexed="true" stored="true"
multiValued="true" omitNorms="true" termVectors="true" />
<field name="organisations" type="string" indexed="true" stored="true"
multiValued="true" omitNorms="true" termVectors="true"
/>
<field name="exchanges" type="string" indexed="true" stored="true"
multiValued="true" omitNorms="true" termVectors="true" />
<field name="companies" type="string" indexed="true" stored="true"
multiValued="true" omitNorms="true" termVectors="true" />
<field name="allText" type="text_general" indexed="true" stored="true"
multiValued="true" omitNorms="true" termVectors="true"
/>
<field name="dateline" type="string" indexed="true" stored="true"
multiValued="true" omitNorms="true" termVectors="true" />
<field name="date" type="pdate" indexed="true" stored="true"
multiValued="true" omitNorms="true" termVectors="true" />
<copyField source="title" dest="allText"/>
<copyField source="text" dest="allText"/>
<copyField source="places" dest="allText"/>
<copyField source="topics" dest="allText"/>
<copyField source="companies" dest="allText"/>
<copyField source="exchanges" dest="allText"/>
<copyField source="dateline" dest="allText"/>
```

The configuration and schema files required for running the example perfectly are available inside the `ajax-solr/examples/solr-home` folder cloned from the `ajax-solr` Git repository.

These files can simply be replaced inside the `<solr_installation>/example/solr/collection1/conf` folder.

Now start Solr.

Talking to AJAX Solr

We will now need to create or connect the web page with this Solr instance. The complete HTML files required for running this example can be found inside the `ajax-solr/examples` folder, cloned from the `ajax-solr` Git repository. Our base HTML page on which we are going to build the search using AJAX Solr is `ajax-solr/examples/reuters/index.0.html`. The following screenshot shows how the basic web page appears:

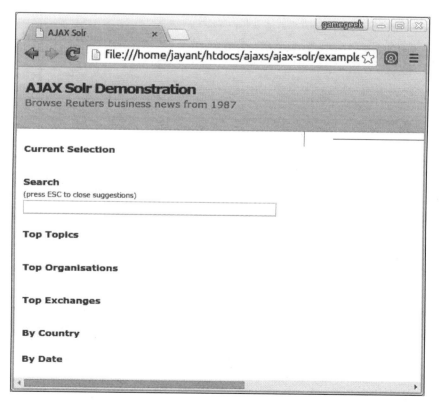

If we look at the code of the page, we can see that the following JavaScript and CSS files are being included in it:

```
<script
src=http://ajax.googleapis.com/ajax/libs/jquery/1.7.2/jquery.min.js
> </script>
<script
src="http://ajax.googleapis.com/ajax/libs/jqueryui/1.8.24/jquery-
ui.min.js"></script>
<link rel="stylesheet"
href="http://ajax.googleapis.com/ajax/libs/jqueryui/1.8.24/themes/smo
othness/jquery-ui.css">
```

We can replace them by downloading our copy of jquery and jquery-ui files.

In order to connect to Solr, we will need to include the following JavaScript in our code:

```
<script src="../../core/Core.js"></script>
<script src="../../core/AbstractManager.js"></script>
<script src="../../managers/Manager.jquery.js"></script>
<script src="../../core/Parameter.js"></script>
<script src="../../core/ParameterStore.js"></script>
```

We need to write the following JavaScript code to ask the Manager object to connect to our Solr instance running on localhost port 8983:

```
var Manager;

(function ($) {

  $(function () {
    Manager = new AjaxSolr.Manager({
      solrUrl: 'http://localhost:8983/solr/collection1/'
    });
    Manager.init();
    Manager.store.addByValue('q', '*:*');
    Manager.doRequest();
  });

}) (jQuery);
```

Let us write this code in a file called reuters.1.js inside the js folder and include it as a JavaScript source in our web page:

```
<script src="js/reuters.1.js"></script>
```

Here we have created an instance of `Manager` and assigned to it the Solr URL that connects to Solr running on our local machine, `localhost:8983`. We have initiated Manager and executed a query `q=*:*`. Since we have not defined any display widget, we will not be able to see the output. However, we can check whether the request was sent by enabling the Firebug status bar on the Firefox web browser.

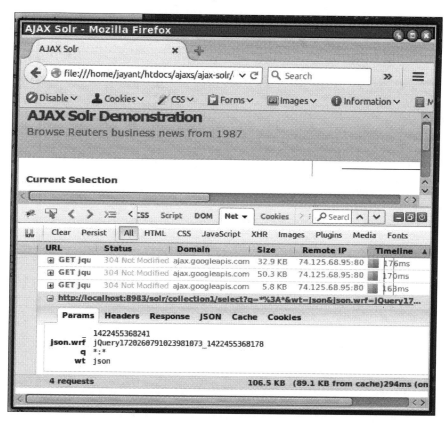

Inside the **Net** tab of Firebug, we can see the requests being sent from the browser. Here we see the following Solr URL being called:

```
http://localhost:8983/solr/collection1/select?q=*%3A*&wt=json&json.wrf
=jQuery1720260791023981073_1422455368178&_=1422455368241
```

Also, we can see the parameters being sent in the call. This step creates the query and specifies the return response format as JSON.

Displaying the result

We can display the documents returned from Solr by creating a display widget. For this, we will need to create a new widget, say `ResultWidget.js`, inside the `widgets` folder. As this is inherited from `AbstractWidget` provided by the AJAX Solr library, we will have to include `AbstractWidget.js` as a JavaScript source in our web page:

```
<script src="../../core/AbstractWidget.js"></script>
```

Let us get a sense of the structure of the code that we will write inside `ResultWidget.js`:

```
AjaxSolr.ResultWidget = AjaxSolr.AbstractWidget.extend({
  //Methods

  init: function () {
    //Manipulation of results. For example, hiding details.
  },

  beforeRequest: function () {
    //Tasks that are supposed to be triggered before Solr responds.
    //For example, displaying loading image.
  },

  afterRequest: function () {
    //Actual code chunk to render the result set.
  }
}
```

Now create a new file inside the widgets folder `ResultWidget.js`. We will have to define `AjaxSolr.ResultsWidget`, which extends the `AbstractWidget`:

```
(function ($) {
AjaxSolr.ResultWidget = AjaxSolr.AbstractWidget.extend({
    start: 0,
```

We would like to show a loader image while the request is being processed. This image is included in the `beforeRequest` function:

```
beforeRequest: function () {
  $(this.target).html($('<img>').attr('src', 'images/ajax-
  loader.gif'));
},
```

After the results are received, the `afterRequest` function is called. Here, we process the result and create the view to be displayed:

```
afterRequest: function () {
    $(this.target).empty();
    for (var i = 0, l = this.manager.response.response.docs.length; i
    < l; i++) {
      var doc = this.manager.response.response.docs[i];
      $(this.target).append(this.template(doc));
```

Here, we are looping through the result set and getting the variable doc out of manager. Now `template` is the function being called to create the HTML code for each result tuple:

```
template: function (doc) {
    var snippet = '';
    if (doc.text.length > 300) {
      snippet += doc.dateline + ' ' + doc.text.substring(0, 300);
      snippet += '<span style="display:none;">' +
      doc.text.substring(300);
      snippet += '</span> <a href="#" class="more">more</a>';
    }
    else {
      snippet += doc.dateline + ' ' + doc.text;
    }

    var output = '<div><h2>' + doc.title + '</h2>';
    output += '<p id="links_' + doc.id + '" class="links"></p>';
    output += '<p>' + snippet + '</p></div>';
    return output;
}
```

The `template` function checks whether the length of the `text` in the document is more than 300. If so, the first 300 characters are displayed and a `more` link is added. The function creates a `div` tag with the document `title` and `id` and returns the output that is appended to the HTML view:

`ResultsWidget.js` is added to our web page with the following code:

```
<script src="widgets/ResultWidget.js"></script>
```

In order to glue this widget to our `Manager`, we will add the `Widget` to our Manager. We also add `id` and `target` div tags:

```
Manager.addWidget(new AjaxSolr.ResultWidget({
    id: 'result',
    target: '#docs'
}));
```

Note the following:

- `id`: It is a required parameter that identifies the widget
- `target`: It is an optional parameter and is normally the CSS selector for the HTML element that the widget updates upon each Solr request

Here we have specified the `target` div tag as `docs`, which is mentioned on our HTML page using the following code:

```
<div id="result">
    <div id="navigation">
        <ul id="pager"></ul>
        <div id="pager-header"></div>
    </div>
    <div id="docs"></div>
</div>
```

To implement the `more` link at the end of each result tag, we implement the following code snippet inside the `init` method:

```
init: function () {
    $(document).on('click', 'a.more', function () {
        var $this = $(this),
            span = $this.parent().find('span');

        if (span.is(':visible')) {
            span.hide();
            $this.text('more');
        }
        else {
            span.show();
            $this.text('less');
        }

        return false;
    });
}
```

At the end of the each result tuple, the `more` link makes the entire result tuple visible, and the `less` link makes the first 300 characters visible. This works on the basis of the code in the `init` function shown earlier. Implementation of the previous code enables the `init` method of `Widget` to be called as soon as the `init` method of `Manager` is triggered.

This code is available in the `index.2.html` and `js/reuters.2.js` files. The execution of the file yields the following output:

AJAX Solr offers extremely convenient ways to achieve different activities and functions using widgets. Some of the features that can be achieved by adding widgets are:

- Display of the customized result set
- Addition of pagination capabilities
- Interactive and fast faceted search
- Free-text search
- Auto-complete capabilities
- Interactive maps
- Addition of calendars
- Interactive tag clouds
- Grouping of search results

Adding facets

Let us add facets and pagination to our example. We will need to define the functions `facetLinks` and `facetHandler` in our `ResultWidget.js` to handle faceting. The `facetLinks` function will be called from the `afterRequest` method. Add the following lines after the `for` loop of the `afterRequest` method:

```
var items = [];
items = items.concat(this.facetLinks('topics', doc.topics));
items = items.concat(this.facetLinks('organizations',
doc.organisations));
items = items.concat(this.facetLinks('exchanges', doc.exchanges));

var $links = $('#links_' + doc.id);
$links.empty();
for (var j = 0, m = items.length; j < m; j++) {
  $links.append($('<li></li>').append(items[j]));
}
```

Let us also define the `facetLinks` function:

```
facetLinks: function (facet_field, facet_values) {
  var links = [];
  if (facet_values) {
    for (var i = 0, l = facet_values.length; i < l; i++) {
      links.push(
        $('<a href="#"></a>')
        .text(facet_values[i])
        .click(this.facetHandler(facet_field, facet_values[i]))
      );
```

```
    }
  }
  return links;
},
```

The `handler` function being called inside `facetHandler` is as follows:

```
facetHandler: function (facet_field, facet_value) {
  var self = this;
  return function () {
    self.manager.store.remove('fq');
    self.manager.store.addByValue('fq', facet_field + ':' +
AjaxSolr.Parameter.escapeValue(facet_value));
    self.doRequest();
    return false;
  };
},
```

This code creates links for browsing by `topics`, `organization`, or `exchanges`. When a link is clicked, the `facetHandler` function is called. This step resets the filter query inside `Manager`, adds a filter query, and sends a Solr request. We can see these links under the title – **U.K. GROWING IMPATIENT WITH JAPAN – THATCHER** as seen in the following figure:

Here we can see two links under the title, namely **trade** and **acq**. Also, the parameters sent to Solr do not contain any filter query. Let us click on a link, say **trade**. We can see that a new Solr query is being executed that contains the filter query for `topics:trade`. The results are refreshed, so now all the results have at least the **trade** link below the title, as shown in the following screenshot:

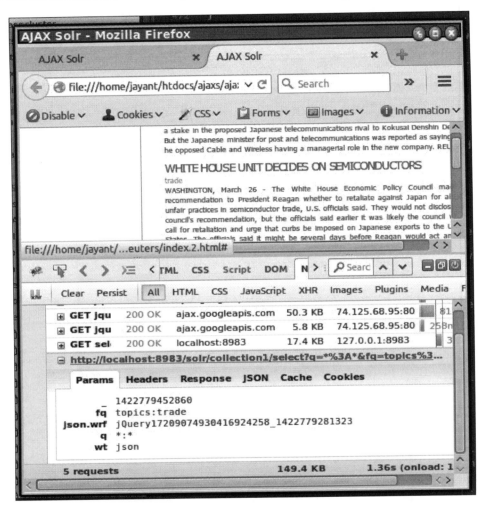

Adding pagination

For adding pagination, we will need to add the `PagerWidget` class to our `manager`. Include the following JavaScript in the main HTML page:

```
<script src="../../widgets/jquery/PagerWidget.js"></script>
```

Add the `pager` widget to `Manager` inside the `reuters.js` file:

```
Manager.addWidget(new AjaxSolr.PagerWidget({
  id: 'pager',
  target: '#pager',
  prevLabel: '&lt;',
  nextLabel: '&gt;',
  innerWindow: 1,
  renderHeader: function (perPage, offset, total) {
    $('#pager-header').html($('<span></span>').text('displaying ' +
    Math.min(total, offset + 1) + ' to ' + Math.min(total, offset +
    perPage) + ' of ' + total));
  }
}));
```

In addition to defining `id` and `target` for this widget, the pager widget exposes some of its own properties, which were defined in the previous code. We have also implemented the abstract method `renderHeader` to display the total results found. This sets the total number of results inside the `pager-header` div tag, which needs to be defined in our HTML code:

```
<div id="pager-header"></div>
```

The `pager` class is defined by the following code inside our HTML:

```
<ul id="pager"></ul>
```

The pagination is shown above the results as follows:

Adding a tag cloud

Let us derive the tag cloud from the facet fields, namely topics, organizations, and exchanges, and display the tag cloud on our web page. For this, add the Solr parameters required for faceting to reuters.js:

```
var params = {
  facet: true,
  'facet.field': [ 'topics', 'organisations', 'exchanges' ],
  'facet.limit': 20,
  'facet.mincount': 1,
  'f.topics.facet.limit': 50,
  'json.nl': 'map'
};
for (var name in params) {
  Manager.store.addByValue(name, params[name]);
}
```

Now, extend the `AbstractFacetWidget` and create a new widget called `TagcloudWidget` by adding the following code in a new file `widgets/TagcloudWidget.js`:

```
(function ($) {
AjaxSolr.TagcloudWidget = AjaxSolr.AbstractFacetWidget.extend({
});
})(jQuery);
```

We have used `AbstractFacetWidget`, which provides many convenient functions specific to the faceting widget.

We will need to add these two JavaScript files to our HTML page:

```
<script src="../../core/AbstractFacetWidget.js"></script>
<script src="widgets/TagcloudWidget.js"></script>
```

Next, add three widget instances to `Manager` for each of the facet fields, `topics`, `organizations`, and `exchanges`. For this, write the following code snippet in the `reuters.js` file:

```
var fields = [ 'topics', 'organisations', 'exchanges' ];
for (var i = 0, l = fields.length; i < l; i++) {
  Manager.addWidget(new AjaxSolr.TagcloudWidget({
     id: fields[i],
     target: '#' + fields[i],
     field: fields[i]
  }));
}
```

Any widget inherited from `AbstractFacetWidget` accepts the mandatory field parameter that identifies the facet field we want the widget to deal with. We need to add the target fields as `div(s)` to our main HTML page:

```
<h2>Top Topics</h2>
<div class="tagcloud" id="topics"></div>

<h2>Top Organisations</h2>
<div class="tagcloud" id="organisations"></div>

<h2>Top Exchanges</h2>
<div class="tagcloud" id="exchanges"></div>
```

We will need to implement the `afterRequest` abstract method in `TagcloudWidget` to handle the response received from Solr. This method is called after receiving a response from Solr, similar to the `afterRequest` method of `ResultsWidget`.

We will add the following code to the `afterRequest` method of `TagcloudWidget`:

```
afterRequest: function () {
    if (this.manager.response.facet_counts.facet_fields[this.field] ===
    undefined) {
        $(this.target).html('no items found in current selection');
        return;
    }

    var maxCount = 0;
    var objectedItems = [];
    for (var facet in this.manager.response.facet_counts.facet_
fields[this.field]) {
        var count =
parseInt(this.manager.response.facet_counts.facet_fields[this.field]
[facet]);
        if (count > maxCount) {
            maxCount = count;
        }
        objectedItems.push({ facet: facet, count: count });
    }
    objectedItems.sort(function (a, b) {
        return a.facet < b.facet ? -1 : 1;
    });

    $(this.target).empty();
    for (var i = 0, l = objectedItems.length; i < l; i++) {
        var facet = objectedItems[i].facet;
        $(this.target).append(
            $('<a href="#" class="tagcloud_item"></a>')
            .text(facet)
            .addClass('tagcloud_size_' + parseInt(objectedItems[i].count /
            maxCount * 10))
            .click(this.clickHandler(facet))
        );
    }
}
```

A number of activities are performed in the previous code snippet. Let us focus on its highlighted portions that are closely related to AJAX Solr.

The first one, `this.manager.response.facet_counts.facet_fields[this.field]`, behaves in the same way as that discussed in the *Displaying the result* section of this chapter. We set the field property `this.field` when adding the widget instance to `manager`. Thus, using this code chunk, we actually inspect the facet data associated with that field in the Solr response.

Note that `clickHandler` is another convenient function offered by `AbstractFacetWidget`. It adds the `fq` parameter, which is associated with the widget's facet field and its corresponding value. If it succeeds, a request is sent to Solr with this filter query.

The following screenshot shows how the tag cloud is displayed when the page is loaded:

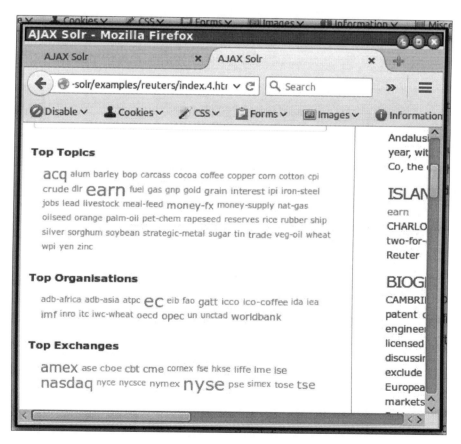

If we click on the topic **earn**, another Solr query is executed and the page is refreshed with the results. As shown in the following image, the Solr query will have a filter query for `topics:earn` in addition to faceting parameters.

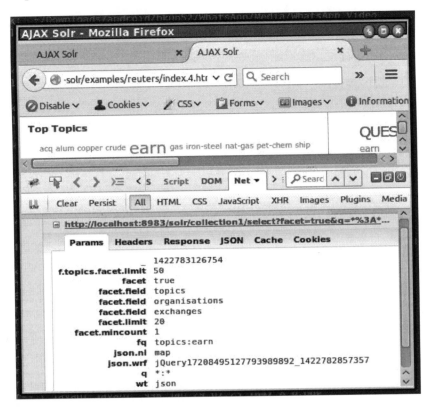

 AJAX Solr can be used to build many custom widgets, such as **freetext**, **filters**, **autocomplete**, **map**, and **calendar**. More details can be obtained from its wiki page at `https://github.com/evolvingweb/ajax-solr/wiki`.

Performance tuning

With AJAX Solr, we end up adding a lot of JavaScript and CSS to our pages. Though the searches would be faster as there is no server between the Solr server and the web browser, front-end optimizations can improve user experience. Here are some tips for that.

- **Controlling and minimizing server traffic**: It is important to minimize the amount of data that flows between the Solr server and the web browser where AJAX Solr is in action. This can be achieved using the following:

  - **Filtering at the server level**: It is not a good idea to fetch the complete set of documents and the associated details from the server and filter them at the browser level so as to render only those results that match with the request. AJAX Solr performs filtering at the server level itself so that the transport channel doesn't get overcrowded with unwanted details. This also helps in minimizing the computation activities performed at the browser level.

  - **Solr schema consideration**: The Solr schema in AJAX Solr allows us to index the chunk of information that we intend to render on the browser. This helps us minimize unwanted data transport and allows the channel to transfer productive information.

  - **Compressing JavaScript and CSS**: Using AJAX Solr, we can compress JavaScript and CSS files. This reduces the data being transferred between the browser and the Solr server and hence speeds up the requests and responses.

- **Proxy server caching**: AJAX Solr supports proxy servers. A proxy server can be set up to act as a reverse proxy cache, which can cache responses sent to the browser. Therefore, responses to repeated queries are faster, as the queries are not executed on the Solr server but served from the proxy server cache. Proxy servers can also be used to cache JavaScript and CSS files. With a proxy server, all responses can be compressed, which speeds up data transfer.

Summary

In this chapter, we discussed AJAX Solr, which is an advanced JavaScript library that can be used to execute queries on a Solr server from a web browser. We saw the different components of AJAX Solr and discussed their internals. We also built a sample application using AJAX Solr and saw how the different components interact with each other. We also saw that, in addition to the display of the results received from Solr, Ajax Solr can be used for pagination, faceting, and building tag clouds.

In the next chapter, we will go through the benefits of using SolrCloud. We will see how SolrCloud can be set up and used to perform distributed indexing and search.

9
SolrCloud

In this chapter, we will learn about SolrCloud. We will look at the architecture of SolrCloud and understand the problems it addresses. We will look at how it can be used to address scalability issues. We will also set up SolrCloud along with a separate setup for central configuration management known as ZooKeeper. We will look at the advanced sharding options available with SolrCloud, memory management issues, and monitoring options. We will also evaluate SolrCloud as a NoSQL storage system.

The major topics that will be covered in this chapter are:

- The SolrCloud architecture
- Centralized configuration
- Setting up SolrCloud
- Distributed indexing and search
- Advanced sharding with SolrCloud
- Memory management
- Monitoring
- Using SolrCloud as a NoSQL database

The SolrCloud architecture

Scaling proceeds in two ways when it comes to handling large amounts of data, horizontally or vertically. Vertical scaling deals with the problems of handling large data by adding bigger and bigger machines. Suppose a single machine which has 4 GB of RAM and 4 CPU can handle a concurrency of 100 queries per second on a data size of say 8 GB. As the amount of data increases, the amount of processing required for serving the queries also increases. Therefore, if the data size goes to 16 GB, the query concurrency that the same machine can handle will be 75 queries instead of 100. For vertical scaling, we would replace the current 4 GB + 4 CPU machine with an 8 GB + 8 CPU machine, which should again be able to serve a concurrency of 100 queries per second on a data size of 16 GB. Horizontal scaling would mean that we add another machine of the same configuration 4 GB RAM + 4 CPU to the system and divide 16 GB of data into two parts of 8 GB each. Each machine now hosts 8 GB of data and can support a concurrency of 100 queries per second. That is, a combined concurrency of 200 queries per second is obtained.

There is a limit to which a system can be scaled vertically. The largest machine available on Amazon as of now has *32 vCPUs* and *244 GB of RAM*. While it may be possible to scale a system in a vertical fashion by adding more hardware, horizontal scaling is still preferable. Maybe a year down the line, Amazon will be able to offer *64 vCPUs with 488 GB of RAM*. What if your data grows exponentially during the one-year period? The larger machine may not be able to satisfy your queries per second requirements. Horizontal scaling is cost-effective as it is possible to retain the existing hardware and add new instead of discarding the existing hardware for an upgraded or better machine. Horizontal scaling not only adds new machines providing additional computing power and memory, but it also provides additional storage. It can be made to act as a distributed system taking care of failover and high availability scenarios wherever required.

Scaling with Solr is as complex. It is possible to add hardware and scale a single Solr or a Solr setup in master-slave architecture in a vertical fashion. For vertical scaling, we will need to continually add more memory and increase the computing power and, if possible, move to SSD drives, which are expensive but a lot more efficient than normal drives. This will improve the disk IO multiple times. Since we need a master-slave architecture for high-availability and failover scenarios, we will need to retain at least two machines, one acting as the master and the other acting as a slave and replicating Solr index data from the master.

However, horizontal scaling is preferable. SolrCloud provides easy scaling in a horizontal fashion.

With SolrCloud, the complete index can be divided into **shards** and **replicas**. A shard is a part of the complete index. A replica is basically a Solr slave that reads data from the master and replicates it. A shard can have more than one replica. SolrCloud has the capability to set up a cluster of Solr servers that also provides fault tolerance and high availability in addition to distributed search and indexing.

SolrCloud offers a centralized configuration, automatic load balancing and failover for queries, and ZooKeeper integration for cluster coordination and configuration. ZooKeeper is a centralized service for maintaining configuration information for a distributed system. It is possible to have a cluster of ZooKeeper services providing high availability and failover. SolrCloud does not have a master node to allocate nodes, shards, and replicas. Instead, it uses ZooKeeper to manage these components.

With SolrCloud, we can add documents to our distributed index via any server in the cluster. The document is automatically routed to the proper shard in the cluster and indexed there. In case of a server or Solr instance going down, another shard will be elected as a leader. The searches are available near real time after indexing.

A full-scale SolrCloud setup is explained by the following architecture:

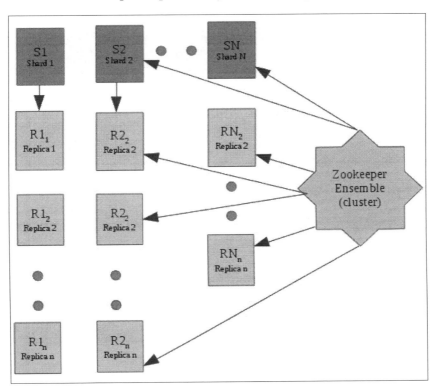

The SolrCloud architecture

The cloud consists of N shards, each of which can be on a different machine. Each shard can have n replicas, again on different machines. The configuration is managed by a separate cluster of ZooKeeper servers known as **Zookeeper ensemble**. The ZooKeeper ensemble will interact with each machine in SolrCloud, namely shard leaders and replicas.

Centralized configuration

While dealing with SolrCloud, the question that comes to mind is how any change in the schema or configuration will be propagated to the different nodes in the cluster. The ZooKeeper ensemble takes care of this.

The ZooKeeper ensemble is another cluster of servers having high availability and failover solutions built into the system. It takes care of the distribution of the schema, configuration and other files, and maintenance of the leader and replica information with regard to SolrCloud. The advantage of this is that whenever any change in the schema or configuration occurs, we need not worry about how it is propagated to all the nodes in the cluster; the ZooKeeper ensemble takes care of the propagation.

It is generally recommended to keep at least three servers for the ZooKeeper ensemble to provide for the failover scenarios. The ZooKeeper service can be run as a separate service, as nodes running SolrCloud, or in separate machines. The ZooKeeper process is lightweight and is not resource intensive.

Setting up SolrCloud

Let us set up SolrCloud. We will look at two ways of setting up SolrCloud. One setup is the ZooKeeper service running inside SolrCloud. This can be considered as a dev or a test setup that can be used for evaluating SolrCloud or for running benchmarks. Another is the production setup where SolrCloud is set up as part of the Apache Tomcat application server and the ZooKeeper ensemble as a separate service. Let us start with the test setup.

Test setup for SolrCloud

We will create a test setup of a cluster with two shards and two replicas. The Solr installation directory comes inbuilt with the packages required to run SolrCloud. There is no separate installation required. ZooKeeper is also inbuilt in the SolrCloud installation. It requires a few parameters during Solr start-up to get ZooKeeper up and running.

To start SolrCloud, perform the following steps:

- Create four copies of the example directory in the Solr installation, namely `node1`, `node2`, `node3`, and `node4`:

  ```
  cp -r example/ node1

  cp -r example/ node2

  cp -r example/ node3

  cp -r example/ node4
  ```

- To start the first node, run the following command:

  ```
  cd node1

  java -DzkRun -DnumShards=2 -Dbootstrap_confdir=./solr/collection1/
  conf -Dcollection.configName=myconf -jar start.jar
  ```

  - DzkRun: This parameter starts the ZooKeeper server embedded in the Solr installation. This server will manage the Solr cluster configuration.

  - DnumShards: This parameter specifies the number of shards in SolrCloud. We have set it to 2 so that our cloud setup is configured for two shards.

  - Dbootstrap_confdir: This parameter instructs the ZooKeeper server to copy the configurations from this directory and distribute them across all the nodes in SolrCloud.

  - Dcollection.configName: This parameter specifies the name of the configuration for this SolrCloud to the ZooKeeper server.

- The output will be similar to the one shown in the following screenshot:

```
3976 [Thread-15] INFO  org.apache.solr.cloud.Overseer  - Update state num
Shards=2 message={
  "operation":"state",
  "state":"down",
  "base_url":"http://127.0.1.1:8983/solr",
  "core":"collection1",
  "roles":null,
  "node_name":"127.0.1.1:8983_solr",
  "shard":"shard1",
  "collection":"collection1",
  "numShards":"2",
  "core_node_name":"core_node1"}
4026 [main-EventThread] INFO  org.apache.solr.common.cloud.ZkStateReader
 - A cluster state change: WatchedEvent state:SyncConnected type:NodeData
Changed path:/clusterstate.json, has occurred - updating... (live nodes s
ize: 1)
```

- We can see the information that we have provided. The shard is active and is named as **shard1**. The number of shards is specified as **2**. Also, we can see that the status is updated as **live nodes size: 1**. This Solr instance will be running on port **8983** on the local server. We can open it with the following URL: `http://localhost:8983/solr/`.

- On the left-hand panel, we can see the link for **Cloud**:

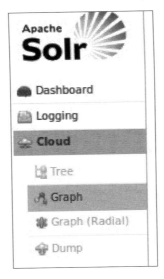

- This was not visible earlier. This option becomes visible when we start Solr with the parameters for SolrCloud. Clicking on the **Cloud** link yields the following graph:

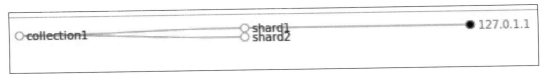

- There are also options available to have a radial view of SolrCloud. This can be seen through the **Graph (Radial)** link. We will continue to examine the SolrCloud graph to know how nodes are being added to the cloud.

- The legend for color coding of the nodes of SolrCloud is visible on the right-hand side of the interface, as shown in the following image:

- As per the legend, the current node is **Leader**. All the other functionalities of the admin interface of SolrCloud remain the same as those of the Solr admin interface.

- To start the second node, let us enter the folder called `node2` and run the following command:

```
java -Djetty.port=8984 -DzkHost=localhost:9983 -jar start.jar
```

  - `Djetty.port`: This parameter is required to start the Solr server on a separate port. As we are setting up all the nodes of SolrCloud on the same machine, the default port `8983` will be used for one Solr instance. Other instances of Solr will be started on separate custom ports.

  - `DzkHost`: This parameter tells this instance of Solr where to find the ZooKeeper server. The port for the ZooKeeper server is Solr's port + `1000`. In our case, it is `9983`. Once the instance of Solr gets connected to the ZooKeeper server, it can get the configuration options from there. The ZooKeeper server then adds this instance of Solr to the SolrCloud cluster.

- On the terminal, we can see that the **live nodes count** has now increased to 2. We can see the graph on the SolrCloud admin interface. It now has two shards, one running on port **8983** and the other on port **8984**:

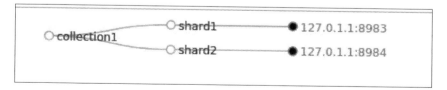

- To add more nodes, all we have to do is change the port and start another Solr instance. Let us start the third node with the following commands:

```
cd node3
java -Djetty.port=8985 -DzkHost=localhost:9983 -jar start.jar
```

- We can see that the **live nodes size** is now **3** and the SolrCloud graph has been updated:

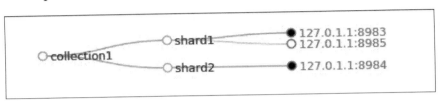

- This node is added as an active replica of the first shard.

- Let us now add the fourth node as well:

```
cd node4

java -Djetty.port=8986 -DzkHost=localhost:9983 -jar start.jar
```

- The **live nodes size** grows to **4**, and the SolrCloud graph shows that the fourth node is added as an active replica of the second shard:

This setup for SolrCloud uses a single ZooKeeper instance running on port 9983, which is the same instance as the Solr instance running on port 8983. This is not an ideal setup. If the first node goes offline, the entire SolrCloud setup will go offline.

> It is not necessary to run the SolrCloud admin interface from the first Solr running on port 8983. We can open up the admin interface from any of the Solr servers that are part of SolrCloud. The options for cloud will be visible in all. Therefore, ideally, we can open SolrCloud from Solr servers running on ports 8984, 8985, and 8986 in our setup.

Setting up SolrCloud in production

The setup we saw earlier was for running SolrCloud on a single machine. This setup can be used to test out the features and functionalities of SolrCloud. For a production environment, we would want a setup that is fault tolerant and highly available. In order to have such a setup, we need at least three ZooKeeper instances. The more, the better. A minimum of three instances are required to have a fault tolerant and highly available cluster of ZooKeeper servers. As all communication between the Solr servers in SolrCloud happens via ZooKeeper, it is important to have at least two ZooKeeper instances for communication if the third instance goes down.

Setting up the Zookeeper ensemble

ZooKeeper can be downloaded from: `http://zookeeper.apache.org/releases.html#download`.

We will set up three machines to run ZooKeeper. Let us name the machines `zoo1`, `zoo2`, and `zoo3`. The latest version of ZooKeeper is 3.4.6. Let us copy the `zookeeper tar.gz` file to the three machines and *untar* them over there. We will have a folder `zookeeper-3.4.6` on all the three machines.

On all the nodes, create a folder named `data` inside the ZooKeeper folder:

```
ubuntu@zoo1:~/zookeeper-3.4.6$ mkdir data
ubuntu@zoo2:~/zookeeper-3.4.6$ mkdir data
ubuntu@zoo3:~/zookeeper-3.4.6$ mkdir data
```

Each ZooKeeper server has to be given an ID. This is specified in the `myid` file in the `data` directory. We will have to create a file called `myid` inside the `data` directory on each ZooKeeper server (`zoo1`, `zoo2`, and `zoo3`) and put the ID assigned to the ZooKeeper server there. Let us assign the IDs 1, 2, and 3 to the ZooKeeper servers `zoo1`, `zoo2`, and `zoo3`:

```
ubuntu@zoo1:~/zookeeper-3.4.6/data$ echo 1 > myid
ubuntu@zoo2:~/zookeeper-3.4.6/data$ echo 2 > myid
ubuntu@zoo3:~/zookeeper-3.4.6/data$ echo 3 > myid
```

Copy the ZooKeeper sample configuration `zoo_sample.cfg` to `zoo.cfg` inside the `conf` folder under the `zookeeper` folder. Open the ZooKeeper configuration file `zoo.cfg` and make the following changes:

```
dataDir=/home/ubuntu/zookeeper-3.4.6/data
server.1=zoo1:2888:3888
server.2=zoo2:2888:3888
server.3=zoo3:2888:3888
```

Let the remaining setting remain as it is. We can see the `clientPort=2181` setting. This is the port where the Solr servers will connect. We have specified the `data` directory, which we just created, as also the ZooKeeper servers that are part of the ensemble, as follows:

```
server.id=host:xxxx:yyyy
```

Note the following:

- `id`: It is the ZooKeeper server ID specified in the `myid` file.
- `host`: It is the ZooKeeper server host.
- `xxxx`: It is the port used to connect to other peers for communication. A ZooKeeper server uses this port to connect followers to the leader. When a new leader arises, a follower opens a TCP connection to the leader using this port.
- `yyyy`: It is the port that is used for leader election.

Let us now start the ZooKeeper instances on all three machines. The following command starts the ZooKeeper instance:

```
ubuntu@zoo1:~/zookeeper-3.4.6$ ./bin/zkServer.sh start
```

We will have to run the command on all three machines. The output indicates that the ZooKeeper instance has started on all the three machines:

```
ubuntu@zoo1:~/zookeeper-3.4.6$ ./bin/zkServer.sh start
JMX enabled by default
Using config: /home/ubuntu/zookeeper-3.4.6/bin/../conf/zoo.cfg
Starting zookeeper ... STARTED
```

Check the logs in the `zookeeper.out` file to verify whether everything is running smoothly. ZooKeeper also comes with a client `zkCli.sh`, which can be found in the `bin` folder. In order to check whether everything is running fine, we can fire a `ruok` command via Telnet on any one of the ZooKeeper servers. If everything is running fine, we would get the output as `imok`. Another command `mntr` can be used to monitor the variables on the ZooKeeper cluster over Telnet.

We have a running ZooKeeper ensemble that we will use for setting up our SolrCloud. We will not delve into the advanced ZooKeeper settings.

Setting up Tomcat with Solr

Let's install Apache Tomcat on all the Solr servers in the `/home/ubuntu/tomcat` folder. On all the Solr servers (`solr1`, `solr2`, `solr3`, and `solr4`), start up Tomcat to check whether it is running fine:

```
ubuntu@solr1:~$ cd tomcat/
ubuntu@solr1:~/tomcat$ ./bin/startup.sh
```

We are using Tomcat version 7.0.53. Check the `catalina.out` log file inside the `tomcat/logs` folder to check whether Tomcat started successfully. We can see the following message in the logs if the start-up was successful:

```
INFO: Server startup in 2522 ms
```

Now, on one server (say `solr1`), upload all the configuration files to the ZooKeeper servers. Our Solr configuration files are located inside the `<solr_installation>/example/solr/collection1/conf` folder. To upload the files onto ZooKeeper, we will have to use the ZooKeeper client. We can copy the `zookeeper` installation folder to one of the Solr servers in order to use the ZooKeeper client. Another option is to use the ZooKeeper client inside the SolrCloud installation. For this, we will have to extract the `solr.war` file found inside the `<solr_installation>/dist` folder. Let us extract it inside a new folder `solr-war`:

```
ubuntu@solr1:~/solr-4.8.1/dist$ mkdir solr-war
ubuntu@solr1:~/solr-4.8.1/dist$ cp solr-4.8.1.war solr-war/
ubuntu@solr1:~/solr-4.8.1/dist$ cd solr-war/
ubuntu@solr1:~/solr-4.8.1/dist/solr-war$ jar -xvf solr-4.8.1.war
```

This will extract all the libraries here. We will need another library `slf4j-api` that can be found in the `<solr_installation>/dist/solrj-lib` folder:

```
ubuntu@solr1:~/solr-4.8.1/dist/solr-war/WEB-INF/lib$ cp ../../../solrj-lib/slf4j-api-1.7.6.jar .
ubuntu@solr1:~/solr-4.8.1/dist/solr-war/WEB-INF/lib$ cp ../../../solrj-lib/slf4j-log4j12-1.7.6.jar .
ubuntu@solr1:~/solr-4.8.1/dist/solr-war/WEB-INF/lib$ cp ../../../solrj-lib/log4j-1.2.16.jar .
```

Now run the following command in the Solr library path `solr-war/WEB-INF/lib` to upload the Solr configuration files onto `zookeeper` on all three servers, namely `zoo1`, `zoo2`, and `zoo3`:

```
java -classpath zookeeper-3.4.6.jar:solr-core-4.8.1.jar:solr-solrj-
4.8.1.jar:commons-cli-1.2.jar:slf4j-api-1.7.6.jar:commons-io-2.1.jar org.
apache.solr.cloud.ZkCLI -cmd upconfig -z zoo1,zoo2,zoo3 -d ~/solr-4.8.1/
example/solr/collection1/conf -n conf1
```

We have specified all the required JAR files in the `-classpath` option.

We used the zookeeper built inside the Solr cloud with the `org.apache.solr.cloud.ZkCLI` package.

- `-cmd`: This option specifies the action to be performed. In our case, we are performing the config upload action.
- `-z`: This option specifies the ZooKeeper servers along with the path (`/solr`) where the files are to be uploaded.
- `-d`: This option specifies the local directory from where the files are to be uploaded.
- `-n`: This option is the name of the config (the `solrconf` file).

In order to check whether the `configs` have been uploaded, move to machine `zoo1` and execute the following commands from the `zookeeper` folder:

```
ubuntu@zoo1:~/zookeeper-3.4.6$ ./bin/zkCli.sh -server zoo1

Connecting to zoo1

[zk: zoo1(CONNECTED) 0] ls /configs/conf1
```

This will list the config files inside the ZooKeeper servers:

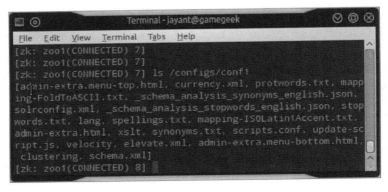

Let us create a separate folder to store the Solr index. On each Solr machine, create a folder named `solr-cores` inside the `home` folder:

```
ubuntu@solr1:~$ mkdir ~/solr-cores
```

Inside the folder `solr-cores`, add the following code in the `solr.xml` file. This specifies the host, port, and context along with some other parameters for ZooKeeper and the port on which Tomcat or Solr will work. The values for these variables will be supplied in the `setenv.sh` file inside the `tomcat/bin` folder:

```
<?xml version="1.0" encoding="UTF-8" ?>
<solr>
  <!-- Values are supplied from SOLR_OPTS env variable in setenv.sh --
>
   <solrcloud>
     <str name="host">${host:}</str>
     <int name="hostPort">${port:}</int>
     <str name="hostContext">${hostContext:}</str>
     <int name="zkClientTimeout">${zkClientTimeout:}</int>
     <bool name="genericCoreNodeNames">${genericCoreNodeNames:true}</
bool>
   </solrcloud>

   <shardHandlerFactory name="shardHandlerFactory"
     class="HttpShardHandlerFactory">
     <int name="socketTimeout">${socketTimeout:0}</int>
     <int name="connTimeout">${connTimeout:0}</int>
   </shardHandlerFactory>
</solr>
```

Now, to set these variables, we will have to define them in the `setenv.sh` file in the `tomcat/bin` folder. Place the following code inside the `setenv.sh` file:

```
JAVA_OPTS="$JAVA_OPTS -server"
SOLR_OPTS="-Dsolr.solr.home=/home/ubuntu/solr-cores -Dhost=solr1
-Dport=8080 -DhostContext=solr -DzkClientTimeout=20000 -DzkHost=zoo1:2
181,zoo2:2181,zoo3:2181"
JAVA_OPTS="$JAVA_OPTS $SOLR_OPTS"
```

Note the following:

- `solr.solr.home`: This is the Solr home for this app instance
- `host`: The hostname for this server
- `port`: The port of this server

- hostContext: Tomcat webapp context name
- zkHost: A comma-separated list of the host and the port for the servers in the ZooKeeper ensemble
- zkClientTimeout: Timeout for the ZooKeeper client

Now, copy the solr.war file from the Solr installation into the tomcat/webapps folder:

```
cp ~/solr-4.8.1/dist/solr-4.8.1.war ~/tomcat/webapps/solr.war
```

Also, copy the JAR files required for logging from the lib/ext folder into the tomcat/lib folder:

```
cp -r ~/solr-4.8.1/example/lib/ext/* ~/tomcat/lib/
```

Once done, restart Tomcat. This will deploy the application solr.war into the webapps folder.

We can see Tomcat running on port 8080 on machine solr1 and access Solr via the following URL:

```
http://solr1:8080/solr/
```

However, this does not have any cores defined.

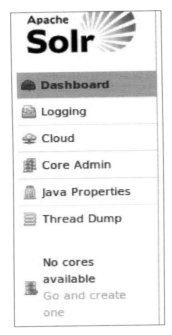

To create the core `mycollection` in our SolrCloud, we will have to execute the CREATE command via the following URL:

```
http://solr1:8080/solr/admin/collections?action=CREATE&name=mycollec
tion&numShards=2&replicationFactor=2&maxShardsPerNode=2&collection.
configName=conf1
```

> We require at least two running nodes to execute this command on SolrCloud. In order to start SolrCloud on multiple nodes, we can use **VirtualBox** and create multiple virtual machines on a single host.
>
> The host name can be mapped onto the IP address in the /etc/hosts file on all the (virtual) machines participating in SolrCloud in the following format:
>
> ```
> #<ip address> <hostname>
> 10.0.3.1   solr1
> 10.0.3.2   solr2
> ```

Note the following:

- `action`: CREATE to create the core or collection
- `name`: The name of the collection
- `numShards`: The number of shards for this collection
- `replicationFactor`: The number of replicas for each shard
- `maxShardsPerNode`: Sets a limit on the number of replicas the CREATE action will spread to each node
- `collection.configName`: Defines the name of the configuration to be used for this collection

The execution of the CREATE action yields the following output:

```
▼<response>
  ▼<lst name="responseHeader">
     <int name="status">0</int>
     <int name="QTime">22625</int>
  </lst>
  ▼<lst name="success">
    ▼<lst>
      ▼<lst name="responseHeader">
         <int name="status">0</int>
         <int name="QTime">13807</int>
      </lst>
      <str name="core">mycollection_shard2_replica2</str>
    </lst>
    ▼<lst>
      ▼<lst name="responseHeader">
         <int name="status">0</int>
         <int name="QTime">13899</int>
      </lst>
      <str name="core">mycollection_shard2_replica1</str>
    </lst>
    ▼<lst>
      ▼<lst name="responseHeader">
         <int name="status">0</int>
         <int name="QTime">20128</int>
      </lst>
      <str name="core">mycollection_shard1_replica1</str>
    </lst>
    ▼<lst>
      ▼<lst name="responseHeader">
         <int name="status">0</int>
         <int name="QTime">20540</int>
      </lst>
      <str name="core">mycollection_shard1_replica2</str>
    </lst>
  </lst>
</response>
```

We can see that two shards and two replicas are created for `mycollection`. The naming of each core is self-explanatory `<collection_name>_<shard_no>_<replica_no>`. We can also see the SolrCloud graph that shows the shards for the collection along with the leader and replicas:

We can see that `mycollection` has two shards, `shard1` and `shard2`. `Shard1` has leader on `solr1` and replica on `solr2`. Similarly, `Shard2` has leader on `solr3` and replica on `solr4`. The admin interface on each node of the Solr cluster will show the shard or core hosted on this node. Go to the admin interface on the node `solr1` and select the core name from the drop-down on the left-hand panel. We should be able to see the details of the index on that node:

```
Instance
            CWD:   /home/ubuntu/tomcat
       Instance:   /home/ubuntu/solr-cores/mycollection_shard1_replica1
           Data:   /home/ubuntu/solr-cores/mycollection_shard1_replica1/data
          Index:   /home/ubuntu/solr-cores/mycollection_shard1_replica1/data/index
           Impl:   org.apache.solr.core.NRTCachingDirectoryFactory
```

Let us also see what happened at the ZooKeeper end. Go to any of the ZooKeeper servers and connect to the ZooKeeper cluster using the `zkCli.sh` script:

```
ubuntu@zoo1:~/zookeeper-3.4.6$ ./bin/zkCli.sh -server zoo1,zoo2,zoo3
Connecting to zoo1,zoo2,zoo3
```

We can see that `mycollection` is created inside the `/collections` folder. On executing a `get`, `mycollection` is linked with the configuration `conf1` that we specified in the `collection.configName` parameter while creating the collection:

```
[zk: zoo1,zoo2,zoo3(CONNECTED) 0] get /collections/mycollection
{"configName":"conf1"}
```

We can also see the cluster configuration by getting the `clusterstate.json` file from the ZooKeeper cluster:

```
[zk: zoo1,zoo2,zoo3(CONNECTED) 1] get /clusterstate.json
{"mycollection":{
    "shards":{
      "shard1":{
        "range":"80000000-ffffffff",
        "state":"active",
        "replicas":{
          "core_node2":{
            "state":"active",
            "base_url":"http://solr1:8080/solr",
            "core":"mycollection_shard1_replica1",
            "node_name":"solr1:8080_solr",
```

```
                "leader":"true"},
            "core_node3":{
                "state":"active",
                "base_url":"http://solr2:8080/solr",
                "core":"mycollection_shard1_replica2",
                "node_name":"solr2:8080_solr"}}},
        "shard2":{
            "range":"0-7fffffff",
            "state":"active",
            "replicas":{
                "core_node1":{
                    "state":"active",
                    "base_url":"http://solr3:8080/solr",
                    "core":"mycollection_shard2_replica2",
                    "node_name":"solr3:8080_solr",
                    "leader":"true"},
                "core_node4":{
                    "state":"active",
                    "base_url":"http://solr4:8080/solr",
                    "core":"mycollection_shard2_replica1",
                    "node_name":"solr4:8080_solr"}}}},
    "maxShardsPerNode":"2",
    "router":{"name":"compositeId"},
    "replicationFactor":"2"}}
```

This shows the complete cluster information—the name of the collection, the shards and replicas, as well as the base URLs for accessing Solr. It contains the core name and the node name. Other configuration information that we passed while creating the cluster are maxShardsPerNode and replicationFactor.

Distributed indexing and search

Now that we have SolrCloud up and running, let us see how indexing and search happen in a distributed environment. Go to the `<solr_installation>/example/ exampledocs` folder where there are some sample XML files. Let us add some documents from the hd.xml file to SolrCloud. We will use the node solr1 for adding documents to the index. Here we are passing the collection name in the update URL instead of the core. The output from the command execution is shown in the following snippet:

```
$ java -Durl=http://solr1:8080/solr/mycollection/update -jar post.jar
hd.xml

SimplePostTool version 1.5
```

```
Posting files to base url http://solr1:8080/solr/mycollection/update
using content-type application/xml..
```

```
POSTing file hd.xml
```

```
1 files indexed.
```

```
COMMITting Solr index changes to http://solr1:8080/solr/mycollection/
update..
```

```
Time spent: 0:00:21.209
```

 Please use `localhost` instead of the `solr1` host if running on a local machine.

The documents are now committed into SolrCloud. To find the documents, perform a search on any node. Let us say we search on the node `solr2`. Execute the following query:

```
http://solr2:8080/solr/mycollection/select/?q=*:*
```

We can see that there are two documents in the result:

So, we actually indexed the documents via the `solr1` server in our SolrCloud and searched via the `solr2` server. The documents were indexed somewhere inside SolrCloud. In order to check where the documents went, we will have to go to each server and examine the overview of the collection. In the present case, the documents were indexed on servers `solr3` and `solr4`, which are replicas.

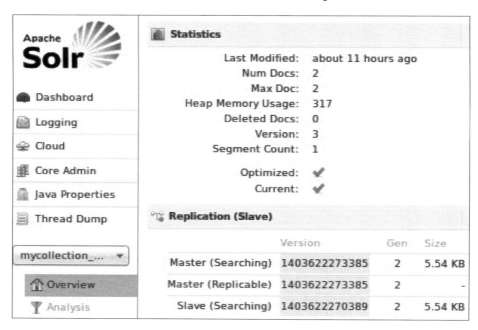

This means that we can index documents from any shard in SolrCloud, and those documents will be routed to a server in the cloud. Similarly, we can search from any shard in the cluster and query the complete index on SolrCloud.

Later in this chapter, we will also look at how and why to send documents to a particular shard.

Let us try indexing via the other machines. Execute the following commands from the `exampledocs` folder on the remaining machines in SolrCloud:

```
java -Durl=http://solr2:8080/solr/mycollection/update -jar post.jar mem.
xml
```

```
java -Durl=http://solr3:8080/solr/mycollection/update -jar post.jar
vidcard.xml
```

```
java -Durl=http://solr4:8080/solr/mycollection/update -jar post.jar
monitor*.xml
```

This will index the documents in the `mem.xml`, `vidcard.xml`, `monitor.xml`, and `monitor2.xml` files into SolrCloud. On searching via, say, the `solr3` machine, we can get all the documents. We indexed all nine documents, and all of them were found during a search on SolrCloud:

```
http://solr3:8080/solr/mycollection/select/?q=*:*
```

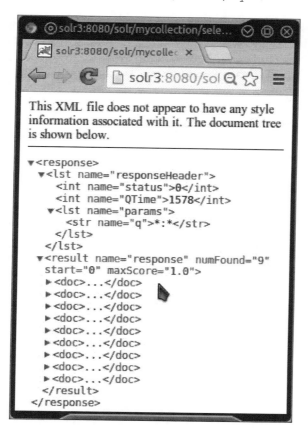

This means that since we have a four-node cluster, we can now index and search via all four nodes. The nodes themselves take care of routing of the documents to their appropriate shards and indexing them. Ideally, this should result in a four-fold increase in the indexing and searching speed. However, in a real-life scenario, the number of queries per second for indexing and search would be a little less than four times. It may also depend on the amount of data in the index, the IO capabilities of the server, and the network bandwidth between the machines in the cloud.

Routing documents to a particular shard

As we have seen, SolrCloud automatically distributes documents to different shards in the index. The queries on the cloud accumulate results from all the different shards and send them back. Why then would we want to route documents to a particular shard?

Suppose that we have a huge cluster of servers as part of SolrCloud—say 100 servers—with 30 shards and 3 replicas for each shard. This gives us ample room to manage a large-scale index expanding to some terabytes of data. A query to get the documents from the index based on a criterion would go to all the 30 shards in the index to get the results. The machine on which the query is executed would accumulate results from all the 30 shards and create the final result set. This would involve huge movement of data between shards and the shard performing the merge operation on the results will have to do some heavy processing, since it would move through 30 different result sets and merge them into a single result set.

It would be better if the query hits fewer shards or probably a single shard and fetches results from that shard without performing any merge operation. This would definitely be faster and less resource and network intensive. Ideally, each query should have an identifier or a set of identifiers pointing to the shards that may contain results from the query. This may not look possible from a broad view. Nevertheless, if the indexing is performed in a fashion that the data is distributed across the shards on the basis of some identifier, it may become possible.

A realistic example is to have documents from different customers indexed in SolrCloud. It would make sense to route the documents on the basis of the customer ID or customer name to the different shards in the cloud. Thus, documents belonging to IBM, Samsung, Apple, and Sony can reside on different shards. While querying, we can specify a prefix in the query so that a query done by IBM hits only the shard on which IBM resides.

Let us create a separate collection in SolrCloud with a routing parameter and then index a few documents into the cloud. We will be indexing the documents in the file `docs.csv`. We will consider the category as the sharding key. Therefore, Solr will create a hash based on the category and distribute the index on the basis of that hash.

To create the collection (let us call it `catcollection`), we have to execute the following command. Note the `router.field=cat` parameter at the end of the `CREATE` command. This is how we specify a router in a collection:

```
http://solr1:8080/solr/admin/collections?action=CREATE&name=catcolle
ction&numShards=2&replicationFactor=2&maxShardsPerNode=2&collection.
configName=conf1&router.field=cat
```

We can see that **catcollection** is created along with the previous collection **mycollection**. This collection again has two shards—**shard1** with **solr3** as **leader** and **solr1** as replica, and **shard2** with **solr4** as `leader` and **solr3** as replica:

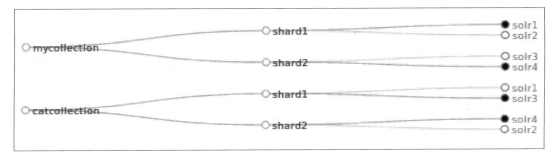

In order to verify whether the routing that we have specified has been successful, we will have to connect to the ZooKeeper server using the `zkCli.sh` script and look at the `clusterstate.json` file:

```
ubuntu@zoo1:~/zookeeper-3.4.6$ ./bin/zkCli.sh -server zoo1,zoo2,zoo3
[zk: zoo1,zoo2,zoo3(CONNECTED) 2] get /clusterstate.json
```

The output will contain both the collections—`mycollection` and `catcollection`—along with all the configuration parameters, as follows:

```
"catcollection":{
  "shards":{
    "shard1":{
      "range":"80000000-ffffffff",
      "state":"active",
      "replicas":{
        "core_node2":{
          "state":"active",
          "base_url":"http://solr1:8080/solr",
          "core":"catcollection_shard1_replica1",
          "node_name":"solr1:8080_solr"},
        "core_node3":{
          "state":"active",
          "base_url":"http://solr3:8080/solr",
          "core":"catcollection_shard1_replica2",
          "node_name":"solr3:8080_solr",
          "leader":"true"}}},
    "shard2":{
      "range":"0-7fffffff",
      "state":"active",
```

```
        "replicas":{
          "core_node1":{
            "state":"active",
            "base_url":"http://solr4:8080/solr",
            "core":"catcollection_shard2_replica1",
            "node_name":"solr4:8080_solr",
            "leader":"true"},
          "core_node4":{
            "state":"active",
            "base_url":"http://solr2:8080/solr",
            "core":"catcollection_shard2_replica2",
            "node_name":"solr2:8080_solr"}}}},
    "maxShardsPerNode":"2",
    "router":{
      "field":"cat",
      "name":"compositeId"},
    "replicationFactor":"2"}}
```

Here the router parameter has the field cat mentioned in it. Also, the range is specified in the range parameter for each shard. shard1 and shard2 will contain documents with hash IDs in the ranges 80000000-ffffffff and 0-7fffffff, respectively. Therefore, when a document is marked for indexing, the router will calculate the 32 bit hash of the content in the cat field and route the document to the shard whose range includes the hash value of the category value:

 The hash values are represented in hexadecimal.

Now let us push the docs.csv file (available with this chapter) to the cloud and see how the documents are distributed across the shards. Execute the following command to push the documents into SolrCloud:

```
$ java -Dtype=text/csv -Durl=http://solr4:8080/solr/catcollection/update
-jar post.jar docs.csv

SimplePostTool version 1.5

Posting files to base url http://solr4:8080/solr/catcollection/update
using content-type text/csv..

POSTing file docs.csv

1 files indexed.

COMMITting Solr index changes to http://solr4:8080/solr/catcollection/
update..

Time spent: 0:00:16.608
```

In order to query a particular shard, we will have to append the `shards=shard<no>` command at the end of the query. Let us see the documents in `shard1` and `shard2`:

```
http://solr1:8080/solr/catcollection/select?q=*:*&shards=shard1
```

```
▼<response>
 ▼<lst name="responseHeader">
    <int name="status">0</int>
    <int name="QTime">0</int>
   ▼<lst name="params">
      <str name="shards">shard1</str>
      <str name="q">*:*</str>
    </lst>
  </lst>
 ▼<result name="response" numFound="4" start="0">
   ▼<doc>
      <str name="id">USD</str>
     ▼<arr name="cat">
        <str>currency</str>
      </arr>
      <str name="name">One Dollar</str>
      <float name="price">1.0</float>
```

We can see that documents belonging to the category `currency` are indexed on `shard1`. Similarly, on executing the query on `shard2`, we can see that the documents belonging to the categories `book` and `electronics` are indexed on `shard2`:

```
http://solr1:8080/solr/catcollection/select?q=*:*&shards=shard2
```

```
▼<response>
 ▼<lst name="responseHeader">
    <int name="status">0</int>
    <int name="QTime">422</int>
   ▼<lst name="params">
      <str name="shards">shard2</str>
      <str name="q">*:*</str>
    </lst>
  </lst>
 ▼<result name="response" numFound="7" start="0" maxScore="1.0">
   ▼<doc>
      <str name="id">0553573403</str>
     ▼<arr name="cat">
        <str>book</str>
      </arr>
```

To send a query to a particular shard, we have to use the `shard.keys` parameter in our query. For example, to send the following query to the shard containing only books, we need to execute the following query:

```
http://solr1:8080/solr/catcollection/select?q=martin&fl=cat,name,descr
iption&shard.keys=book!
```

```
▼<response>
  ▼<lst name="responseHeader">
      <int name="status">0</int>
      <int name="QTime">444</int>
    ▼<lst name="params">
        <str name="fl">cat,name,description</str>
        <str name="shard.keys">book!</str>
        <str name="q">martin</str>
      </lst>
  </lst>
  ▼<result name="response" numFound="3" start="0" maxScore="0.4873799">
    ▼<doc>
      ▼<arr name="cat">
          <str>book</str>
        </arr>
        <str name="name">A Game of Thrones</str>
        <str name="description">Author: George R.R. Martin</str>
      </doc>
    ▼<doc>
      ▼<arr name="cat">
          <str>book</str>
        </arr>
        <str name="name">A Clash of Kings</str>
        <str name="description">Author: George R.R. Martin</str>
      </doc>
    ▼<doc>
      ▼<arr name="cat">
          <str>book</str>
        </arr>
        <str name="name">A Storm of Swords</str>
        <str name="description">Author: George R.R. Martin</str>
      </doc>
  </result>
</response>
```

We can see that all the books that have the word `martin` in their descriptions become a part of the query result. If we try to execute the same query with a different shard key, say currency, we will not be able to get any results:

```
http://solr1:8080/solr/catcollection/select?q=martin&fl=cat,name,descr
iption&shard.keys=currency!
```

```
▼<response>
  ▼<lst name="responseHeader">
      <int name="status">0</int>
      <int name="QTime">2</int>
    ▼<lst name="params">
        <str name="fl">cat,name,description</str>
        <str name="shard.keys">currency!</str>
        <str name="q">martin</str>
      </lst>
  </lst>
  <result name="response" numFound="0" start="0"/>
</response>
```

Adding more nodes to the SolrCloud

Let us see how we can add more nodes to SolrCloud. Create one more machine `solr5`. Copy the Tomcat folder to this machine and create the folder `solr-cores` in the `/home/ubuntu` folder. Alter the `tomcat/bin/setenv.sh` file and change the `-Dhost` parameter to match the machine's host. For `solr5`, it will be:

```
SOLR_OPTS="-Dsolr.solr.home=/home/ubuntu/solr-cores -Dhost=solr5
-Dport=8080 -DhostContext=solr -DzkClientTimeout=20000 -DzkHost=zoo1:2
181,zoo2:2181,zoo3:2181"
```

Also copy the `solr.xml` file from any Solr machine to these machines inside the `solr-cores` folder. Now start Tomcat and check whether it is running by opening the following URL: `http://solr5:8080/solr`.

There are two ways to identify whether this node has been added to SolrCloud. We can check whether the admin interface on `solr5` displays the current **Cloud | Graph**. Another way is to go to the admin | Cloud | Tree | live_nodes folder. This should contain the name of the live nodes. `solr5` should be visible there.

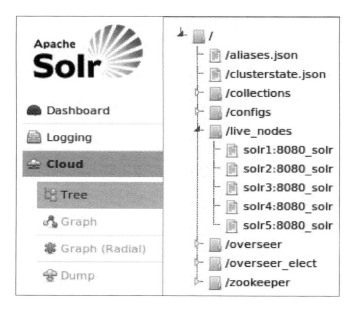

Now, let us add the node as a replica for `shard2` of `mycollection`. For this, we will have to execute the ADDREPLICA command on the collection API, as follows:

```
http://solr5:8080/solr/admin/collections?action=ADDREPLICA&collection=
mycollection&shard=shard2&node=solr5:8080_solr
```

The output from command execution will specify the name of the core that has been created:

```
▼<response>
  ▼<lst name="responseHeader">
     <int name="status">0</int>
     <int name="QTime">7740</int>
  </lst>
  ▼<lst name="success">
     ▼<lst>
        ▼<lst name="responseHeader">
           <int name="status">0</int>
           <int name="QTime">6754</int>
        </lst>
        <str name="core">mycollection_shard2_replica3</str>
     </lst>
  </lst>
</response>
```

In this command, we have specified:

- `action=ADDREPLICA`: This is the action to be performed on the collection.
- `collection=mycollection`: This is the collection on which the action is to be performed.
- `shard=shard2`: This is the shard for which the replica is to be created.
- `node=solr5:8080_solr`: This is the node on which the replica is to be created. The name of the shard is obtained from the `live_nodes` list we saw earlier.

The cloud graph indicates that **solr5** is added as a replica of **shard2** of **mycollection**:

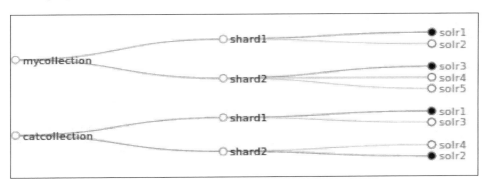

Fault tolerance and high availability in SolrCloud

Whenever SolrCloud is restarted, election happens again. If a particular shard that was a replica earlier comes up before the shard that was the leader, the replica shard becomes the leader and the leader shard becomes the replica. Whenever we restart the Tomcat and ZooKeeper servers for starting SolrCloud, we can expect the leaders and replicas to switch.

Let us check the availability of the cluster. We will bring down a leader node and a replica node to check whether the cluster is able to serve all the documents that we have indexed. First check the number of documents in `mycollection`:

```
http://solr5:8080/solr/mycollection/select/?q=*:*
```

We can see that there are nine documents in the collection. Similarly, run the following query on `catcollection`:

```
http://solr5:8080/solr/catcollection/select/?q=*:*
```

The `catcollection` contains 11 documents.

Now let us bring down Tomcat on **solr2** and **solr3**, or simply turn off the machines. Check the SolrCloud graph:

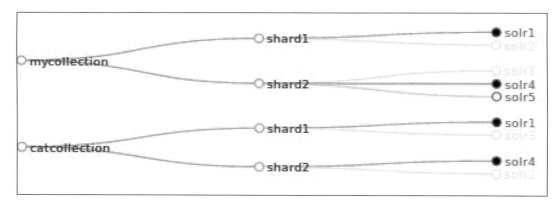

We can see that the nodes **solr2** and **solr3** are now in the Gone state. Here **solr3** was the leader for **shard2** in **mycollection**. Now since it is offline, **solr4** is promoted as the leader. The replica of **shard1** that was **solr2** is not available, so **solr1** remains the leader.

Let us execute the queries we had executed earlier on both the collections. We can see that the count of documents in both the collections remains the same.

We can even add documents to SolrCloud during this time. Add the `ipod_other.xml` file from the `example/exampledocs` folder inside the Solr installation to `mycollection` on SolrCloud. Execute the following command:

```
$ java -Durl=http://solr5:8080/solr/mycollection/update -jar post.jar
ipod_other.xml

SimplePostTool version 1.5

Posting files to base url http://solr5:8080/solr/mycollection/update
using content-type application/xml..

POSTing file ipod_other.xml

1 files indexed.

COMMITting Solr index changes to http://solr5:8080/solr/mycollection/
update..

Time spent: 0:00:07.978
```

Now again run the query to get the complete count from `mycollection`:

```
http://solr5:8080/solr/mycollection/select/?q=*:*
```

The `mycollection` collection now contains 11 documents.

Now start up Tomcat on **solr2** and **solr3**. We can see that after a short time in recovery, both the Solr instances are now added to the cloud. For mycollection, **solr2** continues its role as the replica of **solr1** for **shard1**, and **solr3** becomes the replica of **solr4** for **shard2**:

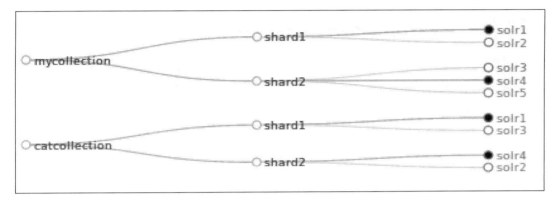

The documents that were added to the cloud while any of the nodes were down are automatically replicated onto the nodes once they come back into the cloud. Therefore, as long as one of the nodes for the shard of a collection is available, the collection will remain available and will continue to support indexing and searching of documents.

Advanced sharding with SolrCloud

Let's explore some of the advanced concepts of sharding, starting with **shard splitting**.

Shard splitting

Let us say that we have created a two-shard replica looking at the current number of queries per second for a system. In future, if the number of queries per second increases to, say, twice or thrice the current value, we will need to add more shards. Now, one way is to create a separate cloud with say four shards and re-index all the documents. This is possible if the cluster is small. If we are dealing with a 50 shard cluster with more than a billion documents, re-indexing of the complete set of documents again may be expensive. For such scenarios, SolrCloud has the concept of shard splitting.

In shard splitting, a shard is divided into two new shards on the same machine. All three shards, the old one and the two new ones, remain. We can check the sanity of the shards and then delete the existing shard. Let us see a practical implementation of the same.

Before starting, lets add a few more documents into **mycollection**. Add the `books.csv` file from the `example/exampledocs` folder to **mycollection**.

```
java -Dtype=text/csv -Durl=http://solr1:8080/solr/mycollection/update
-jar post.jar books.csv
```

To check the number of documents in **mycollection**, execute the following query:

```
http://solr1:8080/solr/mycollection/select/?q=*:*
```

We can see that there are 35 documents currently in **mycollection**. Let us check the count of documents in each shard. Execute the following queries to find the documents in **shard1** of **mycollection**:

```
http://solr1:8080/solr/mycollection/select/?q=*:*&shards=shard1
```

There are **17** documents in **shard1**. Now execute the following query to find the number of documents in **shard2** of **mycollection**:

```
http://solr1:8080/solr/mycollection/select/?q=*:*&shards=shard2
```

We can see that there are 18 documents in **shard2**. Let us also look at how our SolrCloud graph looks. We can see that **shard1** is on **solr3** and **solr4** and **shard2** is on **solr1**, **solr2**, and **solr5**:

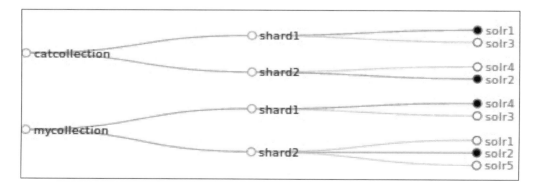

Now let us split **shard1** into two parts. This is done by the `SPLITSHARD` action on the collections API via the Solr admin interface. Execute the command by calling the following URL:

```
http://solr1:8080/solr/admin/collections?action=SPLITSHARD&collection=
mycollection&shard=shard1
```

The output of the command is seen on the browser. We can see that `shard1` is split into two shards `shard1_0` and `shard1_1`:

```
▼<response>
  ▼<lst name="responseHeader">
    <int name="status">0</int>
    <int name="QTime">46981</int>
  </lst>
  ▼<lst name="success">
    ▼<lst>
      ▼<lst name="responseHeader">
        <int name="status">0</int>
        <int name="QTime">12404</int>
      </lst>
      <str name="core">mycollection_shard1_1_replica1</str>
    </lst>
    ▼<lst>
      ▼<lst name="responseHeader">
        <int name="status">0</int>
        <int name="QTime">13421</int>
      </lst>
      <str name="core">mycollection_shard1_0_replica1</str>
    </lst>
    ▼<lst>
```

While the query for shard splitting is being executed, the shard does not go offline. In fact, there is no interruption of service. Let us also look at the SolrCloud graph that would contain information on the split shards.

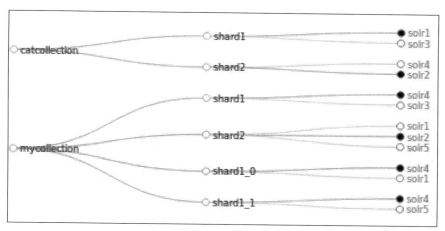

We can see that **shard1** has been split into **shard1_0** and **shard1_1**. Even the shards that have been split have their leaders and replicas in place. **Shard1_0** has **solr4** as the leader and solr1 as the replica. Similarly, **shard1_1** has solr4 as the leader and solr5 as the replica. To check the number of documents in the split shards, execute the following queries:

```
http://solr1:8080/solr/mycollection/select/?q=*:*&shards=shard1_0
```

Shard1_0 contains eight documents.

```
http://solr1:8080/solr/mycollection/select/?q=*:*&shards=shard1_1
```

Also, **shard1_1** contains nine documents. In all, the split shards now contain 17 documents that shard1 had earlier. In addition to splitting shard1 into two sub shards, SolrCloud makes the parent shard, shard1, inactive. This information is available in the ZooKeeper servers. Connect to any of the ZooKeeper servers and get the `clusterstate.json` file to check the status of the shards for `mycollection`:

```
"mycollection":{
    "shards":{
      "shard1":{
        "range":"80000000-ffffffff",
        "state":"inactive",
        "replicas":{
          "core_node1":{
            "state":"active",
            "base_url":"http://solr4:8080/solr",
            "core":"mycollection_shard1_replica1",
            "node_name":"solr4:8080_solr",
            "leader":"true"},
          "core_node4":{
            "state":"active",
            "base_url":"http://solr3:8080/solr",
            "core":"mycollection_shard1_replica2",
            "node_name":"solr3:8080_solr"}}},
```

Now, `shard1_0` and `shard1_1` are marked as active:

```
"shard1_0":{
  "range":"80000000-bfffffff",
  "state":"active",
  "replicas":{
    "core_node6":{
      "state":"active",
```

```
        "base_url":"http://solr4:8080/solr",
        "core":"mycollection_shard1_0_replica1",
        "node_name":"solr4:8080_solr",
        "leader":"true"},
    "core_node8":{
        "state":"active",
        "base_url":"http://solr1:8080/solr",
        "core":"mycollection_shard1_0_replica2",
        "node_name":"solr1:8080_solr"}}},
"shard1_1":{
  "range":"c0000000-ffffffff",
  "state":"active",
  "replicas":{
    "core_node7":{
        "state":"active",
        "base_url":"http://solr4:8080/solr",
        "core":"mycollection_shard1_1_replica1",
        "node_name":"solr4:8080_solr",
        "leader":"true"},
    "core_node9":{
        "state":"active",
        "base_url":"http://solr5:8080/solr",
        "core":"mycollection_shard1_1_replica2",
        "node_name":"solr5:8080_solr"}}}},
```

Deleting a shard

Only an inactive shard can be deleted. In the previous section, we found that since
shard1 was split into **shard1_0** and **shard1_1**, **shard1** was marked as inactive. We can
delete shard1 by executing the DELETESHARD action on the collections API:

```
http://solr1:8080/solr/admin/collections?action=DELETESHARD&collection
=mycollection&shard=shard1
```

The following is a representation of the SolrCloud graph after the deletion of **shard1**:

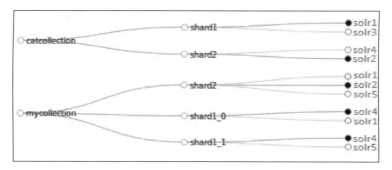

Moving the existing shard to a new node

In order to move a shard to a new node, we need to add the node as a replica. Once the replication on the node is over and the node becomes active, we can simply shut down the old node and remove it from the cluster.

In the current cluster, we can see that **shard2** has three nodes — **solr1**, **solr2**, and **solr5**. We added **solr5** some time back as a replica for **shard2**. In order to remove **solr2** from **mycollection**, all we need to do is use the DELETEREPLICA action on the collections API:

```
http://solr1:8080/solr/admin/collections?action=DELETEREPLICA&collecti
on=mycollection&shard=shard2&replica=core_node3
```

The name of the replica is obtained from clusterstate.json in the ZooKeeper cluster:

```
"mycollection":{
    "shards":{
      "shard2":{
        "range":"0-7fffffff",
        "state":"active",
        "replicas":{
          "core_node2":{
            "state":"active",
            "base_url":"http://solr1:8080/solr",
            "core":"mycollection_shard2_replica1",
            "node_name":"solr1:8080_solr",
            "leader":"true"},
          "core_node3":{
```

```
      "state":"active",
       "base_url":"http://solr2:8080/solr",
       "core":"mycollection_shard2_replica2",
       "node_name":"solr2:8080_solr"},
    "core_node5":{
       "state":"active",
       "base_url":"http://solr5:8080/solr",
       "core":"mycollection_shard2_replica3",
       "node_name":"solr5:8080_solr"}}},
```

The graph now shows **solr2** is removed from **mycollection**:

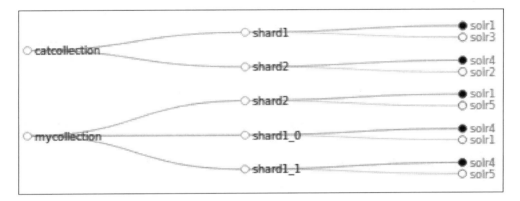

In this case, **solr2**, which is also a node in **catcollection** is still active.

Shard splitting based on split key

Split key-based shard splitting is a viable option. A split key can be used to route documents on the basis of certain criteria to a shard in SolrCloud. In order to split a shard by using a shard key, we need to specify the shard.key parameter along with the collection parameter in the SPLITSHARD action of the collections API.

We can split **catcollection** into more shards using **category** as the split.key parameter. The URL for splitting the shard will be:

```
http://solr1:8080/solr/admin/collections?action=SPLITSHARD&collection=
catcollection&split.key=books!
```

Once the query has been executed, we can see the success message. It says that **Shard2** of **catcollection** has been broken into three shards, as shown in the following SolrCloud graph:

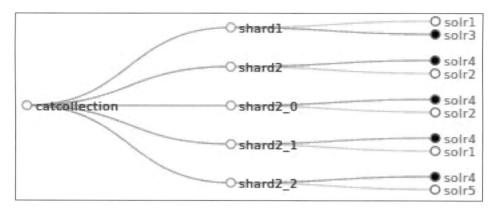

The complete process of splitting a shard into two and moving it to a separate new node in SolrCloud is required in the following scenarios:

- Average query performance on a shard or slowing down of a number of shards. It is important to measure this regularly and keep track of the number of queries per second.

- Degradation of indexing throughput. This is a scenario wherein you were able to index 1000 documents per second earlier, but it goes down to say 800 documents per second.

- Out of memory errors during querying. Even after tuning - query, cache and GC.

Asynchronous calls

Since some API calls, such as shard splitting, can take a long time and result in timeouts, we have the option of running a call asynchronously by specifying the `async=<request_id>` parameter in the URL. `<request_id>` is any ID that can be used to track the status of a particular API call. The `request_id` class and the status of the task are stored in ZooKeeper and can be retrieved using the `REQUESTSTATUS` action on the collections API.

We can delete and recreate catcollection using the following API calls or URLs:

```
http://solr1:8080/solr/admin/collections?action=DELETE&
name=catcollection
```

```
http://solr1:8080/solr/admin/collections?action=CREATE
&name=catcollection&numShards=2&replicationFactor=2&m
axShardsPerNode=2&collection.configName=conf1&router.
field=cat
```

catcollection can be populated using docs.csv file provided by the following command:

```
java -Dtype=text/csv -Durl=http://solr4:8080/solr/
catcollection/update -jar post.jar docs.csv
```

To perform splitting using the async parameter, execute the following command:

```
http://solr1:8080/solr/admin/collections?action=SPLITSHARD&collection=
catcollection&split.key=books!&async=1111
```

```
▼<response>
  ▼<lst name="responseHeader">
      <int name="status">0</int>
      <int name="QTime">106</int>
    </lst>
    <str name="requestid">1111</str>
  </response>
```

We immediately get a response which just shows the requestid that we submitted. The status of the request can be checked by executing the following URL:

```
http://solr1:8080/solr/admin/collections?action=REQUESTSTATUS&request
id=1111
```

```
▼<response>
  ▼<lst name="responseHeader">
      <int name="status">0</int>
      <int name="QTime">19</int>
    </lst>
  ▼<lst name="status">
      <str name="state">completed</str>
      <str name="msg">found 1111 in completed tasks</str>
    </lst>
  </response>
```

Here we can see that the status is marked as completed. These requests and their status are stored in ZooKeeper and are not cleaned up automatically. We can clean up the requests by passing `requestid` as `-1`:

```
http://solr1:8080/solr/admin/collections?action=REQUESTSTATUS&request
id=-1
```

Migrating documents to another collection

Suppose we have a huge collection of over a billion documents and we get a requirement whereby we need to create a separate index with a particular set of documents, or we want to break our index into two parts on the basis of certain criteria. Migration of documents to another collection makes this possible. Effectively, we can specify a source and a destination collection in SolrCloud. On the basis of the routing criteria, certain documents will be copied from the source to the destination collection. We can specify the migration time as the `forward.timeout` parameter during which all write requests will be forwarded to the target collection. The target collection must not receive any writes while the migrate command is running. Otherwise, some writes may be lost.

Let us look at a practical scenario.

We currently have two collections — `catcollection` and `mycollection`. Now `catcollection` contains documents belonging to the categories `books`, `currency`, and `electronics`. Let us move the documents belonging to the category `currency` from `catcollection` to `mycollection`.

The query to get the documents belonging to category `currency` will include the `shard.keys=currency!` parameter:

```
http://solr1:8080/solr/catcollection/select/?q=*:*&rows=15&shard.
keys=currency!
```

We can see that there are 4 documents in the collection. On querying the `mycollection` collection, we find that there are 35 documents in the collection. Now, let us copy the documents from `catcollection` to `mycollection`:

```
http://solr1:8080/solr/admin/collections?action=MIGRATE&collection=cat
collection&split.key=currency!&target.collection=mycollection&forward.
timeout=120
```

Note the following:

- The action is MIGRATE.
- The source collection is catcollection.
- split.key is currency!. All documents that have currency!* as the ID will be moved to mycollection. split.key is identified by the routing parameter that we used earlier. If there is no routing parameter, split.key can be identified by the unique ID of the documents.
- target.collection refers to the target mycollection.
- forward.timeout is the timeout specified during which all write requests to catcollection are forwarded to mycollection.

A success message is displayed once this completes.

```
▼<response>
 ▼<lst name="responseHeader">
   <int name="status">0</int>
   <int name="QTime">28836</int>
 </lst>
 ▼<lst name="success">
   ▼<lst>
     ▼<lst name="responseHeader">
       <int name="status">0</int>
       <int name="QTime">2</int>
     </lst>
     <str name="core">mycollection_shard1_0_replica2</str>
     <str name="status">BUFFERING</str>
   </lst>
   ▼<lst>
```

We can see the routing parameters in the clusterstate.json file. This also includes an expiresAt parameter specifying the time after which the forwarding of requests to the target collection is stopped:

```
"routingRules":{"currency!":{
    "routeRanges":"92a40000-92a4ffff",
    "expireAt":"1404265881748",
    "targetCollection":"mycollection"}}},
```

Once the migration is over, the destination collection, `mycollection`, will contain 4 more documents, with the number totaling to 39. These documents will also be available in the source collection.

Solr collections API reference:
`https://cwiki.apache.org/confluence/display/solr/Collections+API`.

Sizing and monitoring of SolrCloud

It is important to understand that SolrCloud is horizontally scalable. However, each node needs to have a certain capacity. The amount of CPU, disk, and RAM required for each node in SolrCloud needs to be figured out for the efficient allocation of resources. Though no fixed number can be assigned to these parameters as each application is unique, each index within each application has a unique indexing pattern—the number of documents that need to be indexed per second, the size of the documents, and the fields, the tokenization and the storage parameters defined. Similarly, the search patterns would also differ across indexes belonging to different applications. The number of queries per second and the search parameters can be different. The amount of data retrieved from Solr and the faceting and grouping parameters play an important role in the handling of resources used during querying.

Therefore, it is difficult to assign numbers to the RAM, CPU, and disk requirements for each node. Ideally, we should implement sharding on the size of the shard instead of the size of the collection. Routing is another very important parameter in the index. It would save a lot of network IO. The weight of a particular shard depends on the routing parameter, either in terms of the number of documents or the number of queries per second.

It is important to restrict the disk space to two to three times the size of the index. When index optimization happens, it uses up more than twice the disk space.

The ideal way to go about sizing is to put a few normal machines as the nodes of SolrCloud and monitor their resource usage. For each node, we need to monitor the following parameters:

- Load average or CPU usage
- Disk usage

- RAM usage, or RAM utilization across each core
- Core to CPU consumption, or CPU utilization across each core
- Collection to node consumption, or how the requests are being distributed across each node in the collection

Once these parameters are in place, nodes belonging to some shards are found to be overweight. These shards need to be split further in order to properly address scalability issues that may occur in the future.

The health of SolrCloud can be monitored via the following files or directories in the ZooKeeper server:

- `clusterstate.json`
- `/livenodes`

We need to constantly watch the state of each core in the cluster. `livenodes` provides us with a list of available nodes. If any node or core goes offline, a notification has to be sent out. Additionally, it is important to have enough replicas distributed in such a fashion that a core or a node going down should not affect the availability of the cloud. The following points need to be considered while planning out the nodes, cores, and replicas of SolrCloud:

- Each collection should have an appropriate number of shards
- Shards should have a leader and more than one replica
- Leaders and replicas should be on different physical nodes
- Even when using virtual machines, the third step should be considered
- A few standby nodes, which can be assigned as replicas, should be set up, if needed
- An automated process should be followed for setting up standby nodes
- An automated process should be followed for spawning new nodes
- Checks on the network IO should be scheduled to identify the network or cluster traffic and continually optimized

These action points will make the SolrCloud function in an effortless manner.

Using SolrCloud as a NoSQL database

There is a huge market for NoSQL databases, each having its own strength and weakness. Several factors need consideration during the selection of a NoSQL database, namely performance, scalability, security, and ease of development. RDBMS is good but has limitations in terms of scaling to billions of records. Horizontal scaling is a challenge in most RDBMSs.

Search, which was earlier a complex process, is now easy to use and scale. With horizontal scalability, search has also become affordable. NoSQL databases can be key-value, column oriented, document oriented and graph database. The key factors that are used to make a decision regarding the NoSQL database are as follows:

- **Data model**: Refers to how data is stored and accessed or whether the NoSQL database is key-value, document oriented, or column oriented.
- **Distribution model**: Refers to how data is distributed across the cluster to address horizontal scalability. It considers sharding and replication features.
- **Conflict resolution**: Refers to how data is kept consistent across the nodes in the cluster. It ensures that all the nodes apply the operations in the same order and takes care of update and read consistency.

Each NoSQL database needs a search option. MongoDB, Redis, CouchDB, Riak, and other NoSQL databases provide search options, though the search is not as effectively implemented in these databases. Ideally, we need to come down to using Lucene, Solr, or Elasticsearch.

Therefore, instead of adding the search feature to the database, we can add the database to the search function. This means that we can store data inside the Solr index and retrieve it during search. Solr is a document-oriented data store, which is closer to the MongoDB data model. With the latest version of Solr and near real-time functionalities, we obtain the following features:

- Real-time get
- Update durability
- Atomic compare and set
- Versioning and optimistic locking

This brings Solr closer to being a NoSQL database. Talking about the schema less - Solr is effectively '*schemaless*'. We need not run a lengthy alter command to add new fields to the schema. The schema can be altered and new fields indexed in the new schema without affecting the documents that are already present in the index. Altering the schema of existing fields can cause problems. In that case, those fields would need to be re-indexed. However, adding new fields to the index does not affect the existing documents in any way. Any search on those fields would simply ignore the documents in which the fields do not exist.

SolrCloud takes this further by providing horizontal scalability to the Solr database. Solr is 'eventually consistent'.

Eventual consistency is a consistency model used in distributed computing that informally guarantees that, if no new updates are made to a given data item, eventually all accesses to that item will return the last updated value.

Source: `http://en.wikipedia.org/wiki/Eventual_consistency`.

The duration of the presence of inconsistency is known as the inconsistency window. SolrCloud has a very small inconsistency window that depends on the size of the data, the command to be executed, and the network.

This effectively means that Solr can be used as a NoSQL database to store, search, and retrieve data.

Summary

In this chapter, we went through most of the aspects of SolrCloud. We understood the architecture of SolrCloud, constructed a setup for SolrCloud using ZooKeeper servers, and created our collections on the cloud. We saw the advantages of routing and how to implement it. We saw how SolrCloud addresses the horizontal scalability, high availability, and distributed indexing and search requirements for a large-scale Solr deployment. We saw how to manage the shards in SolrCloud and monitor SolrCloud. We can use the monitoring information to size the cores in SolrCloud and scale it further. We also saw that SolrCloud can be used as a NoSQL database.

In the next chapter, we will explore text tagging using the Lucene **Finite State Transducer (FST)**. We will delve into FSTs and how they can be implemented using Lucene and SolrCloud?

10
Text Tagging with Lucene FST

In the previous chapter, we delved into the setup and working of SolrCloud. We saw the working of distributed indexing and search and how they can be used for handling horizontal scalability and high availability issues in a large-scale Solr deployment. We also discussed the use of SolrCloud as a large-scale NoSQL database.

In this chapter, we will understand what text tagging is and how Lucene and, hence, Solr can be used to implement it in indexing. We will discuss the Finite State Transducer (FST) and the algorithms related to it and learn how it can be integrated with Solr. The topics that we will cover are:

- An overview of FST and text tagging
- Implementation of FST in Lucene
- Text tagging algorithms
- Using Solr for text tagging
- Implementing a text tagger using Solr

An overview of FST and text tagging

FSTs are used for **Natural Language Processing** (**NLP**). To understand the function of an FST, let us understand a **Finite State Machine** (**FSM**) first. An FSM is an abstract mathematical model of computation that is capable of storing a status or state and changing this state on the basis of the input. FSMs can be applied to various electronic modeling, engineering, and NLP problems. An FSM is represented as a set of nodes containing the various states of a system and labeled edges between these nodes. Here the edges represent transitions from one state to another and the labels represent the conditions on these transitions. A stream of input can be then processed by the FSM causing a number of state transitions.

The following diagram is an example of an FSM that describes some of the states of our day-to-day life:

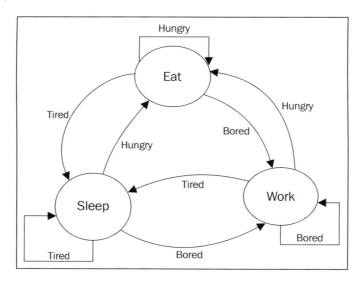

Here **Eat**, **Sleep**, and **Work** are the states in which a person will be. **Bored**, **Tired**, and **Hungry** are the edges showing the conditions under which transitions occur.

An FSM containing a *start* state and an *end* state can be used for language processing by generating or recognizing a language defined by all the possible combinations of conditions generated by traversing each of the edges from the *start* state to the *end* state.

An FST is a special type of FSM. An FST contains an input string and an output string. Therefore, instead of traversing an input string for just accepting or rejecting it, an FST translates the contents of the input string into the output string. That is, an FST accepts an input string and generates an output string. In an FST, each transition has two symbols—one representing the input and the other representing the output. If an FST does not generate an output string, we can assume that the input string has been rejected.

A sample FST is shown in the following figure:

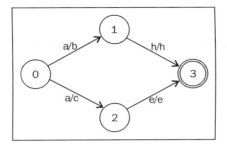

To understand text tagging, let us first look at what **geotagging** is. Geotagging is a solution for identifying place name references in a natural language. The following text is an example of geotagging:

```
I live in a house near Delhi.
```

A geotagger identifies the place **Delhi** in the previous text. This information can be extended to resolve the place name into a particular latitude and longitude combination.

A text tagger has a broader scope. It can identify names and places from unstructured text. An FST can be used as a mechanism for text tagging. A text tagger consults with a dictionary to extract names or tags. Then, it uses simple NLP to eliminate low-confidence tags. It needs to find names with varying word lengths as well as overlapping names. There is a great deal of theory behind FSMs, FSTs, and text tagging. In any case, let us go ahead and see how an FST functions with the help of Lucene.

Implementation of FST in Lucene

The algorithm used for implementing an FST in Lucene is based on the paper *Direct Construction of Minimal Acyclic Subsequential Transducers* published by Stoyan Mihov and Denis Maurel. This algorithm can be used to build a minimal acyclic sub-sequential transducer (a type of FST) that represents a finite relation, given a sorted list of input words and their outputs. As this algorithm constructs the minimal transducer directly, it has better efficiency than other algorithms. It is the perfect fit for a Lucene FST, as all the terms in the Lucene index are stored in a sorted order.

 The following paper was referred to for building the algorithm: http://citeseerx.ist.psu.edu/viewdoc/summary?doi=10.1.1.24.3698.

An FST is implemented in Lucene under the following package:

```
org.apache.lucene.util.fst
```

Let us see a few of the classes inside the package that can be used to work with an FST:

- `Builder<T>`: Can be used to build a minimal FST from pre-sorted terms with outputs
- `FST<T>`: Represents an FSM and uses a compact `byte[]` format
- `Outputs<T>`: Represents the outputs for an FST and provides the basic algebra for building and traversing the FST
- `PositiveIntOutputs`: An implementation of `Outputs` class where each output is a non-negative long value
- `Util`: Contains static helper methods

 The complete Java documentation for the Lucene FST implementation can be obtained from the following link: `http://lucene.apache.org/core/4_8_0/core/org/apache/lucene/util/fst/package-summary.html`.

Let us understand this with an example:

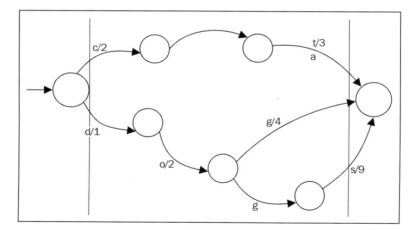

Here is a sample FST that maps three words, cat, dog, and dogs, to their ordinal numbers, which are 5, 7, and 12, respectively. As we traverse the edges of the FST, we sum up the outputs. For example, dog outputs 1 when it hits d, 2 when it hits o, and finally 4 when it hits g. Therefore, the output ordinal will be 7, which is the sum of the outputs corresponding to each hit.

An FST in the Lucene core for the preceding three words would function with reference to the following code:

```
String inputValues[] = {"cat", "dog", "dogs"};
long outputValues[] = {5, 7, 12};

PositiveIntOutputs outputs = PositiveIntOutputs.getSingleton();
Builder<Long> builder = new Builder<Long>(INPUT_TYPE.BYTE1, outputs);
BytesRef scratchBytes = new BytesRef();
IntsRef scratchInts = new IntsRef();
for (int i = 0; i < inputValues.length; i++) {
  scratchBytes.copyChars(inputValues[i]);
  builder.add(Util.toIntsRef(scratchBytes, scratchInts),
outputValues[i]);
}
FST<Long> fst = builder.finish();
```

Once this FST has been built, we can use it for FST-related operations. Lucene supports the following FST operations:

- **Retrieval by key**: The input dog would output 7
- **Retrieval by value**: The input 5 would output cat
- **Scanning**: Iteration over key-value pairs in a sorted order
- **Deduction**: Identification of the n-shortest path by weight

Internally, an FST is stored as a SortedMap class of ByteSequence and Output. If the edges are sorted, it can be represented as:

```
SortedMap<ByteSequence,SomeOutput>
```

This implementation of the FST in Lucene requires less RAM but leads to higher CPU utilization during lookup. This is because in Lucene, the FST has been encoded as byte[]. Higher CPU utilization can be attributed to the fact that the amount of processing required for lookup in this implementation of the FST is more. An FST is memory efficient and loads fast from disk, as it is built from pre-sorted inputs in Lucene.

Text tagging algorithms

The process of text tagging can be explained by the following figure:

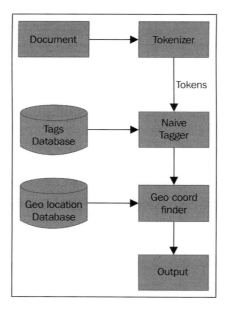

A document is tokenized and the tokens are passed to the naive tagger. The naive tagger uses a tagging algorithm to find the tags. Then, the geo-coordinate finder identifies the geo-locations (lat-long coordinates) corresponding to those tags. They are then available as the output.

There are various text tagging algorithms, each of which has its own benefits. Let us go through some of the algorithms that can be used for text tagging.

Fuzzy string matching algorithm

The fuzzy string matching algorithm can be used to match two strings, *exactly* or *partially*. This means the relationship is fuzzy when there is a set of *n-elements* and another set of *m-elements*, and both partially match the same elements. Using this algorithm, we can identify strings that are similar to a set of other strings. It is like drawing similar terms from the string.

Suppose we want to find the similarity between two words, say `jumps` and `juumpss`, and correct them if necessary. The fuzzy string matching algorithm will return `true` for the first word (`jumps`) as it is correct and will return the correct string (`jumps`) for the other word `juumpss`.

The fuzzy string matching algorithm is characterized by a metric that is a function of the distance between two words. This helps us evaluate the similarity between them. This metric is known as **edit distance**.

Edit distance is defined as the number of operations required to transform one string to another. Using edit distance, we can quantify the dissimilarity between two strings. Edit distance can be used as an NLP mechanism to find corrections for a misspelled word. This is done by identifying words from a dictionary that have the smallest edit distance with respect to the word for which corrections are sought.

Let us see an example to calculate the edit distance. We will find the number of primitive operations, *insertions*, *deletion*, and *substitution*, that are required to convert a string to obtain an exact match with another. This number will be the edit distance between the string and the pattern:

- `Mak` can be converted to `Make` by an insertion operation:

      Mak + e = Make

- `Boooks` can be converted to `Books` by a deletion operation:

      Boooks - o = Books

- `Dish` can be converted to `Fish` by a substitution operation:

      Dish + (- D + F) = Fish

The edit distance between these examples is numerically 1, as only a single operation is required to convert them to the target string.

Let us look at some algorithms used for calculating the edit distance.

The Levenshtein distance algorithm

Levenshtein distance is defined as the minimum number of single-character edits required to convert one word to another. Here the edits are performed by *insertion*, *deletion*, and *substitution* operations that we saw earlier.

`Sitting` can be converted to `Bettings` by the following operation:

      Sitting + (- S + B) = Bitting
      Bitting + (- i + e) = Betting
      Betting + s = Bettings

In the previous example, the Levenshtein distance between `Sitting` and `Bettings` is 3 (2 substitution operations + 1 insertion operation).

If the lengths of the two strings are m and n, the algorithm will have a time complexity of O(mn) and a space complexity of O(mn). In addition, the Levenshtein distance has the following properties:

- It is at least the difference of the sizes of the two strings
- It is at most the length of the longer string
- The distance is 0 if both strings are equal
- The distance is equal to the number of substitutions required for conversion (hamming distance) if both strings are of the same size

Damerau–Levenshtein distance

The Damerau-Levenshtein algorithm is an extension of the Levenshtein distance algorithm. It involves an additional operation, *transposition*. Transposition is the operation whereby the adjacent characters are swapped in order to bring them to a certain form. Let us see an example of transposition:

- The word eat can be converted to ate by two transposition operations:

```
eat => aet (swap e & a)
aet => ate (swap e & t)
```

Therefore, the Damerau-Levenshtein algorithm consists of four operations:

- Insertion
- Deletion
- Substitution
- Transposition

Let us look at an example for calculating the Damerau-Levenshtein distance:

- The word clocks can be converted to bold formatting by the following operation:

```
clocks => substitute c with b => blocks
blocks => transpose l and o => bolcks
bolcks => substitute c with d => boldks
boldks => substitute k with e => boldes
boldes => substitute s with r => bolder
```

The Damerau-Levenshtein distance in this example is 5 (1 transpose + 4 substitution).

Using Solr for text tagging

Now that we know what text tagging is and have seen some algorithms that can be used for text tagging, let us learn how text tagging is done using Solr. There is an open source library, *Solr Text Tagger*, that can be used for text tagging in Solr.

 The library can be referred to at the following link:
`https://github.com/OpenSextant/SolrTextTagger`.

Text tagging via this library involves two layers of FSTs. A word dictionary FST is used to hold each unique word. This enables integers to be used as substitutes for a word (`char[]`). For example, the word `New` will be mapped to `13452` and another word `Delhi` will be mapped to `5223316`:

```
New => 13452
Delhi => 5223316
```

The call to Lucene's FST library `Util.getByOutput(<fst object>, 13452)` will yield the word `New`.

The second layer is a word phrase FST comprising word ID string keys. In the case of `New Delhi`, the word phrase FST will be:

```
New Delhi => [13452, 5223316]
```

The tagging algorithm used in the Solr text tagger is a single-pass or streaming algorithm. The algorithm looks for the original ID of each input term and then creates an FST arc iterator for the name phrase. It then appends the iterator onto a queue of active iterators and tries to advance all iterators. The iterators that do not advance are removed.

 An FST arc iterator is used to access the transitions leaving an FST state.

The Solr text tagger scans the posted text and looks for matching strings in the Solr index. The tags are formed as a linked list containing a start offset and an end offset. A tag starts without a value in an *advancing* state. The tag is advanced with subsequent words, and then eventually, if it does not advance any more, the value is set. Now, the linked list is reduced to tags that are to be emitted.

Let us see an example to understand this:

```
Iterator linked list queue
Head => New Delhi, city
Head+1 => Delhi, city
Head+2 => City
```

In this case, `Head` containing the `New Delhi City` phrase will advance and will be emitted as an output.

Implementing a text tagger using Solr

Let us see how we can implement the *Solr text tagger*. Let us get the latest code for the Solr text tagger from the GitHub repository by cloning the Git repository with the following command:

git clone https://github.com/OpenSextant/SolrTextTagger.git

This will get the code inside a folder called `SolrTextTagger`.

Now inside the `SolrTextTagger` library, run the following command to create the JAR file:

mvn package

The mvn command is available in the Maven repository. This repository can be installed using the following command on Ubuntu machines:

sudo apt-get install maven2

We can also install and use the latest release of maven – maven3.

The mvn command fetches the dependencies required for compiling and creating the JAR file. If any dependencies are not satisfied or remain unavailable, you will need to debug the pom.xml file inside the SolrTextTagger folder and re-run the command.

Alternatively, you can use the solr-text-tagger.jar file available with this chapter.

On successful compilation, we will be able to see the following output on the screen:

```
[INFO] Building jar: /home/jayant/solrtag/SolrTextTagger/target/solr-
text-tagger-2.1-SNAPSHOT.jar
[INFO] ------------------------------------------------------------
[INFO] BUILD SUCCESSFUL
```

```
[INFO] ---------------------------------------------------------------
[INFO] Total time: 54 seconds
[INFO] Finished at: Tue Feb 17 10:43:34 IST 2015
[INFO] Final Memory: 62M/322M
[INFO] ---------------------------------------------------------------
```

The compiled file is available in the target folder inside the `SolrTextTagger` folder:

```
target/solr-text-tagger-2.1-SNAPSHOT.jar
```

This JAR file has to be copied into the `<solr installation>/example/lib` folder from where `solrconfig.xml` will pick it up.

To configure a text tagger with this instance of Solr, we will need to modify the `solrconfig.xml` and `schema.xml` files in our Solr installation. For a fresh installation of Solr, we can go to the `<solr installation>/example/solr/collection1/conf` folder and add or modify the following lines in our `schema.xml`:

```
<field name="name_tag" type="tag" stored="false"
omitTermFreqAndPositions="true" omitNorms="true"/>
<copyField source="name" dest="name_tag"/>
```

Here we are defining a new field `name_tag`, which is of the field type `tag`. In order to populate the field, we have copied the text from our existing field name to the new field `name_tag`.

Next, we will also need to define the behavior of `tag`. This is also done in `schema.xml`, as follows:

```
<fieldType name="tag" class="solr.TextField"
positionIncrementGap="100" postingsFormat="Memory">
     <analyzer type="index">
       <tokenizer class="solr.StandardTokenizerFactory"/>
       <filter class="solr.ASCIIFoldingFilterFactory"/>
       <filter class="solr.LowerCaseFilterFactory"/>
       <filter
class="org.opensextant.solrtexttagger.ConcatenateFilterFactory" />
     </analyzer>
     <analyzer type="query">
       <!-- 32 just for tests, bumps posInc -->
       <tokenizer class="solr.StandardTokenizerFactory"
                  maxTokenLength="32"/>
       <!--
```

```
        NOTE: This used the WordLengthTaggingFilterFactory to test
        the TaggingAttribute.
        The WordLengthTaggingFilter set the
        TaggingAttribute for words based on their length.
        The attribute is ignored at
        indexing time, but the Tagger will use it to only start tags
        for words that are equals or longer as the configured
        minLength.
        -->
        <filter
class="org.opensextant.solrtexttagger.WordLengthTaggingFilterFactory"
minLength="4"/>
        <filter class="solr.ASCIIFoldingFilterFactory"/>
        <filter class="solr.LowerCaseFilterFactory"/>
    </analyzer>
</fieldType>
```

Here, we are defining the analysis happening on the `tag` field type during indexing and search or querying. The attribute `postingsFormat="Memory"` requires that we set `codecFactory` in our `solrconfig.xml` file to `solr.SchemaCodecFactory`. The `postingsFormat` class provides read and write access to all postings, fields, terms, documents, frequencies, positions, offsets, and payloads. These postings define the format of the index being stored. Here we are defining `postingsFormat` as `memory`, which keeps data in memory thus making the tagger work as fast as possible.

During indexing, we use `standard tokenizer`, which breaks our input into tokens. This is followed by `ASCIIFoldingFilterFactory`. This class converts alphabetic, numeric, and symbolic Unicode characters that are not on the 127-character list of ASCII into their ASCII equivalents (if the ASCII equivalent exists). We are converting our tokens to lowercase by using `LowerCaseFilterFactory`. Also, we are using `ConcatenateFilterFactory` provided by `solrTextTagger`, which concatenates all tokens into a final token with a space separator.

During querying, we once again use `Standard Tokenizer` followed by `WordLengthTaggingFilterFactory`. This defines the minimum length of a token to be looked up during the tagging process. We use `ASCIIFoldingFilterFactory` and `LowerCaseFilterFactory` as well.

Now, let us go through the changes we need to make in `solrconfig.xml`. We will first need to add `solr-text-tagger-2.1-SNAPSHOT.jar` to be loaded as a library when Solr starts. For this, add the following lines in `solrconfig.xml`:

```
<lib dir="../../lib/" regex="solr-text-tagger-2\.1-SNAPSHOT\.jar" />
```

You can also use the `solr-text-tagger.jar` file provided with this chapter. It has been properly compiled with some missing classes.

Copy the `solr-text-tagger.jar` file to your `<solr installation>/example/lib` folder and add the following line in your `solrconfig.xml`:

```
<lib dir="../../lib/" regex="solr-text-tagger\.jar" />
```

Also, add the following lines to support `postingsFormat="Memory"`, as explained earlier in this section:

```
<!-- for postingsFormat="Memory" -->
<codecFactory name="CodecFactory" class="solr.SchemaCodecFactory" />
<schemaFactory name="SchemaFactory"
class="solr.ClassicIndexSchemaFactory" />
```

We will also have to define our own request handler, say `/tag`, which calls `TaggerRequestHandler` as provided by the Solr text tagger. Inside the `/tag` request handler, we have defined the field to be used for tagging as `name_tag`, which we added to our `schema.xml` earlier. The filter query is an optional parameter that can be used to match the subset of the documents (for name matching) in our case:

```
<requestHandler name="/tag" class="org.opensextant.solrtexttagger.
TaggerRequestHandler">
    <!-- top level params; legacy format just to test it still works
-->
    <str name="field">name_tag</str>
    <str name="fq">NOT name:(of the)</str><!-- filter out -->
</requestHandler>
```

Now, let us start the Solr server and watch the output to check whether any errors crop up while Solr loads the configuration and library changes that we made.

If you get the following error in your Solr log stating that it is missing `WorlLengthTaggingFilterFactory`, this factory has to be compiled and added to the JAR file we had created:

```
2768 [coreLoadExecutor-4-thread-1] ERROR org.apache.
solr.core.CoreContainer  - Unable to create core:
collection1
.

.

Caused by: java.lang.ClassNotFoundException: solr.
WordLengthTaggingFilterFactory
```

The files that are required to be compiled, `WordLengthTaggingFilterFactory.java` and `WordLengthTaggingFilter.java`, are available in the following folder:

```
SolrTextTagger/src/test/java/org/opensextant/
solrtexttagger
```

In order to compile the file, we will need the following JAR files from our Solr installation:

```
javac -d . -cp log4j-1.2.16.jar:slf4j-api-1.7.6.jar:slf4j-
log4j12-1.7.6.jar:lucene-core-4.8.1.jar:solr-text-tagger-
2.1-SNAPSHOT.jar WordLengthTaggingFilterFactory.java
WordLengthTaggingFilter.java
```

These jars could be found inside `<solr installation>/example/lib/ext` and `webapps/solr.war` file. The WAR file will need to be unzipped to obtain the required JAR files.

Once compiled, the class files can be found inside the `org/opensextant/solrtexttagger` folder. In order to add these files into our existing `solr-text-tagger-2.1-SNAPSHOT.jar`, simply unzip the JAR file and copy the files to the required folder `org/opensextant/solrtexttagger/` and create the JAR file again using the following `zip` command:

```
zip -r solr-text-tagger.jar META-INF/ org/
```

In order to check whether the `tag` request handler is working, let us point our browser to `http://localhost:8983/solr/collection1/tag`.

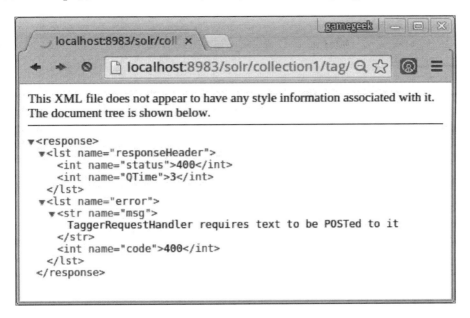

We can see a message stating that we need to post some text into `TaggerRequestHandler`. This means that the Solr text tagger is now plugged into our Solr installation and is ready to work.

Now that we have our Solr server running without any issues, let us add some files from the `exampledocs` folder to build the index and the tagging index along with it. Execute the following commands:

```
cd example/exampledocs
java -jar post.jar *.xml
java -Dtype=text/csv -jar post.jar books.csv
```

This will index all the `xml` documents and the `books.csv` file into the index.

Let us check whether the tagging works by checking the tags for the content inside the `solr.xml` file inside the `exampledocs` folder. Run the following command:

```
curl -XPOST 'http://localhost:8983/solr/tag?overlaps=ALL&tagsLimit=5000&f
l=*&wt=json' -H 'Content-Type:text/xml' -d @solr.xml
```

We can see the output on our command prompt:

The `tagcount` is 2 in the output.

Windows users can download `curl` from the following location and install it: `http://curl.haxx.se/download.html`.

The commands can then be run from the command prompt.

Linux users can pretty print the JSON output from the previous query by using Python's pretty-print tool for JSON and piping it with the curl command. The command will then be:

```
curl -XPOST 'http://localhost:8983/solr/tag?overlaps=ALL
&tagsLimit=5000&fl=*&wt=json' -H 'Content-Type:text/xml'
-d @solr.xml | python -m json.tool
```

The output will be similar to the following image:

Terminal window

```
"response": {
    "docs": [
        {
            "_version_": 1493514260482883584,
            "author": "Isaac Asimov",
            "author_s": "Isaac Asimov",
            "cat": [
                "book"
            ],
            "genre_s": "scifi",
            "id": "0553293354",
            "inStock": true,
            "name": "Foundation",
            "price": 7.99,
            "price_c": "7.99,USD",
            "sequence_i": 1,
            "series_t": "Foundation Novels"
        }
    ],
    "numFound": 1,
    "start": 0
},
"responseHeader": {
    "QTime": 15,
    "status": 0
},
"tags": [
    [
        "startOffset",
        37,
        "endOffset",
        47,
        "ids",
        [
            "0553293354"
        ]
    ],
    [
        "startOffset",
        905,
        "endOffset",
        915,
        "ids",
        [
            "0553293354"
        ]
    ]
],
```

The output contains two sections, `tags` and `docs`. The `tags` section contains an array of `tags` with the `ids` of the documents in which they are found. The `docs` section contains Solr documents referenced by those `tags`.

We take up another `findtags.txt` file and find the tags in this file. Let us run the following command:

```
curl -XPOST 'http://localhost:8983/solr/tag?overlaps=ALL&tagsLimit=5000&
fl=*' -H 'Content-Type:text/plain' -d @findtags.txt | xmllint --format -
```

This will give us the output in the XML format, as follows:

```
<?xml version="1.0" encoding="UTF-8"?>
<response>
  <lst name="responseHeader">
    <int name="status">0</int>
    <int name="QTime">54</int>
  </lst>
  <int name="tagsCount">3</int>
  <arr name="tags">
    <lst>
      <int name="startOffset">905</int>
      <int name="endOffset">915</int>
      <arr name="ids">
        <str>0553293354</str>
      </arr>
    </lst>
    <lst>
      <int name="startOffset">1246</int>
      <int name="endOffset">1256</int>
      <arr name="ids">
        <str>0553293354</str>
      </arr>
    </lst>
    <lst>
      <int name="startOffset">1358</int>
      <int name="endOffset">1368</int>
      <arr name="ids">
        <str>0553293354</str>
      </arr>
    </lst>
  </arr>
  <result name="response" numFound="1" start="0">
    <doc>
      <str name="id">0553293354</str>
      <arr name="cat">
        <str>book</str>
      </arr>
      <str name="name">Foundation</str>
      <float name="price">7.99</float>
```

```
        <str name="price_c">7.99,USD</str>
        <bool name="inStock">true</bool>
        <str name="author">Isaac Asimov</str>
        <str name="author_s">Isaac Asimov</str>
        <str name="series_t">Foundation Novels</str>
        <int name="sequence_i">1</int>
        <str name="genre_s">scifi</str>
        <long name="_version_">1493514260482883584</long>
      </doc>
    </result>
  </response>
```

Here, we can see that three tags were found in our text. All of them refer to the same document ID in the index.

For the index to be useful, we will need to index many documents. As the number of documents increases so will the accuracy of the tags found in our input text.

Now let us look at some of the request time parameters passed to the Solr text tagger:

- `overlaps`: This allows us to choose an algorithm that will be used to determine which overlapping tags should be retained versus which should be pruned away:
  - `ALL`: We have used `ALL` in our Solr queries. This means all tags should be emitted.
  - `NO_SUB`: Do not emit a sub tag, that is, a tag within another tag.
  - `LONGEST_DOMINANT_RIGHT`: Compare the character lengths of the tags and emit the longest one. In the case of a tie, pick the right-most tag. Remove tags that overlap with this identified tag and then repeat the algorithm to find other tags that can be emitted.
- `matchText`: This is a Boolean flag that indicates whether the matched text should be returned in the tag response. In this case, the tagger will fully buffer the input before tagging.
- `tagsLimit`: This indicates the maximum number of tags to return in the response. By default, this is `1000`. In our examples, we have mentioned it as `5000`. Tagging is stopped once this limit is reached.
- `skipAltTokens`: This is a Boolean flag used to suppress errors that can occur if, for example, you enable synonym expansion at query time in the analyzer, which you normally shouldn't do. The default value is `false`.

- `ignoreStopwords`: This is a Boolean flag that causes stop words to be ignored. Otherwise, the behavior is to treat them as breaks in tagging on the presumption that our indexed text-analysis configuration doesn't have a `StopWordFilter` class. By default, the indexed analysis chain is checked for the presence of a `StopWordFilter` class and, if found, then `ignoreStopWords` is `true` if unspecified. If we do not have `StopWordFilter` configured, we can safely ignore this parameter.

Most of the standard parameters that work with Solr also work here. For example, we have used `wt=json` here. We can also use `echoParams`, `rows`, `fl`, and other parameters during tagging.

Summary

We explored text tagging with the help of Lucene and Solr in this chapter. We understood what FSTs are and how they are implemented in Lucene. We also went through some well-known text tagging algorithms and got a brief idea of how text tagging is implemented in Solr. We explored the `SolrTextTagger` package by installing it as a module in Solr and saw some examples of text tagging using this package.

This is the last chapter in this book. In our journey throughout this book, we went through Solr indexing internals where we saw the roles of `analyzers` and `tokenizers` in index creation. We also saw multi-lingual search and discussed the challenges in large-scale indexing and the solutions to these problems. We then saw how Solr's scoring algorithm can be tweaked and customized. We discussed some existing algorithms and concept scoring algorithms. In the next chapter, we explored Solr internals and learnt how the relevancy scoring algorithm works on the inverted index. We delved into the query parsers available in Solr and implemented a Solr plugin for performing proximity search.

Next, we moved on to use cases, where we saw how Solr can be used for analytics and big data processing and for creating graphs. We saw an example of the use of Solr in e-commerce and discussed the relevant problems and solutions. Then, we explored the use of Solr for spatial search. We discussed in depth the geospatial search plugin available with Solr. We went through the problems faced during the implementation of Solr in an advertising system and discussed some solutions to the same.

In the advanced stage, we covered AJAX Solr, an asynchronous library available for executing queries in Solr from the browser. We discussed its features and advantages. We also went ahead and configured SolrCloud. We saw how SolrCloud addresses the problems in horizontal scalability by providing distributed indexing and search. SolrCloud can also be used as a NoSQL database. Finally, we learnt how text tagging can be performed using Solr and Lucene's FST library.

Index

N

Natural Language Processing (NLP) 267
Near Real Time Indexing and Search
    (NRT) 21
nodes
    adding, to SolrCloud 247-249
NoIDFSimilarity class 32
NoSQL database
    conflict resolution 264
    considerations 264
    data model 264
    distribution model 264
    features 265

O

optimizations, Solr 136, 137
OR clause
    working 54-58

P

pagination
    adding 213
Parameter class
    local attribute 198
    parseString attribute 199
    parseValueString attribute 199
    remove attribute 198
    string attribute 198
    val attribute 198
    valueString attribute 199
ParameterStore model
    available parameters 198
    exposed parameters 198
    ParameterHashStore class, using 200
    ParameterStore class, extending 200
parboiled library
    URL 71
parboiled parser
    creating 69-74
Parsing Expression Grammar
    (PEG) parsers
    about 69
    parser actions 70
    ParseRunner class 71

parse tree 70
    value stack 70
pivot faceting
    used, for data analysis 94-98
PointType field type 145
PrefixTree field
    options 147, 148

Q

Quadtree
    about 162
    data, inserting 162
    data, searching 163
query faceting 86-88
query parser
    custom query parser, building 67
queryResultCache 182, 183

R

radius faceting
    about 93, 94
    bounding box filter 90, 91
    distance function queries 92
    for location-based data 89
    geofilt filter 89
    rectangle filter 92
range faceting 86-88
rectangle filter 92
Redis
    Solr, merging with 185-189
relevance calculation algorithm 30, 31
replicas 223
reuters index 202

S

scorer
    on inverted index, working 52, 53
scoring algorithm
    URL 31
search 238-241
search results, quality measurement
    precision 17
    recall 17-19
semantic search
    implementing 130-136

Thank you for buying
Apache Solr Search Patterns

About Packt Publishing

Packt, pronounced 'packed', published its first book, *Mastering phpMyAdmin for Effective MySQL Management*, in April 2004, and subsequently continued to specialize in publishing highly focused books on specific technologies and solutions.

Our books and publications share the experiences of your fellow IT professionals in adapting and customizing today's systems, applications, and frameworks. Our solution-based books give you the knowledge and power to customize the software and technologies you're using to get the job done. Packt books are more specific and less general than the IT books you have seen in the past. Our unique business model allows us to bring you more focused information, giving you more of what you need to know, and less of what you don't.

Packt is a modern yet unique publishing company that focuses on producing quality, cutting-edge books for communities of developers, administrators, and newbies alike. For more information, please visit our website at www.packtpub.com.

About Packt Open Source

In 2010, Packt launched two new brands, Packt Open Source and Packt Enterprise, in order to continue its focus on specialization. This book is part of the Packt Open Source brand, home to books published on software built around open source licenses, and offering information to anybody from advanced developers to budding web designers. The Open Source brand also runs Packt's Open Source Royalty Scheme, by which Packt gives a royalty to each open source project about whose software a book is sold.

Writing for Packt

We welcome all inquiries from people who are interested in authoring. Book proposals should be sent to author@packtpub.com. If your book idea is still at an early stage and you would like to discuss it first before writing a formal book proposal, then please contact us; one of our commissioning editors will get in touch with you.

We're not just looking for published authors; if you have strong technical skills but no writing experience, our experienced editors can help you develop a writing career, or simply get some additional reward for your expertise.

[PACKT] open source
community experience distilled
PUBLISHING

Scaling Apache Solr

ISBN: 978-1-78398-174-8   Paperback: 298 pages

Optimize your searches using high-performance enterprise search repositories with Apache Solr

1. Get an introduction to the basics of Apache Solr in a step-by-step manner with lots of examples.

2. Develop and understand the workings of enterprise search solution using various techniques and real-life use cases.

3. Gain a practical insight into the advanced ways of optimizing and making an enterprise search solution cloud ready.

Apache Solr High Performance

ISBN: 978-1-78216-482-1   Paperback: 124 pages

Boost the Performance of Solr instances and troubleshoot real-time problems

1. Achieve high scores by boosting query time and index time, implementing boost queries and functions using the Dismax query parser and formulae.

2. Set up and use SolrCloud for distributed indexing and searching, and implement distributed search using Shards.

3. Use GeoSpatial search, handling homophones, and ignoring listed words from being indexed and searched.

Please check **www.PacktPub.com** for information on our titles

Instant Apache Solr for Indexing Data How-to

ISBN: 978-1-78216-484-5   Paperback: 90 pages

Learn how to index your data correctly and create better search experiences with Apache Solr

1. Learn something new in an Instant! A short, fast, focused guide delivering immediate results.

2. Take the most basic schema and extend it to support multi-lingual, multi-field searches.

3. Make Solr pull data from a variety of existing sources.

Apache Solr Beginner's Guide

ISBN: 978-1-78216-252-0   Paperback: 324 pages

Configure your own search engine experience with real-world data with this practical guide to Apache Solr

1. Learn to use Solr in real-world contexts, even if you are not a programmer, using simple configuration examples.

2. Define simple configurations for searching data in several ways in your specific context, from suggestions to advanced faceted navigation.

3. Teaches you in an easy-to-follow style, full of examples, illustrations, and tips to suit the demands of beginners.

Please check **www.PacktPub.com** for information on our titles

36888472R00177

Made in the USA
Middletown, DE
19 February 2019